E10

THE BAY PSALM BOOK

The First Book Printed in British North America
———— 1640 ————

ZOLTÁN HARASZTI

Dover Publications, Inc.
Mineola, New York

Copyright

Copyright © 2016 by Dover Publications, Inc.
All rights reserved.

Bibliographical Note

The Bay Psalm Book: The First Book Printed in British North America, 1640, first published by Dover Publications, Inc., in 2016, is a new compilation consisting of *The Enigma of the Bay Psalm Book,* by Zoltán Haraszti, originally published by The University of Chicago Press in 1956 and *The Bay Psalm Book,* first printed in 1640. Stray marks from the original printing have been retained in the interests of authenticity.

Library of Congress Cataloging-in-Publication Data

Names: Haraszti, Zoltán, 1892–1980. Enigma of the Bay Psalm book.
Title: The Bay Psalm book / the first book printed in British North America, 1640. The Enigma of the Bay Psalm Book / by Zoltán Haraszti ; and facsimile of the first edition, 1640.
Description: Dover edition. | Mineola, New York : Dover Publications, 2016. | "An unabridged compilation of The Enigma of the Bay Psalm Book by Zoltán Haraszti originally published by The University of Chicago Press in 1956 and The Bay Psalm Book, first published in 1640"—Title page verso. | Includes bibliographical references and index.
Identifiers: LCCN 2015049488 | ISBN 9780486805269 (hardback) | ISBN 0486805263 (hardback)
Subjects: LCSH: Bible. Psalms—Paraphrases, English. | Music in churches. | Psalmody, | Bible. Psalms. English. Bay Psalm book. | BISAC: RELIGION / Prayer.
Classification: LCC BS1440 .B4 2016 | DDC 223/ .2052—dc23 LC record available at http://lccn.loc.gov/2015049488

Manufactured in China by RR Donnelley
80526301   2016
www.doverpublications.com

Contents

BOOK 1

The Enigma of the Bay Psalm Book.............1
Notes 117
Index of Names..............................141

BOOK 2

The Facsimile 149
Notes on the Reproduction 445

Preface

IN 1640, within ten years of their arrival in America, the Puritans of Massachusetts Bay produced their first book and printed it on their own press. The volume was the Bay Psalm Book—a literary monument of the cultural and religious aspirations of the early settlers of the country.

The work, entitled *The Whole Booke of Psalmes Faithfully Translated into English Metre*, was published in seventeen hundred copies, of which only eleven survive—five complete and the others lacking a varying number of leaves. The fascination of the book was dramatized with uncommon force when, in January, 1947, a copy sold in New York for $151,000, the highest price ever paid for a volume at a public sale. It was also the highest price paid anywhere for a book in the English language, a copy of the First Folio of Shakespeare being a poor second at $77,000.

The volume has often been described; yet, apart from its external features, it has never been examined. It is always spoken of as the first book *printed* in America, never as the first book *written and printed* in America. Moses C. Tyler, the brilliant nineteenth-century historian of American literature, decried it as "a sort of prodigy," and his opinion has been echoed ever since. There have been notable efforts in our time to place the poetry of the New England Puri-

Preface

tans into a just perspective, but the Bay Psalm Book has not profited by them. To be sure, the work is no literary treasure trove; yet much of the ridicule heaped upon it seems undeserved, especially when, on nearer inspection, the despised passages turn out to be literal transcriptions from the King James Version.

This essay tries to correct some of the errors that have grown up around the famous book. It is shown that the Preface, which is a concise theological treatise by itself, was not written by Richard Mather, to whom it has been generally ascribed, but by John Cotton, who was indeed the logical man to do it. This wrong attribution was partly responsible for placing Richard Mather in the forefront of the enterprise—a place which belongs to John Cotton.

Nor was the Bay Psalm Book "the Eliot-Welde-Mather version," as most historians have dubbed it; it was the work of "the chief Divines" of the Bay Colony, as Cotton Mather clearly stated. However, by regarding it merely as a contrivance of the three men who did not write any other verse, scholars have felt exempt from making any attempt to identify the authors. The late George Parker Winship even announced that the Bay Psalm Book was so "consistently uniform" that it might have been composed by a single person! Nothing could be more unfounded. An attentive reading of the book reveals rather a variety of hands; some of them bad, incredibly bad, but quite a few good or even excellent. Thus the writer has succeeded in identifying John Cotton as the author of the Twenty-third Psalm, and in assigning other

Preface

psalms to John Wilson and Peter Bulkeley. But these are the results of a few experiments only. Many others should be made; in fact, the whole translation should be thoroughly studied.

Whatever the literary value of the Bay Psalm Book may be, every exploration of the work has its reward. To quote one more example: For over three hundred years Richard Lyon, one of the two revisers of the Bay Psalm Book and probably the sole author of the first American hymnal, has been an almost entirely unknown figure. To discover who the man was—or to clear up at least part of his still mysterious career —has been a pleasure indeed.

The publication of this facsimile edition will meet a real need. The original copies cannot be used in research that requires their free handling; on the other hand, the small reprint issued in 1862 has nearly disappeared, and the facsimile edition of 1903, too, has become rare. It is hoped, however, that, beyond the circle of special students, the volume will appeal to the general reader. One does not have to be overly sentimental to appreciate the immense symbolical significance of the Bay Psalm Book.

Grateful acknowledgment is expressed here to the Boston Public Library, its Trustees, and its Director, Mr. Milton E. Lord, and to the Old South Church in Boston, its Minister, Dr. Frederick M. Meek, and its Deacons, for permission to reproduce one of the two original copies of the book preserved in the Prince Library. The Old South Church is the legal

Preface

owner of this great collection of Americana, while the Boston Public Library has been its custodian since 1866.

The idea of the publication of a facsimile edition originated with Mr. Barry D. Karl, then with the University of Chicago Press. The present writer was supposed to contribute a brief Introduction; in the writing, however, the paper grew and grew until it became a separate volume. Mr. Karl also read the larger part of the manuscript and made valuable suggestions.

The writer, who is Keeper of Rare Books at the Boston Public Library, is greatly indebted to several of his associates. Miss Harriet Swift, Curator of Americana, Miss Margaret Munsterberg, Mrs. Mary L. Malany, Miss Ellen M. Oldham, and Mr. John L. Spicer were always ready to assist him in his research —the main burden falling on Mrs. Malany.

Dean Eisig Silberschlag and Dr. Joseph Marcus, Librarian, of Hebrew Teachers College, Boston, Massachusetts, were helpful in interpreting the Hebrew text of the Psalms (chap. vi). Dr. J. A. Venn, President of Queens' College, and Archivist of Cambridge University, read the chapter on Richard Lyon, as did Mr. R. C. Anderson of Greenwich, England. Their conjectures will be of great value in further research. And, last but not least, the writer is indebted to Edmund S. Morgan, Professor of American History in Yale University, and his wife Helen M. Morgan, whose comments upon the completed manuscript resulted in the elucidation of many a passage.

Preface

The expert craftsmen of the Meriden Gravure Company, under the supervision of Mr. E. Harold Hugo, prepared the facsimile reproduction of the book with devoted care.

Many are the writer's debts; the responsibility for errors, however, is solely his own.

ZOLTÁN HARASZTI

BOSTON, MASSACHUSETTS
July 1956

Contents

LIST OF ILLUSTRATIONS xiii

I. THE PURITANS' NEED FOR A NEW TRANSLATION 3

II. THE JINGLE OF THOMAS SHEPARD 12

III. JOHN COTTON—NOT RICHARD MATHER . . 19

IV. THE NEW ENGLAND PSALM BOOK . . . 28

V. PROBLEMS FOR THE SCHOLAR 31

VI. EXPERIMENTS IN TEXTUAL ANALYSIS . . . 41

VII. THE SEARCH FOR AUTHORSHIP 56

VIII. THE PSALM-SINGING OF THE PURITANS . . 61

IX. THE PRINTING OF THE BAY PSALM BOOK . 72

X. THE EXTANT COPIES 81

APPENDIX

A. A TRANSCRIPT BY COTTON 93

B. WHO WAS RICHARD LYON? 98

C. THE DRAFT OF THE PREFACE 107

NOTES 119

INDEX OF NAMES 141

List of Illustrations

	FACING PAGE
PROBABLE PORTRAIT OF JOHN COTTON	26
PART OF A PAGE FROM THE DRAFT OF THE PREFACE TO THE BAY PSALM BOOK	26
PART OF A LETTER BY COTTON TO ELMERTON	27
A RICHARD MATHER MANUSCRIPT	27

*The Enigma
of the Bay Psalm Book*

I

The Puritans' Need for a New Translation

ONE of the most important innovations of the Reformation was the singing of the Psalms by the whole congregation instead of by a choir. As soon as the Bible was translated into the vernacular languages, metrical translations of the Psalms began to appear—Luther's *Geystliche Gesangk Buchleyn* in 1524, Marot and Calvin's *Aulcuns Pseaumes* in 1539, and Coverdale's *Goostly Psalmes* also in 1539. People learned them avidly and sang them in their homes, in the field, and in their workshops. The communal singing especially engendered a feeling of unity. Thus psalm-singing, produced by the Reformation, became in turn one of its most powerful weapons. In spreading and deepening the new religious movement, it accomplished more than all the treatises of the theologians.

The German hymnody of the Reformation period was immense. Luther, who loved "the concord of sweet sounds," drew his tunes from the rich tradition of popular and semi-sacred music. His hymns and psalms, the latter being paraphrases rather than translations, possessed simple beauty and great

The Enigma of the Bay Psalm Book

strength. His rendering of Psalm 46, beginning "Ein' feste Burg ist unser Gott," soon evolved into a national anthem of Protestant Germany. In France, curiously enough, psalm-singing began at the Court, with the "sainctes chansonettes" of Clément Marot, poet and courtier of Francis I. Twelve of his psalms, with six more attributed to Calvin, were published in the little volume of 1539; and two years later an enlarged version appeared containing thirty psalms by Marot and fifteen by others.[1] The Sorbonne was alarmed and got the work banned. But by then Calvin had obtained authority from the Council of Geneva to introduce the versified psalms into regular use. It was psalms only, for, unlike Luther, Calvin disapproved of popular hymns and insisted on a close translation of the biblical verses; but he, too, welcomed solemn music, which Louis Bourgeois, Jean Goudimel, and other talented composers supplied.

Coverdale's magnificent prose translation of the Psalter, as adapted by Cranmer for the Great Bible of 1539, was retained, with minor alterations, in the Book of Common Prayer of 1549. His *Goostly Psalmes*, however, with its thirteen psalms and nearly as many hymns, was prohibited soon after its appearance, as Henry VIII, having rejected alliance with the Lutheran princes of Germany (and his marriage with Anne of Cleves), veered again toward Catholicism. It remained for Thomas Sternhold, a courtier like Marot but unfortunately a much less gifted poet, to initiate the metrical version that was to find general acceptance. Thirty-seven of his psalms were published

The Puritans' Need for a New Translation

in 1549, the year of his death. The work was continued by John Hopkins, "a worthy school-maister" of Suffolk, and by several of the exiles, who fled abroad from Queen Mary's reign. They were encouraged by Calvin and urged on by the new editions of the Huguenot Psalter, on which Theodore Beza had been steadily working. After their return to England upon the accession of Queen Elizabeth, they made rapid progress. The complete English metrical version, attached to the Book of Common Prayer, was published in 1562, in the same year as the first complete French Psalter.

The Sternhold-Hopkins version was not the only English translation. Sir Thomas Wyatt and the Earl of Surrey, incomparably better poets than either Sternhold or Hopkins, had translated a number of psalms before. But their verses did not catch on; nor did those of Robert Crowley, John Hall, Francis Seager, and Archbishop Matthew Parker, though the last especially had an engaging simplicity. The very slowness of its development must have helped the Sternhold-Hopkins version, its gradual growth endearing it to the exiles. The mediocrity of its versification was no handicap either. "Had they been more poetically translated," Thomas Warton remarked, "those psalms would not have been acceptable to the common people."[2]

But the tunes were of the greatest benefit to the version. Accented in the same way as the words, they were easy to sing. From 1570 on, the book, with its "apt Notes to synge," was frequently printed as an

The Enigma of the Bay Psalm Book

integral part of the Bible, which thus had both a prose and a verse translation (and when the Prayer Book was included, also a second prose version). Although choral singing continued in the cathedrals and college churches, and congregational singing was restricted to the parishes, the Church, on the whole, favored the new version. The Puritans were the first to manifest dissatisfaction with it, not because of its artistic shortcomings, but because it was too free for their taste; for the version, although "conferred with the Ebrue," was based largely on the Vulgate and Coverdale's prose translation. It was for the Separatists, who from the end of the century on were emigrating to Holland, that a new, stricter version was first prepared. Hebrew scholarship was far more advanced by then; and Henry Ainsworth, pastor of the English church at Amsterdam, had a profound knowledge of the language. After years of labor, in 1612 he published his translation, in prose as well as meter, with copious annotations on the Hebrew text. His work was adopted by both his congregation and that of John Robinson at Leyden.

Having studied the Hebrew text, which few of the earlier translators could do, Ainsworth was able to correct some of the errors of the Sternhold-Hopkins Psalter. Confident that he did not "omit the grace of the Hebrew tongue," or use "such uncouth phrases as the common reader understandeth not," he thought his differences from the earlier English versions justified. "I follow the Original text," he wrote in his preface, "where moe are to be seen than our English

The Puritans' Need for a New Translation

can wel admit of; serving both to shew the sense, and to read with consideration." Believing in the propriety of the singing of psalms by the congregation, he included "singing notes" in his volume, some of them taken from English and others from French and Dutch psalms. The Pilgrims naturally brought with them the psalm book, which, reprinted several times, remained in use at Plymouth till the end of the colony.

The founders of the Bay Colony, on the other hand, whether their Bible was Genevan or King James, had been brought up on the Sternhold-Hopkins version. The book, published by then nearly two hundred times, had taken deep roots in the mind of the people. Yet, like Ainsworth, the ministers were aware of its corruptions. As they later explained:

... it is not unknowne to the godly learned that they [the translators] have rather presented a paraphrase then the words of David translated according to the rule 2 *chron.* 29, 30. and that their addition to the words, detractions from the words are not seldome and rare, but very frequent and many times needles ... and that their variations of the sense, and alterations of the sacred text too frequently, may iustly minister matter of offence to them that are able to compare the translation with the text; of which failings, some iudicious have oft complained, others have been grieved ...

Wishing to enjoy the Lord's ordinance "in its native purity," the ministers decided to make "a plain and familiar translation."[3] Their aim was so much like that of Ainsworth that one may justly ask why they did not accept his version instead of pre-

The Enigma of the Bay Psalm Book

paring a new one. To be sure, they found Ainsworth's tunes "difficult"; but this is hardly the main reason.[4] Nor was it an excess of confidence in their own superior ability that launched them on their venture.

Indeed, the very fact that Plymouth had a satisfactory psalm book made it even more desirable that the Bay Colony should have one of its own. For the Puritans were anxious from the first to emphasize their distinctness from the Pilgrims. On taking his last sight of England in 1629, Francis Higginson had supposedly reminded his fellow passengers: "We do not go to New England as Separatists from the Church of England, though we cannot but separate from the corruption in it...."[5] True, the church which he helped to organize at Salem was modeled upon that of the Pilgrims; it adopted a confession of faith and a covenant and then chose a pastor and teacher who had first renounced their episcopal ordination. Yet the Salem settlers protested against the charge of "rebellion" which returning malcontents had spread against them in England.[6] John White, one of the chief movers of the colonization, desperately defended the emigrants against the accusation of being either Separatists or Semi-Separatists. Nonconformists they were; but that was not separation.[7] Similarly, in their farewell address Governor Winthrop and his companions found it necessary to declare that they esteemed it an honor "to call the Church of England, from whence we rise, our dear mother."[8]

The charge, however, persisted, and henceforth

The Puritans' Need for a New Translation

the apologists of the Bay Colony were occupied year in and year out with defining the precise character of their church—that of "Non-Separatist Congregationalism"—and with proving that, far from having joined the Plymouth Independents, they had formed their own different ideas of church government long before leaving England. In their answer to the reproachful inquiries sent over from England by a group of Presbyterian ministers, the Elders still tried to minimize their exclusiveness toward the other churches ("including Plimouth") of New England. Apart from "particular and individuall circumstances," they replied, "there is no materiall point ... wherein the Churches of New England do not observe the same course."[9] Yet in their discussion of the covenant they professed to be followers of the English divines William Ames, Robert Parker, and Paul Baynes, "neither of whom were Brownists, but bare witnesse against that riged Separation."[10]

Considered in this light, the publication of the Bay Psalm Book acquires a significance far beyond, and independent of, the literary quality of its versification. It is possible then, indeed inevitable, to think of the volume as an expression of the colony's own brand of Calvinism—as a gesture designed to demonstrate that its people were congregationalists and, at the same time, loyal members of the Church of England. The Sternhold-Hopkins version was not Calvinistic enough, and the adoption of the Ainsworth translation would have identified them with the Plymouth Separatists. When in the fall of 1638 a press

The Enigma of the Bay Psalm Book

arrived in the colony, the ministers must have regarded it as a hint from Providence.

With the outbreak of the Civil War in England the situation changed. Westminster Assembly supplanted Convocation, and Presbyterianism took the place of Episcopacy as the state church. The clergy of the Bay Colony did not have to protest their loyalty any longer; several of the leading ministers—John Cotton, Thomas Hooker, and John Davenport—were invited to take part in the assembly, an honor which they declined. In a series of treatises, starting in 1642, Cotton further expounded the nature and organization of their churches. One of the distinctive features of their service was, he proudly told in *The Way of the Churches in New England*, the singing of psalms in their own version: "Before Sermon, and many times after, we sing a Psalme, and because the former translation of the Psalmes, doth in many things vary from the original . . . we have endeavoured a new translation into English meetre, as neere the originall as wee could expresse it in our English tongue . . . and those Psalmes wee sing, both in our publike Churches, and in private."[11]

Puritanism, divided from the beginning, soon broke up into innumerable sects, and the Presbyterians proved even more intolerant than the Anglicans. The colony was forced again to defend itself.[12] In *The Way of the Congregational Churches Cleared*, Cotton argued (as had Mather ten years before) that, in matters of doctrine and organization, they received their light from Masters Parker, Baynes, and Ames; and that it

The Puritans' Need for a New Translation

was an "unworthy calumny" to call them Brownists. "They never begot us," he insisted, "either to God, or to the Church, or to their Schism: a Schism, which as we have lamented in them . . . so we have ever borne witnesse against it, since our first knowledg of it."[13] But these were later developments, outlined here only to show the forces which produced and sustained the Bay Psalm Book.

Under the first day of 1639 Governor Winthrop entered in his journal: "A printing house was begun at Cambridge by one Daye, at the charge of Mr. Glover, who died on sea hitherward. The first thing which was printed was the freeman's oath; the next was an almanack made for New England by Mr. William Peirce, mariner; the next was the Psalms newly turned into metre." This was the earliest notice of the Bay Psalm Book, or, by its full title, *The Whole Booke of Psalmes Faithfully Translated into English Metre*—the first book printed in English America.

II

The Jingle of Thomas Shepard

SIXTY years later, in his *Magnalia*, Cotton Mather related the story of the origin of the work.[1] First he repeated verbatim the translators' grievances against the Sternhold-Hopkins version as voiced in their Preface; then, placing the beginning of the enterprise "about the year 1639," he continued:

> Resolving then upon a New Translation, the chief Divines in the Country, took each of them a Portion to be Translated: Among whom were Mr. Welds and Mr. Eliot of Roxbury, and Mr. Mather of Dorchester. These, like the rest, were of so different a Genius for their Poetry, that Mr. Shepard of Cambridge, on the Occasion addressed them to this Purpose.
>
> You Roxb'ry Poets, keep clear of the Crime,
> Of missing to give us very good Rhime.
> And you of Dorchester, your Verses lengthen,
> But with the Texts own Words, you will them strengthen.[2]

Shepard's humorous little stanza was too good to omit, and Cotton Mather was certainly not the man to do it. However, Cotton Mather did not mean to claim exclusive authorship for Welde, Eliot, and Richard Mather. On the contrary, he clearly stated that each of the chief divines of the country took a portion of the psalm book to be translated. And he referred for a second time to these other translators

The Jingle of Thomas Shepard

in remarking that the three men "like the rest" were of a different genius. One may also note that he inserted his account in the biographical sketch of Henry Dunster, making no mention whatever of the Bay Psalm Book in the sketches of Welde, Eliot, or Mather.[3]

It is not Cotton Mather's fault that scholars, enamored of Shepard's doggerel, have forgotten the rest of the account; that, ignoring the other divines in the picture, they speak only of "three of the ministers."[4] The quatrain itself implies nothing of the kind. One may readily understand that the Cambridge pastor, about thirty-five, was teasing his Roxbury friends, and even Richard Mather, who, although esteemed as "eminently judicious," was not yet the "mighty Man" of later years. But one can hardly imagine Shepard making fun of the august figures of John Cotton or John Wilson, teacher and pastor of the Boston church, the one twenty-four and the other seventeen years his senior.[5] Further, he might well have singled out Welde, Eliot, and Mather precisely because they were inexperienced in versification, but he would not have presumed to teach rhyming to Cotton and Wilson, whose verses were greatly admired.

The position of Cotton and Wilson should be kept in mind. On his arrival in 1633, John Cotton became at once the leader of the clergy, one of the chief architects of the policies of the little theocratic state. A consummate Hebrew, Greek, and Latin scholar, he had been head lecturer at Emmanuel College for six

The Enigma of the Bay Psalm Book

years, long before some of the younger ministers of the colony entered college; and at twenty-seven he was appointed vicar of St. Botolph's at Boston, one of the most beautiful parish churches in England. It was he who in 1630 preached at Southampton the farewell sermon to the Puritans, exhorting them to remember their "Jerusalem at home."[6] In stature and prestige Cotton was the equal of Winthrop, whom he resembled in temper and whose close friend and ally he was. His coming to America was the beginning of a great creative career, well worth, at the end, the richest bishopric; yet he must have felt a pang upon exchanging the thriving capital of Lincolnshire for the small town in the wilderness—his magnificent church, with its vast space, gigantic pillars, and marvelous spire, for a rude meeting house with thatched roof and walls made of mud.[7] With touching simplicity, he expressed his emotions in a poem, the third and fourth stanzas of which follow:

> When I think of the sweet and gracious company
>   That at *Boston* once I had,
> And of the long peace of a fruitful Ministry
>   For twenty years enjoy'd:
>
> The joy that I found in all that happiness
>   Doth still so much refresh me,
> That the grief to be cast out into a wilderness
>   Doth not so much distress me.[8]

The poem, with two others, was printed only after Cotton's death; yet undoubtedly it had been read by friends.

John Wilson, one of the first ministers to come over,

The Jingle of Thomas Shepard

also enjoyed general respect. The son of a canon of Windsor and a grand-nephew of Archbishop Grindal, he was educated at Eton and at King's College, Cambridge, where he was promoted to a fellowship. Instead, he went to Sudbury, in Suffolk, to teach among Nonconformists. During the long years of his ministry in Boston, he was relentless toward Antinomians and other "Opinionists"; yet in private life he was kind and genial. Hawthorne presents him in *The Scarlet Letter*, in a scene with Hester Prynne and her child, as "a grandfatherly sort of personage," which was an exaggeration; but he may have been really "a vast favorite with children." It was for them that he had published, still in England, a volume of fifteen hundred lines about the defeat of the Spanish Armada, the plague of 1603, and the Gunpowder Plot. And he certainly did not stop writing verses in America. "He was another sweet singer of Israel," his son recorded, "whose heavenly verses passed like to the handkerchief carryed from Paul to help and uphold disconsolate ones, and to heal their wracked Souls...."[9] Cotton Mather felt that he should have done Wilson's biography in rhymes, considering that "he had so nimble a Faculty of putting his Devout Thoughts into Verse, that he Signalized himself by the Greatest Frequency, perhaps, that ever Man used, of sending Poems to all Persons, in all Places, on all Occasions; and upon this, as well as upon Greater Accounts, was a David unto the Flocks of our Lord in the Wilderness."[10] Can anyone believe that so irrepressible a versemaker, a David unto his flocks,

The Enigma of the Bay Psalm Book

would keep his hands off the translation of David's Psalms?

Nathaniel Ward of Ipswich, Peter Bulkeley of Concord, and Samuel Whiting of Lynn were some of the "other divines." It would have been strange, even without Cotton Mather's testimony to disprove it, if only the three younger men, none of whom is known to have produced any other verse in English, had been engaged in the translation when many of the other ministers, equally good Hebrew scholars, were practiced writers of poetry.

Another early statement about the authorship of the work was made by Thomas Prince, pastor of the Old South Church in Boston, in the Preface to his revision of the Bay Psalm Book. "By 1636," he wrote, "there were come over hither near thirty pious and learned Ministers, educated in the Universities of England: and . . . they set themselves to translate the Psalms and other Scripture Songs into English Metre. . . . They committed this Work especially to the Rev. Mr. Richard Mather of Dorchester; the Rev. Mr. Thomas Weld, and the Rev. Mr. John Eliot of Roxbury." Thus Prince, too, speaks of the work as a communal enterprise ("they set themselves . . ."), but adds that it was committed "especially" to three men who were "well acquainted with Hebrew . . . and Greek." What the source of his new information was, Prince, writing one hundred and twenty years after the event, does not say. It is doubtful that he had any. He probably merely repeated, in his own way, Cotton Mather's account—

The Jingle of Thomas Shepard

as did Daniel Neal, the English historian of the Puritans, forty years before.[11]

In their absorption in Shepard's joke, scholars have paid little attention to the errand of John Josselyn, who, upon his arrival in Boston in 1638, delivered to Cotton, "for his approbation," the verse translations of Psalms 16, 25, 51, 88, 113, and 137 sent by Francis Quarles. Why to Cotton—unless he had asked for them, or unless the English poet had learned that he was involved in the project?[12]

It is necessary to place Shepard's quatrain in its proper perspective, for the overemphasis put upon this puny verse was undoubtedly responsible for another capital error which, in turn, has made the theory of "the triumvirate of Bay Psalmists" seem unassailable.

As is well known, no manuscript of the translation of any of the psalms exists; the draft of the Preface, however, has been preserved in the Prince Collection, now in the Boston Public Library. The manuscript covers nine quarto pages and consists of about three thousand words, as against twenty-three hundred of the corresponding portion of the Preface.[13] The draft is therefore more voluminous than the printed text. Here and there some of its sentences were shortened and some of its passages were eliminated before it reached the printer; but, with the exception of a few lines, nothing was added to it. Unfortunately, the condensation was accomplished at the expense of the style; the discourse, with its many "objections" and "answers," required a more leisurely pace. The au-

The Enigma of the Bay Psalm Book

thor seems to have been interested only in the theological vindication of the translation, for the manuscript ends at the point where the description of the method employed in the work begins.[14]

The manuscript is unsigned; however, the *Catalogue of the Prince Library*, published by the Boston Public Library in 1870, tentatively described it: "This appears to be a rough draft of the preface for the 'Bay Psalm Book' printed in 1640. It ... was written, probably, by Rev. Richard Mather, one of the editors of the Bay Psalm Book, the handwriting being apparently his." It *was* a draft of the Preface—not a rough but a finished one. One half of the entry being thus not only true but an understatement, the correctness of the other half, the attribution to Richard Mather, seems to have been taken for granted. It was made by Joseph Otis Williams, who did the cataloguing of the manuscript section of the Prince Library.[15] Justin Winsor, then Superintendent of the Boston Public Library, indorsed the attribution, and on its strength Mather has been regarded ever since not only as one of the principal translators but also as the promoter of the whole venture.[16]

The announcement will come therefore as a surprise: the manuscript was not written by Richard Mather but by John Cotton. And since the printed text, as will be shown, is almost identical with the draft, it is John Cotton and not Richard Mather who must be considered the author of the Preface to the Bay Psalm Book.

III
John Cotton—Not Richard Mather

DESCRIBED on the title-page as "a discourse declaring not only the lawfullnes, but also the necessity of the heavenly Ordinance of singing Scripture Psalmes in the Churches of God," the Preface is an important part of the work.

One wonders at first what prompted the ministers to dwell upon the subject after congregational singing had been in practice for over eighty years. However, the singing of psalms had always had its opponents from both the right and the left. Some high-churchmen maintained that the Sternhold-Hopkins version had never received either royal approbation or parliamentary sanction; and the earliest Separatists, like Henry Barrow, denounced the use of English meter.[1] The subject was to be debated even in the Westminster Assembly and, to help the partisans of singing, Nathaniel Homes, the millenarian rector of St. Mary Stayning in London, reprinted the Preface to the Bay Psalm Book in his *Gospel Musick* of 1644 as "the Iudgement of our worthy Brethren of New-England."

Doubt about Richard Mather's authorship of the Preface first arose in the writer's mind when, in

The Enigma of the Bay Psalm Book

preparation for this essay, he reread the draft. In the quiet flow of the manuscript he missed the blunt force of Mather's writing; the tone was rather the slow persuasiveness of John Cotton, a man of "meek words," who (excepting his bitter controversy with Roger Williams) seldom raised his voice. Even the nature of their quotations was different; to reinforce an argument, Mather often referred to contemporaries, whereas Cotton looked for guidance mainly to Moses and the Prophets. Mather, apart from a brief stay at Oxford, was not college-educated; though expert in doctrine, he remained an essentially practical man. The finer theological subtleties were more the element of Cotton, a Puritan scholastic steeped in medieval habits of thought.

This was only an impression, but it was enough to make the writer look with suspicion at the injunction at the end of the draft: "And so goe on in shewing what other things have bene attended to in this Translation according to the Letter which was read at Dortchester." Would it have been likely for Mather to speak of the meeting of the translators as one held "at Dortchester"? Other participants from Boston, Roxbury, Cambridge, or elsewhere would have named the town; but the minister who lived there was more apt to use the expression "at my house," "at the parsonage," or something like it.[2]

The packet of six psalms sent by Quarles to Cotton suddenly reminded the writer of the latter's *Singing of Psalmes, a Gospel Ordinance*, printed in 1647—the only tract of its kind published by anyone in the

John Cotton—Not Richard Mather

colony, and one containing a vigorous defense of the translation.[3] Its very title repeats the description, printed on the title-page of the Bay Psalm Book, of the Preface, and the text begins the same way: "To prevent the godly-minded from making melody to the Lord in Singing his Praises with one accord ... Satan hath mightily bestirred himselfe, to breed a discord in the hearts of some ..." Cotton's treatise is ten times as long as the Preface to the Bay Psalm Book; yet the similarity of their ideas and language became at once obvious. Then a comparison of the parallel passages disclosed the close relationship of the three documents. A few examples must suffice for illustration:

Draft: This Commaundement and Practise, was it Ceremoniall, or morall? Something in it indeede was Ceremoniall, as that the Levites were the choise singers, and that they played with Instruments. . . .

Preface: For this commandement was it cerimoniall or morall? Some things in it indeed were cerimoniall, as their musicall instruments etc. . . .

Treatise: Singing with Instruments was typicall, and so a ceremoniall worship, and therefore is ceased. But singing with heart and voyce is a morall worship . . . [pp. 5–6].

All three documents emphasize—at great length and in almost identical words—that it was God's ordinance to make the whole Scripture available in the tongue of every nation; that thus the Psalms had to be translated into English; and that if they were to be sung, they had to be rendered into English meter. Only a line will be quoted here: "As God hath hid from us the Hebrew Temple Tunes . . . ," the draft

The Enigma of the Bay Psalm Book

states; "As the Lord hath hid from us the hebrew tunes . . . ," the Preface affirms; "And yet withall [God] hath hid from us the Hebrew Tunes . . ." (p. 56), the treatise repeats.

As to what kind of songs were to be sung—Scripture psalms or songs indited by some personal gift—all three sources agree:

Draft: . . . Protestant Churches . . . who have gotten victory over the beast, are described with Harpes in their hands, to sing the song of Moses and of the Lamb, Rev. 15. 3.

Preface: . . . when he [John] brings in the protestant Churches getting the victory over the Beast with harps in their hands and singing the song of Moses. Rev. 15. 3.

Treatise: The Song of those who had gotten victory over the beast (Rev. 15.) is said to be the Song of Moses and of the Lambe, ver. 3 [p. 27].

The thesis that the whole congregation should sing together is reinforced by the same point:

Draft: In Exodus, not onely Moses but the Children of Israel are said to sing this song, and as the word is in the originall They spake saying, not Moses alone. . . .

Preface: Not only Moses but all Israell sang that song, they spake saying (as it is in the orig.) *Ex.* 15. 1.

Treatise: In *Exod.* 15. 1 Moses and the children of Israel are said to sing a Song of Thanksgiving to the Lord [p. 40].

To be sure, many of the parallel passages were drawn from the Bible, and therefore their similarity could be considered inevitable. But the use of the same quotations is important in itself.

Some passages occur only in the Preface and the treatise. An example:

John Cotton—Not Richard Mather

Preface: There are many verses together in several psalmes of David which run in rithmes (as those that know the hebrew and as Buxtorf shews *Thesau.* pa. 629). . . .

Treatise: . . . and some of them run in meeter also, as those know that know the Hebrew, and as Buxtorf sheweth in his *Thesaur.* pag. 629 [p. 56].

Even more revealing are the excerpts found only in the draft and the treatise, for the draft was, after all, of a more private character. Yet, writing his treatise seven years later, Cotton used it apparently without the slightest qualm:

Draft: And all the children of the New Testament being now growne up as Elders or as heires come to ripe Age, in comparison of the Saints of the Old Testament, who were counted as children under Age. *Gal.* 4. 1, 2, 3.

Treatise: . . . fitted to the solace of the outward sences of children under age (such as the Israelites were under the Old Testament, *Gal.* 4. 1, 2, 3.) yet now in the growne age of the heires of the New Testament . . . [p. 6].

On the question as to whether women may sing as well as men, the three documents affirm:

Draft: And Miriam and all the women are said to come out with Timbrells and daunces, and Answer was returned to the men in other wordes, though to the same purpose.

Preface: All as well as Moses [sang], the women also as well as the men.

Treatise: It is certain, the Law, yea the Lawgiver Moses did permit Miriam and the women that went out after her to sing forth the praises of the Lord, as well as the men, and to answer the men in their Song of thankesgiving [p. 43].

Besides the sameness of the argument, one may also note that Miriam's name occurs only in the draft

The Enigma of the Bay Psalm Book

and the treatise. Equally characteristic are the passages containing the Hebrew words:

Draft: And therefore it is, that the Apostle speaketh to the whole Church, and to all the members of it, that they should all of them Teach and Admonish one another in Psalmes, and Hymnes, and Spirituall songs, singing with grace in their hearts to the Lord. (*Col.* 3. 16. *Eph.* 5. 19.) Which Psalmes, and Hymnes, and Spirituall songs doe conteyne all the severall sorts of Davids Psalmes: some being called by David himself *mizmorim*, that is Psalmes, others *tehilim*, that is Hymnes, others *shirim*, that is, Spirituall songs.

Preface: Therefore not some select members, but the whole Church is commaunded to teach one another in all the severall sorts of Davids psalmes, some being called by himself *mismorim:* psalms, some *tehilim:* Hymns, some *shirim:* spirituall songs.

Treatise: Taken from the Commandement, or exhortation of the Apostle, *Eph.* 5, 19 . . . and to the like purpose, *Col.* 3: "Let the word of Christ dwell in you richly . . . teaching and admonishing one another in Psalmes and Hymnes and spirituall Songs, singing with grace in your hearts to the Lord." . . . Now those three be the very Titles of the Songs of David . . . : some of them are called *mismorim*, that is, Psalmes: some *tehilim*, that is, Hymnes; some *shirim*, that is, Songs, spirituall Songs [p. 16].[4]

Again, the Apostle's exhortation and the reference to the Epistles to the Colossians and to the Ephesians are mentioned only in the draft and the treatise—surely, a sufficient indication that the two were written by the same hand.

Many other passages could be cited; indeed, the whole material of the draft and the Preface was incorporated into the *Singing of Psalmes*. It is possible

John Cotton—Not Richard Mather

to imagine, of course, that in composing his treatise Cotton took over another man's ideas and phrases; notions about plagiarism were less strict in the seventeenth century. But it is difficult to believe that this would happen in the small community of the colony.

It was only after the internal evidence of Cotton's authorship was established that the writer thought of an external one. The former is so much more interesting! But now a brief search yielded such proof in abundance.

The manuscript section of the Prince Collection includes John Cotton's correspondence with his fellow ministers, over fifty letters, twenty of which are by him. The first of these he wrote before leaving England, and the last not long before his death. The handwriting shows few changes; nevertheless, the letters of the time of the printing of the Bay Psalm Book seem the most applicable. There are several such, all signed. The one written to the Reverend Mr. Elmerton, of Cranbrook, in Kent, England, on August 26, 1640, especially invites comparison. It is a treatise rather than a private letter, discussing the subject of justification by faith; and for this reason it was copied out carefully, like the draft of the Preface to the Bay Psalm Book. The identity of the handwriting in the two manuscripts seems obvious at first sight; and a close examination turns the impression into certainty. The characters—the capitals *A*, *B*, *E*, *G*, *I*, *T*, and the minuscules *f*, *g*, *h*, *r*—all have their counterparts, with traits which set them apart from the writing of anyone else. The same words occurring

The Enigma of the Bay Psalm Book

in both places look like facsimiles of each other; and, further, the spacing between the words and the lines is also the same.

(One should note that some of the capitals appear in two forms in Cotton's manuscripts. Thus the *C* with the descending stroke at the top, the ornate *P*, and the conventional *S* in the draft—different from those in the letter to Elmerton—may be found in two of Cotton's signed letters to Peter Bulkeley, dated January 4, 1640 and August 7, 1641, one discussing the Covenant and the other, the doctrine of redemption. Indeed the *B* has two forms in the same letter to Elmerton.)

In contrast, the handwriting of Richard Mather, as it appears in his signed letters and manuscripts, is something wholly different. A glance at his autograph of "A Modell of Church-Government," his proposal for the Cambridge Platform of 1648, now preserved at the American Antiquarian Society, is sufficient to show this beyond a doubt. Its writing is characterized by the same slant, bold loops under the *y*'s, and a tendency to cursiveness that one finds in all Mather manuscripts. For the convenience of the reader, a page of the draft of the Preface, a page from Mather's "Modell," and a part of Cotton's letter to Elmerton are reproduced here in facsimile.[5]

The question remains: Who did the revision of the draft for the press?

In the upper corner of the first leaf there is an inscription, written in two lines: "For my reverend brother/Th[omas] Shepard." This too is in Cotton's

Courtesy of Connecticut Historical Society

PROBABLE PORTRAIT OF JOHN COTTON
The portrait was done apparently in 1649, when Cotton was sixty-five. It was later repainted.

The Answer is easy: That these Saints rejoyces
1. These Spirituall Songs by ye extraordinary gift of the
Spirit, whereby they were enabled to dictate Rule & Metre of
Gods owne framing Composed. As ye like extraordinary
gift of ye Spirit was found in ye Church, were found
not requisite to allow ye like liberty in composing Psalmes
for ye Churches uses upon y.t occasion.
If it be replyed, noe allow ministers to pray renewed
prayers entitled by ye Ordinary gift of ye Spirit: & why
not to sing Composed Psalmes by ye like gift? O Answer
i.s, there i.s like proportion betweene Prayer
& Thanksgiving. & therefore of a minister may pray
a prayer renewed by ye ordinary gift of ye Spirit, soe
may in like sort frame hymn with a thanksgiving renewed
by ye ordinary gift of ye Spirit. But to Compose a
Psalme requireth a further gift, even spirituall History,
as well as spirituall Grace, which is not found in every ye.

Cornerstone, the Head of ye Corner: vote both nothing by conformity to him either in Grace, or suffermgs: It is more acceptable to the Lord to teach children itn witt & Confidence boyes & of ofspno, then to teach men, wth profitating of Confidence to thwarants mbortions of ye Sonnes of men. And yet ebon yo filens from teaching now in a way of publique ministry, crysth with a lowd voyce, that there be such corruptings in publique administrations, ad a ton = — son — Confidens would rather those Conscience in pueris infrueolis, & mone while after the Ante to thate to fall, then both to Support it by an Endeav = -full hand. The Lord supports yo spirit in all yo2 Employmts, & offer them to ye best furtherance of yu & tworshipp in the flying.

If it is hopes me to route ms Wilford Named in go tho to whom I am So much beholding for his loving & often Intertaynmt. I know not where the road, but now perhaps you may nch bring a this to him. I pray to yo him and inlarg. Forgett me not (Searo brethren) in yo2 carnett Prayers before ye Lord: vere cannot forgett you. So taking leave of yor

yoᴱ bnworthy, yet very loving freind & brother
John Cotton_.

Boston. this 26. of 6. 1640.

Courtesy of Boston Public Library

PART OF A LETTER BY COTTON TO ELMERTON

(Facsimile slightly reduced)

A Modell of Church-goverment

The Synod at Cambridge (aheing nominated sundry of the *Elders, to draw vp each of them a seuerall modell of church-goverment, and amongst others (being nominated pud for one for y^t purpose to goe and get out of ye seuerall modells y^t ye govt might be out reposed, such as ye Synod should joyntly agree vpon; I therefore vpon y^is occasion and Call drew vp y^is y^t followes, & presented it to ye Synod at y^ir next meeting, wch being then by ye Synod deliberately read and prused, they afterward agreed vpon y^t wch now is published and printed as the Platformne agreed vpon by ye Synod; wch most of y^ings and y^is of myne being compared, it may appeare that the doctrine sprnin by me expressed & delivered was well approoved of by y^t Reuered & juditious Assembly:

R: M:

Courtesy of American Antiquarian Society   *(Facsimile slightly reduced)*

A RICHARD MATHER MANUSCRIPT
Introduction to his Draft of the Cambridge Platform.

John Cotton—Not Richard Mather

hand; the characters are larger and more formal, but their kind may be found in some of his letters. The instruction at the end, in brackets, "And so goe on in shewing what other things have bene attended to in this Transaction according to the Letter which was read at Dortchester," was evidently addressed to the Cambridge pastor. It may be justly assumed that Shepard complied and added the section about abbreviations, dilations, use of synonyms (such as "folk" for "people," "God" for "Jehovah," "reioice" for "shout for ioye"), and other such matters.[6] He may also have done the final editing—not to the advantage of the piece. As noted before, the draft lost its spotaneity in the condensation and, at times, even its lucidity. Living near the press, Shepard probably acted as proofreader and adviser to the printer.

The last paragraph of the Preface, following the portion supplied by Shepard, may also be by Cotton. These are the lines that, taken from an earlier passage of the draft, reaffirm the faithfulness of the translation, asking possible critics to consider that "Gods Altar needs not our polishings."

IV

The New England Psalm Book

CONTEMPORARIES realized that not all was well with the Bay Psalm Book, that, as Cotton Mather expressed it, "a little more Art was to be employ'd" upon it. In 1647 a second edition appeared in England, but by then the ministers had decided upon a revision. The work was committed to Henry Dunster, president of Harvard and "a very good Hebrician," who with "some Assistance" from Richard Lyon (sent over by Sir Henry Mildmay as an attendant to his son, a student at the college) "Revised and Refined" the translation.[1]

The revision was printed by Samuel Green at the Cambridge press in 1651 under the title *The Psalms Hymns and Spiritual Songs of the Old and New Testament, faithfully translated into English metre*.[2] The hymns and spiritual songs, which preceded and followed the psalms, were extensive. They included the Songs of Moses, of Deborah and Barak, of Hannah, David's Elegy, the whole Song of Songs, the Songs of Isaiah, the Lamentations of Jeremiah, the Prayer of Habakkuk, and the Song of the Virgin. The book was intended, as is stated on the title-page, "For the use, edification, and comfort of the Saints, in publick and private, especially in New-England." Adopted at once in the Bay Colony, and also by the new churches

The New England Psalm Book

outside, it became known as the New England Psalm Book.

Many of the psalms were considerably rewritten, but the larger number remained essentially the same. Even in the case of rewriting, there were few changes in the vocabulary; only the rhymes were corrected— or spoiled. Thus, under a new name, the Bay Psalm Book materially survived; or, to quote Cotton Mather again, it was "brought into the Condition wherein our Churches ever since have used it." The work won popular favor even among the Puritans of England and Scotland and was reprinted more than fifty times during the next hundred years.[3]

Dunster and Lyon were content with their accomplishment. "Wee have with speciall care & diligence translated," they claimed extravagantly, "into such Meeters as are most usuall and suitable for such holy Poems, in our own language, having a special ey both to the gravity of the phrase of Sacred writt, and sweetness of the verse." The supposition is that Dunster supplied the Hebrew knowledge, Lyon the poetical talent. Further, Lyon is believed to have written the hymns and spiritual songs.[4]

Yet the new psalm book did not seem to give complete satisfaction either. "I heartily join with those Gentlemen," Cotton Mather commented, "who wish that the Poetry hereof were mended." Of course, Cotton Mather was not a disinterested observer. Since early youth he had been dreaming of his own psalm book "for Use among the People of God"; and in 1718 he completed at last his *Psalterium Americanum*.[5] "Of all the more than twice Seven Versions

The Enigma of the Bay Psalm Book

which I have seen," he wrote in the Introduction, "it must be affirmed, that they leave out a vast heap of those rich things, which the Holy Spirit of God speaks in the Original Hebrew; and that they put in as large an Heap of poor Things, which are intirely their own. All this has been meerly for the sake of preserving the Clink of the Rhime." And he declared with his customary bashfulness: "This Translation may deserve some Thanks from the Religious part of Mankind, for having tendered a plain, clear, fair sense of many Passages, which have hitherto been so Translated, that People could scarce tell how well to understand them." Although the earlier translations suffered from excessive Hebraisms, his own version was, naturally, "much more agreeable to the Original, than the Old one, or than any that has yet been offered unto the World."[6]

Unfortunately, "Mankind" proved less grateful for Cotton Mather's endeavor than he had expected. His flock at the North Church may have sung his blank verses, but the rest of the colony stuck to the old version. The New England Psalm Book held its ground even against the new version by Tate and Brady and the one by Isaac Watts. However, by the middle of the eighteenth century the work had run its course. One church after another voted for a change. Thomas Prince vainly tried to stop the trend. His own "revised and improved" edition, published in 1758, was adopted by his own congregation alone; and by 1786 even his people turned to Watts's psalms and hymns.[7]

V

Problems for the Scholar

THE Bay Psalm Book was by then merely a memory. In 1829 Samuel Kettell the anthologist described its versification as "harsh and unmusical to the last degree." But it remained for Moses C. Tyler to deliver the deadly thrust that put the book beyond the pale of literary consideration:

In turning over these venerable pages, one suffers by sympathy something of the obvious toil of the undaunted men who, in the very teeth of nature, did all this; and whose appalling sincerity must, in our eyes, cover a multitude of such sins as sentences wrenched about end for end, clauses heaved up and abandoned in chaos, words disembowelled or split quite in two in the middle, and dissonant combinations of sound that are the despair of such poor vocal organs as are granted to human beings. The verses, indeed, seem to have been hammered out on an anvil, by blows from the blacksmith's sledge. Everywhere in the book, is manifest the agony it cost the writers to find two words that would rhyme—more or less; and as often as this arduous feat is achieved, the poetic athlete appears to pause awhile from sheer exhaustion, panting heavily for breath.[1]

It would not have been easy to defend the book in the face of such an indictment. But no one has even tried. On the contrary, as if to preclude the dreaded charge of provincialism, scholars have outdone each

The Enigma of the Bay Psalm Book

other in their ridiculing of the work. The most sympathetic merely wondered why the ministers had to rush into print with their "uncouth" translation instead of being content with the Sternhold-Hopkins version. Yet the latter had once its own fair share of abuse. Thomas Warton called it "obsolete and contemptible," "an absolute travesty," in every part of which "we are disgusted with a languor of versification and a want of common prosody."[2] And Thomas Campbell thought that "Sternhold and Hopkins degraded the spirit of Hebrew psalmody by flat and homely phraseology; and mistaking vulgarity for simplicity, turned into bathos what they found sublime."[3] Nevertheless, the Sternhold-Hopkins version managed to survive, reaching its six-hundredth edition by the end of the nineteenth century.

One does not have to compare the poetry of the New England Puritans with that of England; nobody would expect that a small colony could produce similar values. It should be sufficient glory, indeed, that one of the great prose works of the century—*The Bloudy Tenent of Persecution*—was written by an American, even if he was banished to live among the Indians. On the other hand, it is proper to consider the poetical efforts of the Puritans in the spirit of the age. We have done less than this, Professor Harold S. Jantz insists, because of the traditional premise that early Puritan verse is "provincial, awkward, dull, and often involuntarily funny." We have misapplied, he writes, "the critical standards of eighteenth-century smoothness and nineteenth-century romantic lyri-

Problems for the Scholar

cism to seventeenth-century Baroque verse which had no interest in being either smooth or romantic"; and he suggests that the early New England poets should be regarded as "belated conceptists, fifty or more years after the decline of that poetic fashion in Europe." He is even able to distinguish several groups: the early Baroque, which includes the founding fathers; the high Baroque, comprising the younger immigrants; and the late Baroque, with the native poets and late-comers—appellations which would have greatly surprised those pious ministers.[4]

Yet in discussing the Bay Psalm Book, Professor Jantz does not seem to apply his own criteria. He does not feel obliged to, since none of his "triumvirate of Bay Psalmists"—Welde, Eliot, and Mather—were poets. "The painful accuracy," he casually remarks, "with which the three rendered the original Hebrew Psalms into English produced rhythmic effects which even at that time aroused a certain holy risibility." But what if the translation was made not by those three men alone but also by John Cotton, John Wilson, Nathaniel Ward, Peter Bulkeley, Thomas Shepard, John Norton, and others of the founding fathers and younger immigrants? Professor Jantz is willing to admit that "the reverend versifiers do here and there attain to fairly reputable verse, as for instance in Psalms 103 and 107."[5] And the *other* instances?—for the expression implies the existence of such. Or is the poetry of the Puritans so rich that they can be quietly discarded?

In no other part of early Colonial poetry is "our

The Enigma of the Bay Psalm Book

lack of basic factual knowledge," of which Professor Jantz complains, so complete as concerning the Bay Psalm Book. And this applies to both the principles and the details of the translation.

The worst reproach brought against the work is its extreme literalness. Yet the desire for faithfulness was not a unique obsession with the clergy of the Bay Colony—it was the general trend of high Calvinism. The reaction against the fourfold interpretation of the Bible began with the early Reformers. Already Wyclif and John Huss insisted that the Bible should be its own interpreter. Tyndale urged: "The Scripture hath but one sense, which is the literal sense, and that literal sense is the root and ground of all, and the anchor that never faileth."[6] Luther, too, warned that "every word should be allowed to stand in its natural meaning"; but his liberal trust in "the rule of faith" led to a return to the medieval speculations. Calvin and his followers were more rigorous: the Second Helvetic Confession declared, "We acknowledge only that interpretation for orthodox and genuine which is taken from the Scriptures themselves, that is, from the spirit of that tongue in which they were written. . . ." And the English Puritans, ever on guard against "Popish practices," were even more uncompromising than their Continental brethren. Thomas Cartwright reasserted that "the Scriptures are the rule, the line, the squyre and light, whereby to examine and trie all judgements and sayings of men and of angels, whether they be such as God approveth, yea or no."[7] In their desperate search for

Problems for the Scholar

the strict grammatical sense, for the true meaning of God's words, the translators of the Bay Psalm Book were men of their time.

Nor is literal translation necessarily a crime, even on purely aesthetic grounds. There are no universally acknowledged rules of translation. Some allow considerable freedom to the translator if his work sounds like an original poem; others insist on the exact rendering of every shade of every word. Great names could be quoted from both camps; but, curiously enough, the modern bias seems to be toward grammatical accuracy. "The clumsiest literal translation," a writer has recently pronounced, "is a thousand times more useful than the prettiest paraphrase."[8] The Bay Colony ministers opposed the extremists on both sides—those who would tolerate only a prose translation of the Psalms as well as those who indulged in free imitation. Without knowing it, they were really engaged in a dispute over the theory of translation!

Of course, they carried their Hebraisms too far. As Cotton Mather wisely observed eighty years later: "If you Translate a French Book, suppose, into English, you turn it into English Phrase, and make not a French English of it; For, *Il fait froid*, for instance, you do not say, *It makes Cold*, but, *It is Cold*."[9] Yet one cannot always judge a translation by ear alone. Without special scrutiny, it is impossible to decide whether certain tortured expressions are the ministers' own inventions or were borrowed from some respectable source, whether they are willful

The Enigma of the Bay Psalm Book

distortions or contain a variation of meaning never revealed before.

The translators must have begun their work with a minute study of the prose psalter included in the Bible. But which version of the Bible did they use? The question can be answered only by a checking of the scriptural quotations in their tracts and sermons. The results of a cursory review seem enlightening. Those of the younger generation, who had received their education after the publication of the King James Version in 1611, adopted exclusively this text. Thus the writings of Richard Mather, John Eliot, Thomas Shepard, John Norton, and their contemporaries have no trace of the Geneva Bible.[10] The older men, on the other hand, used both the Geneva Bible and the King James Version but in varying proportion. Peter Bulkeley undoubtedly preferred the first. Once, quoting from the King James Version, he affectionately added: "and our Geneva reade. . . ."[11] John Wilson seems to have depended on both. Cotton's case was exceptional. In spite of his age, he used more often the King James than the Genevan. But this was probably due to his long residence at Cambridge University, and partly to his desire to conform to the prevailing practice.[12] However, a fuller investigation is needed, for the matter is important in tracing the authorship of the individual translations.

It is only sensible to assume that the ministers, men trained at the universities, did not go at their task blindly, without learning what the earlier translators had accomplished—at least in regard to pre-

Problems for the Scholar

cision if not literary skill. They respected Sternhold and Hopkins, and said so. "Wee have cause to blesse God in many respects," the Preface to the Bay Psalm Book stated, "for the religious indeavours of the translaters of the psalmes into meetre usually annexed to our Bibles." It was to the paraphrasing and alterations of sense that they objected. The Pilgrims' Psalter they naturally knew well; as noted before, they found its tunes "difficult," but otherwise did not criticize it.[13] They also had copies of the translation started by King James but really done by the Earl of Stirling; and they must have known George Wither's rendering into "lyrick-verse." George Sandys's *Paraphrase upon the Psalms*, 1636, might have scared them away by its very title, although they were interested in his translation of Ovid.[14] Richard Brathwaite's *Psalmes of David*, 1638, had again a better chance.[15] The question is: To what extent did they consult these earlier metrical versions?

Whether the ministers had recognized that one of the main characteristics of Hebrew prosody was parallelism, they did not say, but in their translation they acted upon the principle. The Preface noted that "there are many verses together in several psalmes of David which run in rithmes"; and Cotton's *Singing of Psalmes* further emphasized that "the verses observe a certain number and measure of syllables, and some of them run in meeter also."[16] One could not ask for more. The subject was fairly new; Johann Reuchlin's *De Accentibus Linguae Hebraicae*, with the monk Boeschenstein's chapter on the

The Enigma of the Bay Psalm Book

musical rendering of the Hebrew accents (*teamim*) appeared only in 1518. Deriving his information mainly from Buxtorf's *Thesaurus*, Cotton spoke with familiarity about the "musical Accents" of the psalms. Modern scholarship has not progressed much farther; it is still unable to identify the rhythms and tonal intervals of the melodies (*neginoth*). The comparative study of the music of ancient Egypt and Babylonia and of the surviving music systems of Syria, Persia, and other Near Eastern countries has produced only vague theories about the music of the Temple.[17]

There was certainly no lack of source material for research. Whatever the emigrating Puritans might have left behind, their books were not a part of it. Nor did they ever stop ordering new ones; every ship that sailed for the colony included a large consignment of books in its cargo. John Harvard's library, when the college received it in 1638, comprised 400 volumes; John Cotton thought that his books were worth £150, although, he adduced, they had cost him more; and there were few ministers, even in the outlying parishes, without their Hebrew grammars, concordances, and the huge folios of the leading Reformers. Theological works formed the largest section of these libraries, and among them were many expositions of the psalms. The translators of the Bay Psalm Book must have examined the commentaries of Calvin, Musculus, Osiander, Rivetus, and many others, all of which they possessed.[18]

It is doubtful that the problems of "higher

Problems for the Scholar

criticism" worried them much. Under the influence of the humanists, the Reformers were open to the new ideas about the historical dates of the various books of the Bible. The first sentence of Calvin's *Commentary* reads: "He who collected the Psalms into one volume, whether Ezra or someone else. . . ." However, by the seventeenth century a dogmatic revival set in, which insisted on David's authorship of all the psalms. The ministers of the Bay Colony sympathized with this turn, but they could hardly ignore the contrary evidences. Thus they followed the Hebrew Psalter in dividing their translation into five books, with the note after the second: "The prayers of David, the Son of Jesse, are ended," although a number of psalms by Asaph and the Sons of Korah were included in the first two books, and eighteen more psalms ascribed to David came afterward. And, in spite of the attributions of nearly thirty psalms to other persons, they spoke of "Davids words" and "Davids poetry," using the name interchangeably for the whole work. One may justly ask how they could explain Psalms 126 and 137 without recognizing their post-Exilic origin or account for the repetitions of certain psalms and for the use of "Jehovah" in some of the books and "Elohim" in others,[19] without realizing that the Psalter was a composite of earlier collections.

Only Ainsworth's translation marked the fivefold division, but the prose versions too added the "finis" clause after Psalm 72. At that point Ainsworth noted that "Davids prayers are not set last in order."

The Enigma of the Bay Psalm Book

However, it was only in the next generation that scholars, led by Grotius, began to discuss in earnest these contradictions and confusions.

These are some of the problems that the student of the Bay Psalm Book has to keep in mind.

VI
Experiments in Textual Analysis

As an illustration of the literary inferiority of the Bay Psalm Book, Professor Tyler presents part of Psalm 58, which, as one may remember, is a prayer for the delivery of the righteous from unjust judges. Why not start with this? First the King James Version and then the Bay Psalm Book are quoted. No matter how familiar the former is, it is only fair to print both texts in the original spelling. Put in modern spelling and punctuation, much of the oddity of the Bay Psalm Book, too, would disappear.[1]

The wicked are estranged from the wombe, they goe astray as soone as they be borne, speaking lies.

>The wicked are estranged from
>the womb, they goe astray
>as soone as ever they are borne;
>uttering lyes are they.

There is nothing queer—one notes incredulously—about the lines of the Bay Psalmists. They repeat the King James Version almost verbatim. Next:

Their poison is like the poyson of a serpent; they are like the deafe adder that stoppeth her eare:
Which will not hearken to the voyce of charmers, charming never so wisely.

>Their poyson's like serpents poyson:
>they like deafe Aspe, her eare
>that stops. Though Charmer wisely charme,
>his voice she will not heare.

The Enigma of the Bay Psalm Book

The Bay Psalmists write "deafe Aspe" (as Ainsworth did) instead of "deafe adder"—surely a permissible change and, incidentally, one used by the Jewish Version of 1917.[2] Nor is there any essential difference between the "hearken" of the King James Version and the "heare" of the Bay Psalm Book; in fact, all the earlier translators chose "hear." There is, however, the clumsy inversion, "her eare that stops," blocking the flow of the verse. But inversions were more frequent and therefore less reprehensible in the seventeenth century. And finally comes the sixth verse, the ridiculous sound of which in the words of the Bay Psalmists must have been the reason for Tyler's selection of the piece:

> Within their mouth doe thou their teeth
>   break out, o God most strong,
> doe thou Iehovah, the great teeth
>   break of the lions young.

Yet a glance at the King James Version shows that the Bay Psalmists were not so absurd after all: "Breake their teeth, O God, in their mouth: breake out the great teeth of the young lyons, O Lord." The earlier translators spoke of the "jawbones," "tusks," "fangs," and "grinders" of the young lions; the Bay Psalmists relied instead on the King James Version. Their only addition was the adjective "most strong" after "O God," to have it rhyme with "young." Here, too, they contracted an inversion, but this rather strengthens the utterance.

These few verses comprise sixty-nine words in the King James Version and sixty-eight in the Bay Psalm

Experiments in Textual Analysis

Book. In Sternhold-Hopkins they require ninety-five words. This is the proportion throughout: the Bay Psalm Book consists of about the same number of words as the prose translations, whereas the Sternhold-Hopkins version uses nearly one-third more. The ministers of the Bay Colony wanted "to keep close to the original text," making "a plain translation" rather than smooth their verses "with the sweetness of any paraphrase." Yet they wished to have meter and rhyme! No wonder that, without any elbow-room to move about, they had to resort to inversion. It is instructive to see that Dunster and Lyon in their effort to achieve "a little more of Art" were forced to use nearly as many words as Sternhold and Hopkins.

One turns with curiosity to Psalm 1—*Beatus ille*—which may be considered as an introduction to the whole book. Touchingly simple, it is a bold assertion of faith in the moral government of the world. What did the Bay Psalmists do with this beautiful poem? Let us quote again the King James Version and then the Bay Psalm Book:

Blessed is the man that walketh not in the counsell of the ungodly, nor standeth in the way of sinners, nor sitteth in the seat of the scornefull.

> O Blessed man, that in th'advice
> of wicked doeth not walk:
> nor stand in sinners way, nor sit
> in chayre of scornfull folk.

Like the Geneva Bible, the Bay Psalm Book has

The Enigma of the Bay Psalm Book

"wicked" instead of "ungodly." It speaks of "chayre" instead of "seat," in contrast to all the prose versions but in consonance with Sternhold and Hopkins, who borrowed it from the Vulgate's *cathedra*. The next verse:

> But in the law of Iehovah,
>   is his longing delight:
> and in his law doth meditate,
>   by day and eke by night.

The last two lines were copied from the Ainsworth Psalter; no other translation has the tell-tale "eke." Ainsworth's influence is also felt in the third verse. The Bay Psalmists say "in his season yeilds his fruit," where all other versions translate "bringeth forth his fruit" and Ainsworth himself has "shall give his fruit." But Ainsworth includes among his notes: "When it beareth or yeildeth fruit." The fourth verse ends:

> but they are like unto the chaffe,
>   which winde drives to and fro.

The felicitous "the winde drives to and fro" comes from the Sternhold-Hopkins version, which, like the Vulgate, used "dust" (*pulvis*) instead of "chaffe."

The fifth and sixth verses contain two expressions original to the Bay Psalm Book and far closer to the Hebrew sense than those of any of the other translations. For the King James Version's "Therefore the ungodly shall not stand in the iudgement . . . ," the Bay Psalmists offer:

> Therefore shall not ungodly men,
>   rise to stand in the doome

Experiments in Textual Analysis

Ainsworth indicates "rise to stand" (together with "shall not stand") as a proper meaning for the Hebrew *yakumu*, without employing it in his own translation. And finally the last verse, "For the Lord knoweth the way of the righteous: but the way of the ungodly shall perish."

> For of the righteous men, the Lord
>   acknowledgeth the way:
> but the way of ungodly men,
>   shall utterly decay.

Again the Hebrew word *yodeᶜa* means "acknowledges" rather than "knoweth." Modern biblical scholars, who probably have never set eyes on the Bay Psalm Book, recognize "rise to stand" and "acknowledges" as preferable to the phrases used in the other versions. The last line, "shall utterly decay," was taken again from Ainsworth.

The translation, as has been seen, is a compendium of selections from many sources. But, with remarkable skill, the author chose the best words and expressions for both style and fidelity. Come what may, this writer affirms that the Bay Psalm Book translation of Psalm 1 is admirable.

The famous Psalm 23, the praise of Jehovah as Protector of the pilgrim, begins: "The Lord is my shepheard; I shall not want. He maketh me to lie down in greene pastures: He leadeth mee beside the still waters."

> The Lord to mee a shepheard is,
>   want therefore shall not I.

The Enigma of the Bay Psalm Book

> Hee in the folds of tender-grasse,
> doth cause mee downe to lie:
> To waters calme mee gently leads.

For the charming "green pastures" the ingenious "folds of tender-grasse" was substituted. The translator must have been fond of the Bishops Bible, which had: "He wyll cause me to repose myselfe in pasture full of grasse, and he wyll leade me unto calme waters." The words "cause me," "grasse," and "waters calme" all come from there. However, "grasse" became "tender-grasse"—taken evidently from William Whittingham's translation in the Sternhold-Hopkins version. And then one suddenly recalls John Cotton's poem on the death of Thomas Hooker, with its line "Viret, like Rain [was wont] on tender grass to shower...."[3]

The rendering of the third verse agrees with the King James Version. In the fourth, one is sorry to see "valley of the shadow of death" changed into "valley of deaths shade" (under the influence of Calvin's *Commentary*, which quotes the Jewish grammarians to the effect that *zalmaveth* meant "death-shade"). In any case, the loss is nothing compared to Whittingham's "Though I were even at deaths door."

The fifth verse holds a fresh surprise! Instead of "Thou preparest a table before me" of the King James and all other prose versions, one reads, "For mee a table thou hast spread," as in the second translation of the psalm in the Sternhold-Hopkins Psalter, made by Sternhold himself. But the very words occur also in Cotton's poem on God's Providence: "In all my meals my table thou hast spread...." Surely, two

Experiments in Textual Analysis

lines of a short psalm which appear also in two of his three existing poems must reveal Cotton's hand in the translation—as indeed one expects that he would reserve the Twenty-third Psalm for himself.

The last verse merely emphasizes the translator's dependence upon the King James Version:

Surely goodnes and mercie shall followe me all the daies of my life: and I will dwell in the house of the Lord for ever.

> Goodnes & mercy surely shall
> all my dayes follow mee:
> and in the Lords house I shall dwell
> so long as dayes shall bee.

Everyone has his favorite psalms; the present writer is particularly fond of the songs of nature. Here are some magnificent verses from Psalm 8, according to the King James Version:

When I consider thy heavens, the worke of thy fingers, the moone and the starres which thou hast ordained;
What is man, that thou art mindfull of him? and the sonne of man, that thou visitest him?
For thou hast made him a little lower than the Angels; and hast crowned him with glory and honour.

And this is what the Bay Psalmists made of it:

> when I thy fingers work, thy Heav'ns,
> the moone and starres consider:
> which thou hast set. What's wretched man,
> that thou dost him remember?
> or what's the Son of man, that thus
> him visited thou hast?
> For next to Angells, thou hast him
> a litle lower plac't
> and hast with glory crowned him,
> and comely majesty.

The Enigma of the Bay Psalm Book

"Wretched man" (the "poore wretch" of the James-Stirling version) is an innovation for "man," and the Hebrew text may supply the reason: the original word is *enosh*, which means not just "man" but "the weak one." Ainsworth had the rather pleasing "fraylman" with "Adams son" instead of "the son of man," both of which were adopted by Richard Brathwaite in 1638. The rhyme "hast" and "plac't" makes one wince; yet it may have been acceptable in the seventeenth century. In any case, it was probably copied from Wither's translation.

Psalm 19, too, is a nature song, as well as a song of praise. Says the King James Version: "Day unto day uttereth speach, and night unto night sheweth knowledge"; and the Bay Psalmists, quite on their own, have it:

> Day speaks to day, knowledge
> night hath to night declar'd.

The writer submits that this is not only a beautiful but an inspired translation. And then the next image: "Which [the Sun] is as a bridegrome comming out of his chamber, and reioyceth as a strong man to runne a race," is rendered as

> Who Bridegroom like from's chamber goes
> glad Giants-race to run.

This, too, is excellent. The use of "giant" instead of "strong man" goes back to the Prayer Book Version, or rather to the Septuagint (*hos gígas*); the Hebrew original, *gibbor*, means only "a strong man." Sternhold metrified it as follows:

Experiments in Textual Analysis

> In them the Lord made for the Sun
>   a place of great renowne:
> Who like a bridegroom ready trim'd
>   doth from his Chamber come.

There is really nothing as funny as that in the whole Bay Psalm Book. Thomas Warton, in pointing out that "ready trim'd" was nothing more than "freshshaved," uses these lines as an example of Sternhold's way of "impairing a splendid description by an impotent redundancy."

Psalm 36 invokes the mercies of the Creator on a journey to the Jordan Valley. Behind the traveler rise the mountains of Jerusalem, and before him lie the deeps of the Dead Sea; God will nourish him with food and fresh water in the desert: "Thy righteousnesse is like the great mountaines; thy iudgements are a great deepe; O Lord, thou preservest man and beast."

> Thy judgements a great deep, like great
>   mountains thy righteousnes:
> Thou savest man & Beast, o Lord.

One wishes that the Bay Psalmists had used here the Bishops Bible's more majestic "mountaynes of God," based on the Vulgate's *montes Dei*. But it was a question of interpretation; for the Hebrew words are *Keharere El*, and *El* may mean both "God" and, as an adjective, "mighty" or "great."

Everyone knows the opening line of Psalm 42: "As the Hart panteth after the water brookes, so panteth my soule after thee, O God. . . ." One approaches the Bay Psalm Book with misgivings:

The Enigma of the Bay Psalm Book

> Like as the Hart panting doth bray
> after the water brooks,
> even in such wise o God, my soule,
> after thee panting looks.

"Panting doth bray" is embarrassing. But the Geneva Bible also has "braieth," and the Bishops Bible even starts the same way: "Lyke as the Hart brayeth." Hopkins, too, insisted on the sound: "Like as the Hart doth breath & bray, / the well-springs to obtaine. . . ." One should remember that, at the time, the verb was used about many animals, not only the ass. Spenser made even the tiger bray ("The Lyons rore; the Tygres loudly bray . . ."). The Hebrew word is *taᶜarog*, which, like the Arabic *ᶜaraja*, means "heavy breathing in ascent." Jerome mistook it for a derivative of *ᶜaragah*, "a garden bed," and gave the fanciful rendering: "As the garden is made ready for irrigating waters, so is my soul made ready for thee, O God." (The present-day Vulgate contains, of course, the correct translation.)

A powerful declaration of faith in God—written probably in the days of Isaiah to celebrate the deliverance of Jerusalem from the Assyrians—Psalm 46 begins: "God is our refuge and strength: a very present helpe in trouble." The Bay Psalmists render it:

> God is our refuge, strength, & help
> in troubles very neere.

This is close to the Geneva Bible. The next verse has

> though th'earth removed were.
> Though mountaines move to midst of seas

Experiments in Textual Analysis

One notes the word "move" instead of "rushe" or "be carried" of the earlier translations—and one which was accepted by the Revised Version of 1885! But the most notable verse is the ninth, which has been celebrated as a promise of universal peace: "He maketh warres to cease unto the end of the earth: hee breaketh the bow, and cutteth the speare in sunder, he burneth the chariot in the fire." The Bay Psalm Book renders it, very creditably, as

> Unto the utmost ends of th'earth
>   warres into peace hee turnes:
> the speare he cuts, the bowe he breaks,
>   in fire the chariots burnes.

However, the meaning of the psalm has been questioned: the original word *milhamoth* (plural of *milhamah*) signifies both war and an army, and the Hebrew Psalmist may have intended to declare that the Lord will kill the hosts of the enemy rather than that He turns war into peace. The translation of *ᶜad ketzé haʾaretz* would then be "throughout the land of Israel" and not "unto the utmost ends of the earth." One may note that the Jewish Version of 1917 upholds the universal application of the verse.

The question of the six psalms (Psalms 16, 25, 51, 88, 113, and 137) which Francis Quarles sent to John Cotton deserves special attention. Were they incorporated in the translation? And if so, is it possible to recognize them, by stylistic evidence, as the work of the skilled English poet? Unfortunately, lack of space forbids the examination of all the psalms involved.

The Enigma of the Bay Psalm Book

Psalm 25, an impassioned appeal to Jehovah, goes along smoothly, close to the King James Version. The sixth verse, "Remember, O Lord, thy tender mercies, and thy lovingkindnesses: for they have beene ever of old," reads

> Thy bowels, Lord, & thy mercyes
> minde; for they are for aye.

One prefers "lovingkindness," the Vulgate's *misericordia*, to "bowels"; yet the Hebrew word is *rahameka*, derived from *rehem*, "womb," which is rendered by the King James Version as "thy bowels" in Isa. 63:15. Sternhold merely wrote: "thy mercies manifold / I pray thee Lord remember."

The fifteenth verse, "Mine eyes are ever towards the Lord: for hee shall plucke my feete out of the net," is given as

> Mine eyes continually are
> upon Iehovah set:
> for it is hee that will bring forth
> my feet out of the net.

"Will bring forth my feet" lacks the pungency of "plucke my feete," but it is more accurate. It may have been original with the Bay Psalm Book, or it may have been taken over from Brathwaite ("To bring my feet out of the net"). It is worth noting that the Jewish Version translates the line exactly the same way.

Then the phrasing of the next verse, "Turne thee unto me, and have mercy upon me: for I am desolate and afflicted," gives a sudden jolt:

Experiments in Textual Analysis

> Unto me-wards turne thou thy face,
>   and on mee mercy show:
> because I solitary am
>   afflicted poore also.

The awkwardness of the first line is pathetic. The forceful "I am desolate," too, was changed to the poor "I solitary am." However, the translation may have been right, for the Hebrew *yahid* means "a lonely one." Indeed, the Jewish Version gives: "For I am solitary and afflicted"—the second agreement with the Bay Psalm Book in the same psalm. Was it a mere coincidence?

Psalm 51, the great *Miserere mei*, would be difficult to pass over. As in Sternhold-Hopkins (and nowhere else), there are two versions. It is more charitable to concentrate on the first. The sixth verse, "Behold, thou desirest trueth in the inward parts: and in the hidden part thou shalt make me to know wisedome," reads:

> Behold, thou dost desire the truth
>   within the inward part:
> and thou shalt make mee wisdome know
>   in secret of my heart.

"The inward part" is the equivalent of the Hebrew *tuhoth;* the "secret of my heart," which comes from the Geneva and Bishops Bibles, stands for *satum,* "secret." In the tenth and eleventh verses the Psalmist prays: "Create in mee a cleane heart, O God; and renew a right spirit within mee. Cast mee not away from thy presence; and take not thy holy Spirit from me." In the Bay Psalm Book:

The Enigma of the Bay Psalm Book

> A cleane heart (Lord) in me create,
>   also a spirit right
> in me renew. O cast not mee
>   away out of thy sight;
> Nor from me take thy holy spirit.

The second version—for it cannot be entirely ignored—here produces something extraordinary:

> Create in mee cleane heart *at last*
>   God: a right spirit in me new make.
> Nor from thy presence quite me cast,
>   thy holy spright nor from me take.

Evidently, in their effort to approximate the Hebrew word *hadesh*, "to renew," the Bay Colony ministers did not want to lag behind their Plymouth brethren: "A right spirit in me new make" was borrowed from the Ainsworth poem.

The seventeenth verse, stressing the importance of spiritual rather than material sacrifice, expresses the deepest thought of the Hebrew Psalmist. The first version in the Bay Psalm Book reads

> The sacrifices of the Lord
>   they are a broken sprite:
> God, thou wilt not despise a heart
>   that's broken, & contrite.

"Sprite" (the "sprete" of the Prayer Book) was invented by Ainsworth.

One is almost ready to credit the first version of the psalm to the English poet. However, he is supposed to have also done Psalm 137—the most atrocious piece in the whole volume. This is how this song of beauty and vengeance begins:

Experiments in Textual Analysis

> The rivers on of Babilon
>   there when wee did sit downe:
> yea even then wee mourned, when
>   wee remembred Sion.

And then it goes on, from bad to worse:

> Because there they that us away
>   led in captivitee,
> Requir'd of us a song, & thus
>   askd mirth: us waste who laid,
> sing us among a Sions song,
>   unto us then they said.

No one but the Bay Psalmists could have fabricated such inversions! With a praiseworthy lack of squeamishness, Alexander B. Grosart included these "hitherto utterly over-looked" psalms in Quarles's collected works,[4] with no more justification than John Josselyn's brief testimony;[5] and American scholars surrendered the treasures without a word of protest.

The ministers of the Bay Colony were under no illusion of having produced memorable poetry. They knew that their verses were "not always so smooth and elegant" as might have been expected. But they were not abashed. "Conscience rather than Elegance, fidelity rather than poetry" was their aim. And the results were inevitable. The strain to attain the literal sense—almost as mystic as the allegories of the Schoolmen—choked the imagination of the translators, making their naturally lucid English cramped and obscure. Yet, in spite of themselves, they achieved many a fine line.[6]

VII

The Search for Authorship

WHAT do these few experiments prove? One can hardly expect the solution of the whole enigma, yet they allow some general conclusions.

The prevailing view of the "triumvirate of Bay Psalmists" can be safely discarded. The determination of the authorship of the individual translations is a difficult task; but assertions about its impossibility should not deter the student. The Twenty-third Psalm was almost certainly done by John Cotton, and there is no reason why the authors of other translations could not be similarly identified.[1] To begin with, phrases from the Geneva and Bishops Bibles offer a sound cue for setting aside certain psalms as the work of the older men. Not that the younger ministers, followers of the King James Version, could not have utilized the other versions; but the Psalms, more than any other part of the Bible, commanded the emotional attachment of early upbringing.[2]

One must be aware, of course, of the possibility of composite authorships; the translations, if they were submitted to a meeting of the ministers as was the Preface, might have undergone substantial changes. The uneven character of some, in which very good lines alternate with very bad ones, seems to argue

The Search for Authorship

for such a practice. For the most part, however, each translation is uniform in style.

The most obvious way of starting the search for authorship may be through key words taken from the known works of the ministers. The poems of John Wilson would have filled, according to his son, "a large Folio"; however, the manuscripts are lost and only a few of his compositions got into print. The elegy on the death of Joseph Brisco, issued as a broadside in 1657, is one of them.[3] In it are the lines:

> To those that do Blaspheme his Holy Name,
> and unto those that reverence the same . . .

The couplet has an echo of the Psalms; Psalm 74 is actually an appeal to God to punish the blasphemers of His sanctuary. The Bay Psalm Book renders some of its verses:

> How long shall the oppressing foe
> o mighty God, defame?
> thine enemy for evermore
> shall he blaspheme thy name?

One notes Wilson's rhyme, "Name" and the space-filling "the same." It occurs also in one of his poems on Thomas Shepard:

> and oh how should we bless his Name
> That on his Son powr's the same . . .[4]

The Name (for Jehovah) appears often in the Psalms, usually rhyming with "fame," "defame," "frame," and so on; but the artificial conjunction with "the same" turns up also in Psalms 69, 72, 86, 89, 118, and 148. Other ministers *could* have used the psalm's

The Enigma of the Bay Psalm Book

phrase and the rhyme, but the fact that Wilson *did* use them points in his direction.

Or one may consider Peter Bulkeley's long lamentation on the death of Thomas Hooker.[5] Its third and fourth lines read:

> A Man of God, which came from God to men,
> And now from them is gone to God agen.

The rhyme "men" and "agen" occurs only once in the Bay Psalm Book—in Psalm 90:

> and then thou sayst yee sonnes of men
> doe yee returne agen.

Bulkeley speaks of "Lebanus," as does Psalm 29 of the Bay Psalm Book. The younger ministers would have said, after the King James Version, "Lebanon"; the older ministers, on the other hand, might have used either "Lebanus" or "Lebanon" or both, for the early versions of the Bible gave the first, except the Genevan (so dear to Bulkeley), which had the second. Indeed, Psalm 29 of the Bay Psalm Book includes also "the mountaine of Lebanon." And there is a further resemblance: Psalm 29 extolls Jehovah as the God of Storm and Peace; and Bulkeley presents Hooker as a man of wrath and consolation, and employs similar images! (Psalm: "Iehovahs voyce doth make / the desert shake . . ."; Bulkeley: "And fear did Lebanus his Cedars shake . . . ," etc.).

These are only random probings and far from exhaustive even in the case of the two writers. They are certainly encouraging and should be tried in many more instances.

The Search for Authorship

There is still another approach that may yield good results—the comparison of the Bay Psalm Book with the New England Psalm Book. According to the extent of the revision, the psalms may be divided into three groups: those substantially rewritten, those partly altered, and those barely touched. The Twenty-third Psalm belongs to the last group. The original translation was good; and one may doubt, at any rate, that Dunster would have taken it upon himself to discard Cotton's verses. Of the other psalms discussed in the preceding section, Psalms 1, 42, and 46 received the same courteous treatment on the part of the revisers. One may confidently look for the work of the older ministers in this group, the more so since residues of the Geneva and Bishops Bibles are more conspicuous there.

Whatever their merit, the verses of the leaders deserved consideration. Psalms 110, 112, and 137 are cases in point. The original versions were obviously too crude; yet the revisers, no doubt to spare the sensitiveness of the writers, printed them with a few changes—and then added their own translation. Dunster and Lyon were in a position to know who wrote what; and they could not be greatly blamed if they felt freer with the work of those who had died (like Shepard) or returned to England (like Welde and Peters). Versifiers were as touchy then as they are today, and the remarkable thing is that apparently no enmities ensued from the publication of the new edition. That two years later Dunster lost his position as President of Harvard College was due to

The Enigma of the Bay Psalm Book

his heretical views on infant baptism, not to his tampering with the iambics of the ministers.[6]

Incidentally, the alternate version of Psalm 112 bears the initials of Richard Lyon—the only psalm whose authorship can be authenticated by external evidence. But even this single definite example of Lyon's participation in the revision seems to have been overlooked. Those twenty-four lines, with their intricate rhyme scheme, may furnish valuable hints for ascertaining the separate contributions of the two men and their manner of handling the original translations.

Only a line-by-line examination can reveal the peculiar qualities of the work and provide answers, if possible, to the questions of authorship. The study should be undertaken in any case. In the enormous literature on the Hebrew Psalter, entire volumes have been devoted to the dating of a few psalms, to the elucidation of abstruse topographical and historical allusions. The fraction of a similar effort may penetrate the mist surrounding the Bay Psalm Book. And it may show that what has seemed from afar a huge boulder is in fact a crudely wrought but respectable edifice.

VIII

The Psalm-singing of the Puritans

THE musical aspects of the Bay Psalm Book also deserve further investigation, as does indeed the entire subject of the music of the early Puritans. Historians have maintained that the early settlers of New England were hostile to all music but psalm-singing and that some were opposed even to that. "The history of music in New England, for the first two centuries," George Hood wrote in 1846, "is the history of Psalmody alone." Yet he meant no disparagement. "Between music and religion, in the churches of our land," he went on, "there has ever been a beautiful and intimate connection."[1] Hood's opinion was reaffirmed by his successors. "Music with the Puritans," F. L. Ritter added, "became a kind of sacred people's-song." The writer observed that the Cavaliers brought some secular music with them to Virginia and later to South Carolina, but this exercised little influence on American musical development; it was "from the crude form of a barbarously sung simple psalmody" that our musical culture emerged.[2] W. S. B. Matthews, Charles C. Perkins, Louis C. Elson, John Tasker Howard, and many others may be quoted to the same effect.

The Enigma of the Bay Psalm Book

They agreed that in the early days of New England instrumental music was looked upon "as a snare of the devil"; that "secular music of all kinds was sternly interdicted"; and that the Puritans often believed that music was "a useless and harmful instrument."[3]

Torn out of context, these statements may sound inimical—the very last thing of which the authors could be accused. If anything, they overrated the musical taste and training of the first settlers. Thus Hood accepted, without any questioning, that psalmody was "studied, known and approved" at Harvard College "for many years after its first founding"; and that numerous "musical theses," destroyed when the college library was burned down, had been printed at that time.[4] The fault of these writers was not partisanship but inaccuracy and lack of adequate research.[5]

Opinion about the English Puritans' musical interests, or, rather, indifference, had been very much the same. Henry Davey at the end of the last century created therefore quite a stir with his *History of English Music*, insisting that the Puritans' dislike of church music did not extend to secular music; that Cromwell, Milton, Bunyan, and many of their other leading men were ardent music lovers; and that English music-publishing really began during the Commonwealth.[6] Taking his own cue from Davey, Percy A. Scholes, in *The Puritans and Music in England and New England*, hoped to prove even more conclusively the fallacy of nineteenth-century historians. Undoubtedly he laid the ghosts of some obstinate

The Psalm-singing of the Puritans

errors; yet concerning the music of the colonists, where proof was most needed, the English scholar offered little that was new. Nor was he altogether objective, ignoring as he did some of the most revealing sources unfavorable to his position. Toward the end, Scholes admitted that he had "not gone deeply into research on questions of church music."[7]

Psalm-singing was, of course, not the only music of the Puritans. "There were popular ballads and folk-songs . . . ," Van Wyck Brooks writes, "sailors' chanties along the coast, ballads of village murders, rockaby songs, sugar-makers' songs, sung by weavers and carpenters, by farm-wives and wandering fiddlers, by hunters, trappers, guides and lumbermen, snatches and refrains and longer pieces, brought from the old world or natural outgrowths of the American soil."[8] The researches of folklorists—for it is to them rather than to music historians that one has to turn for evidence—have corroborated the confident assertion. A number of poems represented in Francis James Child's great collection, *The English and Scottish Popular Ballads* (Boston, 1882–98), were known to the early settlers, and they were transmitted orally.[9] The new press at Cambridge had no intention of perpetuating the profane beauties of "The Elfin Knight" or "The Golden Vanity"; its broadsides were mainly reserved for funeral verses to be pinned on the palls of coffins.

Nor did the students at Harvard College restrict their singing to psalms. Professor Morison calls attention to the notebook of Seaborn Cotton, a son of

The Enigma of the Bay Psalm Book

John Cotton, which contains three well-known English ballads—"The Love-Sick Maid," "The Last Lamentation of the Languishing Squire," and "The Two Faithful Lovers"—with fragments of others. They were copied before 1651, the year of young Cotton's graduation.

The most fertile breeding-ground of the popular song was the tavern. To be sure, in the early days of the colony the tavern was an institution very different from the one it became later. Located near the meeting house it was the gathering-place of worshipers and of the militia on training days. The town meeting, town council, and the courts usually assembled there. Indeed, the General Court required that every town sustain an ordinary. When John Cotton deprecated "the drunken, carnall Poets singing their carnall Sonnets in their Tavernes and Alehouses," he still had memories of the old country in mind.[10] By the end of the century, however, many of the taverns had changed into dens for the "idle." The Reverend Benjamin Wadsworth warned his people at the First Church against them, noting that "those wedded to bad Company have often a greater relish for Play-books, Romances, filthy Songs and Ballads than for the Holy Scriptures."[11] According to Cotton Mather, every other house in Boston was an alehouse. Visible Saints too frequently resorted to them, and not only for bare necessities of life. Increase Mather had to admonish his flock: "Tarry not in Taverns or Ordinary's or in Houses where Strong Drink is sold. . . . It is a sad thing, that Professors

The Psalm-singing of the Puritans

and Church-members should many of them be guilty of Scandalizing the world in this respect."[12]

A modern history of the music of early New England would assimilate the mass of material collected by the folklorists, yet the emphasis would still be decidedly on psalmody. Letters, diaries, inventories, and other records must be further searched—and the already known documents freshly examined.

The first abundant source for such a history is the Pilgrims' Psalter. Its "singing notes," as Ainsworth remarked, were taken from English psalms "when they fitted the measure of the verse," and from French and Dutch psalms when the long verses required "the gravest and easiest tunes." But many of the melodies of the English psalm books, too, came from the Huguenot Psalter. Ainsworth used, in all, thirty-nine tunes, representing fifteen types of stanza.[13] The Pilgrims, as mentioned before, learned them in Holland. Describing their departure for America, Edward Winslow feelingly recalled: "Wee refreshed ourselves after our teares with singing of Psalmes, making joyfull melody in our hearts, as well as with the voice, there being many of the Congregation very expert in Musick."[14] It was to the Pilgrims —and to the people of Salem and Ipswich who had adopted Ainsworth's Psalter—that the Reverend Thomas Symmes referred in writing a century later: "There are many persons of credit now living, children and grandchildren of the first settlers of New England, who can very well remember that their

The Enigma of the Bay Psalm Book

Ancestors sung by Note, and they learnt so to sing of them."[15]

However, the most authentic information of the music of the early Puritans may be gathered from the Bay Psalm Book itself. The singing of the Psalms was, indeed, foremost in the minds of the translators —the Preface starts out with the very words, and is devoted entirely to the subject. In defending "not only the lawfulness but the necessity" of singing psalms, the Preface took it for granted that the use of English tunes was justified. How could anyone object to them when "the Lord hath hid from us the hebrew tunes, lest wee should think our selves bound to imitate them"? The legitimacy of English tunes, in turn, bolstered the argument for the translating of the Psalms into English meter: "Every nation without scruple might follow," it argued, "as the graver sort of tunes of their owne country songs, soe the graver sort of verses of their owne country poetry." Musical instruments were a different matter. Innumerable passages of the Old Testament show that a variety of them—a large and small harp, a trumpet, and several kinds of flutes—were a part of the Temple service; their use, however, was "cerimoniall" rather than "morall," and they were not needed any longer in "the ripe age of the Church."

The Bay Psalm Book had no musical notations, but the "Admonition to the Reader" at the end discussed exclusively the tunes. "The verses of these psalmes," it stated, "may be reduced to six kindes, the first whereof may be sung in very neere fourty

The Psalm-singing of the Puritans

common tunes, as they are collected out of our chief musicians, by Tho. Ravenscroft." These verses of the "first kinde" were written in common meter, that is, in alternating lines of eight and six syllables. The second kind could be sung "in three tunes as Ps. 25, 50, and 67 in our english psalm books." Their pattern was: two lines of six, one line of eight, and one line again of six syllables. The third kind, the "Admonition" went on, could be sung "indifferently" as Psalms 51, 100, and the Ten Commandments in the English psalm books. Their verses were in long meter: in four lines of eight syllables each. These three kinds, the translators declared, "comprehend almost all this whole book of psalmes, as being tunes most familiar to us." The remaining handful of psalms employed three metrical schemes: four lines of six syllables alternating with four lines of four syllables; six lines of eight syllables; and eight lines of eight syllables. Thus any psalm could be sung to a variety of tunes, the choice being restricted only by the need to match the metrical system of psalm and tune.[16]

There were over a hundred tunes in Ravenscroft's Psalter—more than half by the compiler. The congregations of the Bay Colony were satisfied with many less. And they could hardly have had much interest in the complicated four-part settings, with their harmonic progressions, supplied by such composers as George Kirbye, Giles Farnaby, John Dowland, and Ravenscroft himself.

One of the most conspicuous innovations of the

The Enigma of the Bay Psalm Book

New England Psalm Book must have already been prompted by the deterioration of singing. The psalms described at the end of the Bay Psalm Book as associated with the fourth kind of tunes—Psalms 97, 99, 128, 147, and 148—were reprinted almost verbatim; but the singing of these verses must have overtaxed the musical faculties of the congregation, for the New England Psalm Book provided a new version in common meter for each. For six psalms written in long meter—Psalms 51, 85, 100, 117, 133, and 138—the Bay Psalm Book itself included substitute versions in common meter, all of which were retained in the New England Psalm Book. In addition, the latter furnished new versions in common meter for four more—Psalms 5, 86, 115, and 119. Thus they were all assimilated to the simpler common tunes.

But it is the Boston edition of 1698, the first known edition to have musical notations, that presents the best retrospective view of the changes that had taken place during the preceding half-century. The Bay Psalm Book still spoke of "neere fourty common tunes"; the little volume of 1698 contained only thirteen—eight short and five long. It gave also directions "for ordering the Voice."[17] To begin with, the compass of the tune must be observed, and then "place your first Note so . . . that the rest may be sung in the compass of your and the peoples voices, without Squeaking above, or Grumbling below." Six of the short tunes (Oxford, Litchfield, Low Dutch, York, Windsor, and Cambridge) were listed as

The Psalm-singing of the Puritans

suitable for consolatory psalms or for psalms of prayer, confession, and funerals. They could be started on "a cheerful high pitch," since their compass did not exceed five or six notes. The other two short tunes (St. David and Martyrs), used for psalms of thanksgiving, had to begin low, since they rose an octave above the first note. And finally, four of the five long tunes began on a low note; and one (the tune for Psalm 100) started "indifferent high," falling four notes below the first.[18]

No outline of early New England music, however meager, would be complete without mentioning Samuel Sewall. The Judge and his family, contrary to our general notions about the Puritans, loved music. On December 1, 1699, he jotted in his diary, "Was at Mr. Hillers to enquire for my wives virginals," which implies that Hiller either sold or repaired such instruments.[19] Sewall was a dauntless singer of psalms who filled the office of precentor at the Old South Church for twenty-four years. In his later years he made mistakes in setting the tune either too low or too high; and when in the winter of 1718 the incident repeated itself, he understood that his voice was "much enfeebled" and accordingly resigned. Luckily, his successor restored York tune to its station with "much Authority and Honor."[20]

But not all precentors were so conscientious as Sewall, nor were all congregations so easily righted as the Old South Church. The decline of singing was gradual. In 1667 the churches of Salem and Ipswich admitted that they could not sing the Ainsworth

The Enigma of the Bay Psalm Book

tunes "so well as formerly"; and in 1692 the Plymouth church itself went on record that "many of the psalms in Mr. Ainsworth's translation had such difficult tunes, that none in the church could set." All three turned to the New England Psalm Book.[21]

For most of the congregations even these simpler tunes proved too much. By the beginning of the new century, the state of psalm-singing had degenerated so much that the clergy became alarmed. Their tracts and sermons described the situation as approaching bedlam. "Everyone sang as best pleased himself," Thomas Symmes noted in 1720, "and every Leading-Singer would take the Liberty of raising any Note of the Tune, or lowering of it, as best pleas'd his Ear, and add such Turns and Flourishes as were grateful to him."[22] Others were even gloomier. "The tunes," Thomas Walter lamented in 1721, "are now miserably tortured, and twisted, and quavered, in some Churches, into an horrid Medly of confused and disorderly Noises." They were left "to the Mercy of every unskilful Throat to chop and alter, twist and change, according to their infinitely divers and no less odd Humours and Fancies." No two churches sang alike; no two men in the congregation quavered together. In the ears of a good judge, it sounded "like Five Hundred different Tunes roared out at the same time. . . ."[23] Walter's opinion was indorsed by fifteen ministers headed by Increase and Cotton Mather.

The clergy fought valiantly for the redemption of the psalmody. The controversy over singing by note

The Psalm-singing of the Puritans

("the regular way") or by rote ("the usual way") kept the congregations in violent excitement for years. The "reformation," which led to the establishment of the first singing schools and societies, marks the beginning of conscious musical culture in New England.[24]

IX

The Printing of the Bay Psalm Book

THE story of the printing of the book—and that of the first English press of America—must now be briefly told. A good deal has been written on the subject; however, the records are incomplete, and one has to be careful in separating fact from fancy.

It was in the summer of 1638 that Jose Glover, a well-to-do dissenting minister, embarked with his family on the "John of London" for America, bringing with him a press, a quantity of paper, and the necessary equipment of types.[1] With him came Stephen Day of Cambridge, with his wife, two sons, a stepson, and three menservants.[2] Glover assumed the cost of transportation for Day and his party, amounting to 44 pounds and also delivered him "kettles and other iron tooles" to the value of 7 pounds. As security, Day gave him a bond for 100 pounds obliging himself and his men "to labor and worke with and for the said Josse Glover and his assignes in the trade which the said Stephen now useth in New England. . . ."[3] Day was described in the bond as a locksmith and Glover as a clerk; there was no mention of any plan of starting a press. On the contrary, it was definitely stated that Day was to

The Printing of the Bay Psalm Book

continue his trade in the New World.[4] The absence of any reference to printing may have been a form of secrecy resulting from a desire to avoid the suspicions of the government which would not have liked to see a printing press established by the Puritans in America.[5]

Glover's family included his wife, the former Elizabeth Harris, and five children, three from an earlier marriage. They were accompanied by a number of servants of both sexes and brought with them a large amount of furniture and costly utensils. Unfortunately, Glover died on the voyage, "the Lord seeing it meet that this reverend and holy servant of his should fall short of shores of New England."[6] Upon her arrival, his widow, accustomed to comfortable living, acquired the mansion that Governor Haynes, who had just emigrated to Connecticut, had built in the Market Square at Cambridge. For the Days she found more modest lodgings on Crooked Lane, a few hundred yards away.[7]

The precise date of the opening of the press is not known. The enterprise is first mentioned, as a possibility, in a letter by Edmund Browne, later to become minister of Sudbury, who on September 7, 1638, informed his patron in England: "Wee have a Cambridge heere, a College erecting, youth lectured, a library, and I suppose there will be a presse this winter." The Glovers and Days may have been still on the ocean at that time; but by December 10 the press was in Cambridge. On that day Hugh Peter, pastor of Salem, notified Patrick Copeland, pastor in

The Enigma of the Bay Psalm Book

Bermuda: "Wee have a printery here and thinke to goe to worke with some speciall things, and if you have anything you may send it safely by these" (meaning the bearers of his letter, chiefly Capt. William Peirce).[8] Yet it is a matter of conjecture whether the press was actually in operation then. It was certainly working during the following winter, as Governor Winthrop's first entry in his journal for 1638/39 proves. Since the new year, according to the old-style reckoning, started on March 25, the first two months and twenty-four days of 1638/39 should be counted for 1639. However, Winthrop's reference to the Psalm Book, which bears the imprint of 1640, indicates that the entry, or at least part of it, was a later interpolation by him.[9]

Two records in College Book III, preserved in the Archives of Harvard, show that Glover received some help for the establishment of the press. The first states that "Mr. Joss: Glover gave to the Colledge a font of printing Letters," and the second: "Some Gentlemen of Amsterdam gave towards the furnishing of a Printing-Press with Letters gave fourty nine pound and something more."[10] Historians have tried to account for the motives of the donors. Professor Morison suggests that, under the pressure of Archbishop Laud's campaign, the authorities of Holland became unfriendly to the Puritans who were issuing their English tracts from Dutch printing houses; and that these gentlemen from Amsterdam hoped that Glover's press "might well become the nucleus of a large printing establishment, producing for the

The Printing of the Bay Psalm Book

English market prohibited books."[11] There must have been some expectations in that direction, as Hugh Peter's letter to the Bermuda pastor indicates; however, with all the malcontents watching them, the cautious Puritans could hardly have presumed to accomplish in the colony, and on the scale of "profitable" business, what could not be done in a foreign country. The Amsterdam gentlemen were simply Puritan sympathizers; and one may well explain the establishment of the press in Edward Johnson's words as the "further compleating the Colonies in Church and Common-wealth-work."[12]

It was apparently as a locksmith that Stephen Day was known in his home town, the English Cambridge, where in 1618 he married the widow of a baker. Considering the date, his own two sons could not have been more than nineteen and eighteen when they came to America. The elder, Stephen, died a year later; it was the younger boy, Matthew, who became associated with his father at the press. Stephen Day's name does not appear on the title-page of any of the books issued at Cambridge, and it has been suggested that his son Matthew was the real printer. Certain it is that in 1647 Stephen Day retired from the press, and in the next two years, until his death in May, 1649, Matthew was the recognized foreman. During the rest of his life—and he lived until 1668—Stephen Day made no attempt to return to the craft, and styled himself again a "locksmith." Yet his role as the first printer of the English colonies in America cannot be dismissed. On December 10,

The Enigma of the Bay Psalm Book

1641, the General Court, granting him 300 acres of land, named him "the first that set upon printing."[13]

In any case, by the summer of 1641 the "printery" came under the management of Henry Dunster, president of the college, who had married Mrs. Glover and took at once great interest in her business affairs. He supervised the press even after her death two years later; and when the president's new lodging was erected in 1645 or 1646, he transferred it there. The printing plant, however, remained private property till 1654 when, upon his retirement, Dunster sold it to the college. Forced to resign from his office on account of his views on infant baptism, Dunster moved with his second wife and four children to Scituate, in Plymouth Colony. It was at this point that Glover's heirs started suit against him, demanding restitution of their property. Dunster made counter-charges of the great expenditures incurred on behalf of his first wife, the education of the children, and so on. Probing into the affairs of the press was part of the lawsuit, and so it happens that most of the information relating to the introduction of printing into English America may be found in the court records of Middlesex County and the Dunster Manuscripts at Harvard.

In an affidavit Stephen Day—by then a farmer, prospector for iron, and doubtless a locksmith again—attested that "the Charges which Mr. Glover expended in England for the procureing of the Printing Presse was besides fraeght and other petty expences at least twenty poundes," further stating that "the

The Printing of the Bay Psalm Book

same materials that were brought over hither... are worth in this place at least 40 poundes." In another affidavit he testified that the paper which Glover provided for the press cost him 60 pounds; that this paper, excepting 6 pounds' worth which his wife sold, was used for printing until Dunster handed over the press to the college; and that upon his retirement Dunster took away the remainder. He added that, according to his information, this remainder amounted to about 12 reams.[14]

There is also a folded sheet among the Dunster Manuscripts covered with estimates about the paper and cost of the printing of the early publications. It has neither date nor signature but was evidently prepared by Stephen Day and Samuel Green (who upon Matthew Day's death became the printer) for use in the Glover-Dunster suit. The two men thought that Dunster's profits amounted to 192 pounds—114 for books published in Day's time and 78 for those in Green's time.[15] Their account included the following figures about the Bay Psalm Book:

```
Psa booke 33 sheets 1700 collated
    sold at 20d a piece              £141.13.04
    to abate for printing              33.00.00
                                     ----------
                                      108.13.04
Spent 116 Rheams paper
    worth 5s a Rheam                   29.00.00
                                     ----------
                                       79.13.04
```

There must have been an error in the calculation. The 148 leaves of the book required not 33 but 37

The Enigma of the Bay Psalm Book

sheets, which for the 1,700 copies printed amounted to 126 rather than 116 reams.[16] Both paper and printing were costlier, therefore, than Day and Green figured, and consequently the net profit was smaller by 6 or 7 pounds.

The case was tried before Governor Endicott and four other magistrates. After a detailed balancing of the accounts, on June 24, 1656, the jury found that Dunster owed the estate £117.8.2, besides books and other debts amounting to £57. These sums included £50 charged against him for "the printing presse and paper."[17]

The press for which, according to Day, Glover paid "at least twenty poundes" is supposed to be still in existence—preserved under a glass case at the Vermont Historical Society at Montpelier. The authenticity of the piece, however, is questionable. In 1659 the Corporation for the Propagation of the Gospel sent to Cambridge a second press; and a third was brought over in 1665 by Marmaduke Johnson, Green's assistant. Ten years later this third press was acquired by John Foster, the first printer in Boston; but there is no way of proving that, of the remaining two, it was the original Day press that finally migrated to Vermont. However, the press with which Glover embarked for America must have been of the kind that may be seen now at Montpelier. Such a machine was in common use in England at the time, with a platen measuring about fifteen by ten inches.[18]

The first product of the Cambridge press, the Freeman's Oath, was a broadside, no copy of which

The Printing of the Bay Psalm Book

exists.[19] There is no copy of the second publication, the "Almanack made for New England" by Captain Peirce, either. Judging from the almanacs published for 1646, 1647, and 1648, of which single copies have survived, it consisted of eight leaves. The publication of the Bay Psalm Book was, of course, a much more considerable undertaking.

With the facsimile reprint before him, the reader needs no detailed description of the volume. It is a small quarto, the signatures being *4 **4 A-V4 W4 X-Z4 Aa-Ll4. The text was printed with a roman type, the size of "a small-bodied English," which Isaiah Thomas thought was a very good letter and probably new.[20] A font of smaller type, both roman and italic, is used on the title-page, and a still smaller one, under the title of Psalm 18. Day had, in addition, some Hebrew and Greek characters, and an assortment of larger types for headings and initials. The title-page is surrounded by cast ornaments, and similar pieces are placed also at the head of each division showing an awkward effort at elegance.

The composition is rather poor. No space is allowed between the psalms, and sometimes a title is at the bottom of a page. The press-work is uneven; and an examination of the extant copies might reveal many variations. The printer seems to have been wholly unacquainted with punctuation: periods were often omitted where they should have been used, and they were used where only a comma was necessary; words of one syllable were at times divided with a hyphen, and those of two or more syllables without one.

The Enigma of the Bay Psalm Book

Singularly enough, at the head of every left-hand page is printed "Psalm," and at the head of every right-hand page, "Psalme." The spelling seems too irregular even for the time. The leaf of errata lists only seven mistakes, but the number could probably be multiplied by ten. "The rest [of faults], which have escaped through oversight," the reader is graciously told, "you may amend, as you find them obvious."[21] Yet with all its shortcomings, the printing was not worse than most provincial printing in England when, after the outbreak of the Civil War, innumerable private presses sprang up everywhere.

This is the work which, written by stern Puritan ministers and printed by a locksmith, has maintained itself as one of the most coveted volumes in the world.

X

The Extant Copies

BY 1640 the population of the Bay Colony was about ten thousand—and, in determining the size of the edition of their psalm book, the clergy may have allowed a copy for every family. Of the seventeen hundred copies thus printed, eleven have survived—five complete and six lacking a varying quantity of leaves. This is a fairly large number, considering that most of the early publications of the Cambridge Press are lost or exist only in a single copy, like the first edition of the New England Psalm Book. The preservation of so many copies of the Bay Psalm Book is partly due to the collecting zeal of Thomas Prince, who accumulated five for his library.

With one exception, all the existing copies are in public institutions, and all but one are in America. They are listed here as follows:

1. John Carter Brown Library, Providence, Rhode Island. Perfect, but a small portion of the margin of the title-page and the lower, blank part of the leaf of errata are cut out. In the original calf binding, rebacked. Richard Mather's note "Richardus Matherus eius liber" appears several times on the flyleaves and covers.

2. Yale University Library. Small portions of the fore-margins of eight leaves have been repaired, with the addi-

The Enigma of the Bay Psalm Book

tion of a few letters or numbers on the errata leaf. Bound by Francis Bedford, in dark-brown crushed levant morocco, the sides studded with gold stars and corner and center ornaments.

3. Prince Collection, Boston Public Library. A small part of the bottom of leaf Ee is torn off. Rebound in 1850. This is the tallest, although not the widest copy. A leaf measures $7\frac{1}{4} \times 4\frac{3}{8}$ inches, as against $6\frac{7}{8} \times 4\frac{1}{2}$ inches of the John Carter Brown copy.

4. Prince Collection, Boston Public Library. A small portion of the bottom of the "Finis" leaf is torn off and the leaf of errata is lacking. Rebound in 1850.

5. Lenox Collection, New York Public Library. The upper corner of leaf G is torn off, with portions of three lines. Twelve leaves, mended and re-margined, were inserted from another copy. Bound by Francis Bedford, in red morocco.

6. Bodleian Library, Oxford. Perfect, but greatly soiled. Bound in green calf *ca.* 1820. The volume was a bequest from Thomas Tanner, Bishop of St. Asaph, in 1735. When Tanner removed his books from Norwich to Oxford, where he served as Canon of Christ Church, they fell into the river and were submerged for twenty hours.

7. American Antiquarian Society, Worcester, Massachusetts. Lacks the title-page and the leaf of errata. A corner from the first page of the Preface and the upper portion of the next to last page are torn off. In the original vellum binding. Isaiah Thomas' copy.

8. Henry E. Huntington Library, San Marino, California. Lacks the first four and the last three leaves. In the original calf binding. It belonged once to the Shuttleworth family. Since then it was owned by a Boston bookseller; Bishop John Hurst of Washington, D.C.; Dodd, Mead & Co., New York; and E. Dwight Church of Brooklyn.

9. Rosenbach Foundation, Philadelphia. Bought in Ireland in 1934. Lacks eight leaves, including the title-page. In original binding.

The Extant Copies

10. Harvard College Library. Lacks the first six and the last four leaves. It was a gift from Middlecott Cooke of Boston. Rebound in 1900.

11. Mr. A. Van Sinderin, Brooklyn, New York. Lacks the title-page and eighteen leaves. In the original calf binding.

Numbers 1–4 and 11 were the five copies that once belonged to Thomas Prince. A friend and disciple of Cotton Mather, Prince was the first great American book collector. The early Puritans loved their books, and many of them, ministers and magistrates, assembled substantial libraries; but Prince went at his task systematically, thinking not only of his own needs but of those of posterity. From his college days he hunted for books relating to New England. The partial dispersal of Cotton Mather's library, after his death in 1728, gave Prince an especially rich opportunity. At least one copy of the Bay Psalm Book—Richard Mather's own—must have come into his possession at that time. "I made the Collection from a public View and Desire," he wrote in his will in 1758, "that the Memory of many important Transactions might be preserved." In bequeathing his books to the Old South Church, he stipulated that the collection must be "kept entire." Even his bookplate emphasized that the volumes were "to remain forever" in what he called "The New-England Library."

The collection, housed in the steeple of the church, suffered some losses during the Siege of Boston in 1775–76. In 1814 it was removed to the parsonage on Milk Street, a part of it being sent to the Massachusetts Historical Society. Then in 1866 the whole

The Enigma of the Bay Psalm Book

collection was, to assure its greater usefulness, deposited in the Boston Public Library, where it has been ever since. But by that time only two of the five copies of the Bay Psalm Book were left. The other three had passed into private hands. Edward A. Crowninshield, a wealthy bibliophile of Boston and Salem, acquired one in 1849;[1] an incomplete copy went, at the same time, to George Livermore of Cambridge;[2] and finally the third was obtained, ten years later, by Dr. Nathaniel B. Shurtleff, physician, antiquarian, and a future mayor of Boston.[3]

The way in which the three copies were alienated from the Prince Library is a strange story, important details of which have remained unknown until recently.

Crowninshield's bold adventure is commemorated in one of the two copies of the Bay Psalm Book—Number 4—still in the Prince Library. On a flyleaf, former Lieutenant-Governor Samuel T. Armstrong, a deacon of the church,[4] wrote in pencil: "This book was bound at the cost of Mr. Ed. Crowninshield and given in Exchange for No. 259 in the Catalogue. Jan. 1850 S.T.A."[5] If the grammar is correct, the note means that Crowninshield gave the book in exchange for the copy which he had received and that, in addition, he had it newly bound. However, this was not the case. Crowninshield gave only the binding and not the book, the title-page of which still has the shelf-number it had in the parsonage of the Old South Church. The new binding was cardboard covered with imitation leather, which could hardly have cost

The Extant Copies

him more than a dollar. But it would have been better if Crowninshield had spared himself this generous outlay of money. The margins would have escaped the binder's knife, and the volume would be twice as valuable today.

As for Livermore's copy, no record of the barter seems to exist. It is not unlikely that he was responsible for the binding of the second copy—Number 3—still in the Prince Library, which is of the same kind as the one supplied by Crowninshield. Yet it was through Livermore's activity that the earliest information about the "exchanges" transpired.

Henry Stevens, Vermont-born London bookseller, had been looking for a copy of the Bay Psalm Book for years, on commission from James Lenox, the famous New York collector. Then, to his amazement, in January, 1855, he picked up an unknown copy in a London auction room. But the volume turned out to be incomplete. "Knowing," he recalled, "that my old friend and correspondent, George Livermore of Cambridge, N. E., possessed an imperfect copy, which he and Mr. Crowninshield, after the noble example of the 'Lincoln Nosegay,' had won from the Committee of the 'Old South' in Boston, together with another and perfect copy, I proposed an advantageous exchange, and obtained the four missing leaves."[6] In fact, Livermore traded away not only four but twelve leaves to Stevens, who sold the copy thus completed to Lenox. As part of the latter's great collection of treasures, the volume is now in the New York Public Library.[7]

The Enigma of the Bay Psalm Book

"The Lincoln Nosegay," mentioned by Stevens, was the title of a pamphlet published by the Reverend Thomas F. Dibdin about 1814. In it the famous antiquarian advertised for sale nineteen volumes, several of the choicest Caxtons among them, which he had purchased for an unusually low price from the library of Lincoln Cathedral. It is a fair guess that it was Dibdin's exploit at Lincoln that inspired Livermore and Crowninshield, who were great admirers of the loquacious Englishman, to get their copies of the Bay Psalm Book. In fact, Dibdin's paper was reprinted in 1849—early enough to start them on their enterprise.[8] Yet not everyone appreciated Dibdin's smart deal. "The guardians of the temple slept, and Mammon prevailed," the historian of English cathedral libraries commented. In quoting the "noble example of 'the Lincoln Nosegay,'" Stevens therefore could not have had anything redolent in mind.[9]

Crowninshield's library, upon his death in 1859, was acquired by Henry Stevens, who offered the Bay Psalm Book to the British Museum; and when they were reluctant to purchase, sold it, washed and rebound, to George Brinley of Hartford for 150 guineas. At the Brinley sale in 1879, where it was of course the star item, the volume was bought by Cornelius Vanderbilt for $1,200. This is the copy for which the Friends of the Library of Yale University paid in 1947 the fabulous price of $151,000. After Livermore's death, in 1865, his books were deposited at Harvard and, in 1894, sold at auction. His copy of the Bay Psalm Book, lacking by then the title-page and eighteen leaves, realized $425. It was purchased

The Extant Copies

by Alfred White of Brooklyn, from whom it was inherited by the present owner.

Dr. Shurtleff, too, was a book collector, and he had known Crowninshield's library well. As the author of an obituary of Crowninshield, he extolled his late friend as "a great lover of literature," whose "taste in bibliography was exquisite." In describing the library, he spoke with special warmth of its "perfect copy of the old Bay Psalm Book, probably the only one owned by a private individual in New England."[10] Dr. Shurtleff's temptation to get such a perfect copy was great. He could have purchased now the Crowninshield copy from bookseller Stevens; instead, he wrote a letter—on December 30, 1859, less than two months after the sale of the Crowninshield library—to Loring Lothrop, a deacon of the Old South Church:

MY DEAR SIR:

I am very desirous of obtaining one of the duplicate copies of the old Bay Psalm Book belonging to the Old South Church Library, having a strong veneration for the old volume. I think I have books in my library, such as would be not only appropriate for the Library of the Old South Church but also valuable for reference and for the use of those who may rely upon the library for works suitable to be consulted. Among the books which I happen to think of, are the original editions of Winthrop's New England, and Belknap's New England Biography, appropriate I think for Prince's New England Library, and which I would gladly give in exchange [for] one of the duplicates. If you will have the kindness to give this request the proper direction, you will much oblige your friend etc.

NATH. B. SHURTLEFF

The Enigma of the Bay Psalm Book

Deacon Lothrop, a former master of the Girls' High School, quickly responded.[11] Within a fortnight Dr. Shurtleff was in possession of the best copy of the Bay Psalm Book—the one once owned by Richard Mather.

Dr. Shurtleff was right in describing his two books as "not only appropriate for the Library of the Old South Church but also valuable for reference." He carefully avoided, however, mentioning the relative monetary values—a curious omission, considering that in the catalogue of the Crowninshield library the Bay Psalm Book was estimated at $525, while Winthrop's *New England* was rated at $5 and Belknap's *American Biography* (this was the correct title) at $3.[12]

Mayor Shurtleff died in October, 1874, and a year later his library was put up for auction. However, the prospective sale of the Bay Psalm Book aroused considerable commotion in the Boston papers.[13] The Old South Church had to take action. On December 2, 1875, Deacons Avery Plumer and Frederick D. Allen filed a complaint with the Supreme Court of Massachusetts against Dr. Shurtleff's estate; and the same day an injunction restrained the auctioneers from selling the volume.[14] In the ensuing lawsuit the widow maintained that the Bay Psalm Book came into her husband's possession "by sale or barter," in proof of which she quoted his letter to Deacon Lothrop. The exchange, she declared, was "fair and proper, and made by her testator in good faith." She further argued that, by not having filed their bill within six

The Extant Copies

years, the deacons "have been guilty of such *laches* and want of due diligence that they are not entitled to any relief."[15]

The trial took place on April 15, 1876. As to the fairness and propriety of the exchange, any apprentice in a Boston bookstore could have given expert opinion.[16] But the voiding of the claim because of the lapse of time was a different matter, and, in accordance with the Statute of Limitations, the court dismissed the complaint.[17] The deacons appealed to the full court but afterward dropped the charge and paid the expenses. The road was thus cleared for the sale of the book. On October 12, 1876, it was sold to Sidney S. Rider, a Providence book-dealer for $1,025. From him the volume went to C. Fiske Harris, upon whose death in 1881 it was acquired, with a copy of the 1647 edition, for the John Carter Brown Library at Providence. The price was $1,500 and a number of "valuable" books.[18]

Thus the story ends well. Two of the copies have found their way to public institutions, and one could not wish for better places for them. The third, still in private hands, has done useful duty in doctoring up the copy in the New York Public Library. To be sure, the original "exchanges" could have taken place in a less imaginative manner, such as the payment of a decent price; but the thing itself was bound to happen sooner or later. The possession of five copies of the Bay Psalm Book by any library was extraordinary even a hundred years ago; today it would be a monstrosity.

The Enigma of the Bay Psalm Book

Luckily, the Prince Library still has two copies. It is with pleasure that one of these is offered now—in an excellent reproduction—to scholars, to help them in their work; to book lovers, to give them enjoyment; and to the general public, for whom it was intended when first published more than three hundred years ago.

Appendixes

APPENDIX A
A Transcript by Cotton

IN 1643 there was published in London the *Church-Government and Church-Covenant*, which has been described as "the first elaborate definition and exposition of the New England theory of the Church and its administration to be put forth in print."[1] The work consists of three treatises: *The XXXII Questions;* then *An Apologie of the Churches in New-England for Church Covenant;* and *An Answer of the Elders of the Severall Churches in New-England unto Nine Positions* . . . , the last two with separate title-pages.

All three treatises are without the name of the author; however, the first two were written by Richard Mather, as John Cotton and Nathaniel and Increase Mather testified, and the third has been attributed to John Davenport. There is a preface by Hugh Peter, Roger Williams's successor as pastor of the church at Salem, who as one of the agents of the colony was sent to England in 1641.

A large part of a manuscript of the first essay, now in the Library of the University of Virginia, has been accepted, on the authority of "an unknown librarian," as Richard Mather's autograph. This is an error, however. The manuscript is a transcript made

The Enigma of the Bay Psalm Book

by John Cotton. The writing has no resemblance to Mather's signed autographs, and it agrees completely with those of Cotton. But besides the penmanship, there is also considerable circumstantial evidence to prove that the manuscript is in Cotton's hand.

In his reply to a charge by Roger Williams that he, as one of the Elders, was responsible for *The XXXII Questions*, Cotton wrote:

> ... the answer to that Question [the 31st], and to all the other thirty-two Questions, were drawne up by Mr. Mader, and neither drawne up nor sent by me, nor (for ought I know) by the other Elders here, though published by one of our Elders there. Howsoever, the substance of that Answer doth generally suite with all our mindes, as I conceive. In particular; The Answer which our reverend and beloved brother Mr. Mader did returne unto that Question, I have read it, and did readily approve it (as I doe the substance of all his Answers) to be judicious, and solide.[2]

Nathaniel Mather, who in 1650 returned to Europe and became vicar at Barnstaple, Devonshire, stated in his introduction to a tract by his father:

> ... the Answerer whereof [*The XXXII Questions*] was Mr. Richard Mather, and not any other Elder or Elders in New-England, who likewise is the Author of the discourse concerning Church-Covenant printed therewith, which latter he wrote for his private use in his own Study, never intending, nor indeed consenting to its publication, nor so much as knowing unto this day how the copy of it came abroad into those hands by whom it is made publick, save that he conjectures some procured a copy of it from Mr. Cotton, to whom (such was their intimacy in his lifetime) he communicated it, as he writes in a late Letter to

A Transcript by Cotton

a Son of his now in England who it seems had enquired of him concerning those Treatises. . . .[3]

Richard Mather, then, informed his son that he had "communicated" his work to his intimate friend Cotton; and he also conjectured that someone had procured from Cotton the copy which was published in England. He spoke specifically of the treatise on *Church-Covenant;* but Cotton, as is clear from his statement, was equally interested in his answer to the Thirty-two Questions. It was concerning the latter that Increase Mather recorded:

Of which Book my Father Mather was the Sole Author. And he wrote it in the Primitive Times of these Churches (viz. in the year 1639) as himself assured me. What he wrote was approved of by other Elders, especially by Mr. Cotton, unto whom he Communicated it.[4]

Richard Mather's letter to his son Nathaniel and his information given to his younger son Increase seem to tell the whole story. Cotton transcribed Mather's work for his own use—a practice fairly common at that time and especially reasonable in this case when the author did not intend publication. Cotton's protest that it was not he who had sent the copy to London fits in well with the rest. It was not his copy but one made from his own that actually went to London and was used there in the printing shop. Cotton's own transcript has survived and is now in Virginia.

The autograph is by the same hand as the draft of the Preface to the Bay Psalm Book. It might be asked, therefore, whether the draft, too, is not a

The Enigma of the Bay Psalm Book

transcript of a lost manuscript by Richard Mather. There are, however, clear indications that the draft is an original manuscript. Cotton would have had far less reason to make a transcript of such a work, for the Preface was promptly printed. He would not have written on a transcript, in a formal hand: "For my reverend brother/Th Shepard," or repeated the instruction at the end: "And soe goe on in shewing what other things have been attended to . . ." etc. Above all, he would not have expropriated almost its entire content for the treatise that he was to publish, under his own name, seven years later. At least, there is no such example of piracy, from a contemporary, in the literature of early New England.

Indeed, John Cotton has not fared well at the hands of the cataloguers of his manuscripts. The Prince Collection contains two other extensive papers by him (original in both composition and handwriting), which have been attributed to Richard Mather. One is a tract entitled "The Scope of Revelation," dated 1639 and extending to fourteen pages; and the other, a sermon on Acts IX:17, "That thou mightest be filled with the Holy Ghost," eleven pages long.[5] In addition, there are a number of letters and manuscripts by Cotton listed in the *Prince Catalogue* as if their authorship were unknown or unknowable. Among them is a four-page letter to Peter Bulkeley on the working of faith by the Holy Ghost; one to Richard Saltonstall on the keeping of a rash vow; and the very important "Exceptions against some things in the Synod at Cambridge, 1649."[6] (This last cer-

A Transcript by Cotton

tainly could not have been fastened on Richard Mather, the author of the Cambridge Platform.)

It was a vicious circle. Once the draft of the Preface was accepted as Richard Mather's autograph, the other similar autographs had to be ascribed to him or (when this seemed impossible) left hanging. And it may have worked also the other way. If the autograph of the *Church-Government* was Richard Mather's—as the authorship was undoubtedly his—then the other autographs, including the draft of the Preface, must have appeared as his, too. Herein lies the importance of recognizing the Virginia manuscript for what it is: a transcript made by John Cotton. It clears up the entire confusion.

APPENDIX B
Who Was Richard Lyon?

RICHARD LYON, the collaborator of President Dunster in the revision of the Bay Psalm Book, has been one of the most shadowy figures in the early history of New England. Almost all our knowledge about him has been derived from Cotton Mather's account. And historians seem to have been satisfied. Despite considerable anxiety to ascertain more facts about William Mildmay, with whom Lyon is supposed to have come to America in 1644 and left in 1651, no one has made any inquiry about Richard Lyon. Mildmay, the eldest son of Sir Henry Mildmay, graduated from Harvard. Lyon was of common stock and did not receive any degree. Yet he was one of the two men who rewrote the Bay Psalm Book and was probably the chief author of the first American hymnal. Next to Anne Bradstreet, he composed and printed more verse in America than any of the early Colonists.

Our lack of information concerning the identity of Richard Lyon has been a strange gap in the history of the period. It is not without excitement, therefore, that the present writer submits here his findings. If they are correct, they will solve part of the mystery.

Cotton Mather's brief paragraph, mentioned in this essay, reads:

Who Was Richard Lyon?

The Psalms thus turn'd into Meetre were Printed at Cambridge, in the Year 1640. But afterwards, it was thought, that a little more of Art was to be employ'd upon them: And for that Cause, they were committed unto Mr. Dunster, who Revised and Refined this Translation; and (with some Assistance from one Mr. Richard Lyon, who being sent over by Sir Henry Mildmay, as an Attendant unto his Son, then a Student in Harvard Colledge, now resided in Mr. Dunster's House:) he brought it into the Condition wherein our Churches ever since have used it.[1]

The next early reference is to be found in John Oldmixon's *The British Empire in America*. The second edition contains the lines:

Here [Harvard College] also was bred William Mildmay, Esq; Son to Sir Henry Mildmay, and elder Brother to Henry Mildmay Esq; of Shawford, in Hampshire, where his Posterity, very nearly related to the Author, reside at this Day. Mr. Mildmay's Tutor here was Mr. Richard Lyon.[2]

Oldmixon, a compiler rather than an original writer, obviously took this glimpse of Lyon, like so much else, from Cotton Mather. One notes, however, that he speaks of him as a "Tutor," instead of "an Attendant," of William Mildmay. The difference is important, for the former word conjures up a person more mature and better-schooled than the latter. Yet the designation has been accepted. John L. Sibley, in the first volume of his *Graduates of Harvard University*, still described Lyon as "Tutor or Attendant" of Mildmay; but historians ever since have consistently referred to him as a tutor.

The most concise records on Mildmay and Lyon

The Enigma of the Bay Psalm Book

are in the *Alumni Cantabrigienses*, compiled by John Venn and J. A. Venn. Under the name of William Mildmay, the work contains the following entry:

Adm. Fell.-Com. at Emmanuel, Sept. 26, 1640. S. of Sir Henry, of Wanstead, Essex (grandson of Sir Walter). B. in London, 1622. Matric. 1641. Sent to New England in charge of a tutor, Mr. Richard Lyon, 1644. Graduated B.A. at Harvard, 1647. Returned to England, 1651. Married Mary, dau. of John Brewster, of Barking, Essex. Died June 1, 1682. Buried at Danbury, Essex. M.I. (Vis. of Essex, 1634; J. G. Bartlett.)[3]

Lyon is called again a "tutor"; and, further, it is stated that Mildmay was sent to America in 1644, together with Lyon. Mildmay graduated from Harvard in 1647, and since the curriculum extended to three years, it seemed merely natural to assume that he must have entered the college in 1644. However, there is no documentary evidence to prove this; on the contrary, there is every reason to believe that the two young men came over later, in 1646.

Seven students graduated from Harvard in 1647, William Mildmay (Gulielmus Mildmay) listed at the end. "As the names in the early classes, except in cases of degradation for misdemeanors," Sibley wrote, "purport to be arranged according to family rank, Mildmay's position at the bottom of the class has been the subject of considerable curiosity."[4] It has been indeed. For one would expect special consideration for William Mildmay, the eldest son of a Knight.[5] The College Laws of 1642–46 even prescribed: "Every Scholar shall bee called by his Sir-

Who Was Richard Lyon?

name onely till hee bee invested with his first degree; except hee bee fellow-commoner or a Knights Eldest Sonne or of superiour Nobility."[6] To account for his humiliation, historians have decided, therefore, that William Mildmay must have been an unusually stupid fellow, something of "a half-wit." That he started his academic course in 1641 at Emmanuel and was twenty-five by the time of his graduation from Harvard seemed to corroborate the opinion.[7]

Yet it has been wholly gratuitous to send him down in history as a dullard. No one knows when and why Mildmay left Emmanuel. He may have joined the army, and his father may have sent him later to America to get him away from the perils of the Civil War—at a time when he himself was in danger.[8] There is nothing to tell against Mildmay, except his position at the bottom of the class list. And this great puzzle can be solved by the simple fact that he entered Harvard not as a Freshman but as an upper classman, to be precise, as a Senior.

This made all the difference. The college lists were compiled during the Freshman year, and it was a rule, remaining in force till well into the eighteenth century, that "if a student entered a certain class after the names of the members of that class had been recorded, his name was not inserted." This applied— the editors of the Harvard College Records write— both to a Freshman who came after his class had been "placed" and to a student who at entrance was admitted to an upper class.[9] It was a favor to Mildmay to have his name included at all.[10]

The Enigma of the Bay Psalm Book

Tidying up the facts about William Mildmay is the first step to the identification of Richard Lyon. The Mildmay family had a special interest in Emmanuel, founded in 1585 by Sir Walter Mildmay, chancellor of the exchequer under Queen Elizabeth. It would seem logical, therefore, that Sir Henry, looking for a companion to his son, would choose someone connected with the college. Emmanuel is the place where one has to search for traces of Richard Lyon; and the *Alumni Cantabrigienses* contains an entry under the name (spelled "Lions"): "Adm. sizar at Emmanuel, Michs. 1645. Of Lancashire. Matric. 1645. . . ."

Having read the entry on Mildmay, one is inclined to be skeptical at first. Matriculated in 1645, Lions (Lyon) seems to have been too young to serve as tutor of William Mildmay, who had matriculated four years before; and having been at Cambridge in 1645, he could not have come to America in 1644. The picture, however, changes if he was employed as "an Attendant," and not as a tutor. He was admitted as a sizar at Emmanuel, that is, as a student doing various services to defray his college expenses—just the kind of impecunious fellow who would have accepted the commission offered by Sir Henry. And once it is clear that William Mildmay was sent over in 1646, instead of 1644, the one obstacle to Lyon's coming with him disappears. The identity of Lions of Emmanuel College with Lyon, the attendant to William Mildmay, becomes even more likely through the circumstance that after his matriculation nothing is heard of him at Emmanuel.[11]

Who Was Richard Lyon?

There is another primary source of information about Richard Lyon besides Cotton Mather's story. It is the Account Book of Thomas Chesholme, steward of Harvard College from 1649 to 1660, first published by Professor Morison in 1935.[12] The credit and debit columns of "Mr. Willyam myldmay and mr. lyons" contain some amusing items. Mildmay's charges for "commons and sizings" ("commons" meaning board and "sizings" meaning beer and bread at the morning and afternoon "bevers," and extras at meals)[13] were consistently higher on every quarter day than those for Lyon. Either he lived better or had a greater appetite. The payments were made by Lyon in silver, beef, wheat and rye, sugar, etc. On February 14, 1651, Edward Goff paid to his account one pound "for a saddell of mr. lyons," while Brodstreat (Bradstreet) paid ten shillings for his "dixenary," whether Latin or Hebrew is not told. Evidently, ready to leave, Lyon was selling his belongings.

Differences in spelling of names were frequent in the seventeenth century. Yet it is not without significance that the earliest contemporary source (written fifty years before Cotton Mather's account) gives the name as "lyons," with an *s* at the end—like the entry in the *Alumni Cantabrigienses*.

Lyon (Lions) was working at the time with Dunster on the revision of the Bay Psalm Book. Mildmay, having received his master's degree in 1650, could have left earlier; but if his father had sent him to America to have him out of harm's way, he may just as well have stayed on until his companion finished

The Enigma of the Bay Psalm Book

his work—till 1651, when the New England Psalm Book appeared.

The revision of the translation probably began in 1647.[14] Richard Lyon must have been quite young then, but this did not have to be a handicap. Dunster had the necessary knowledge of Hebrew; Lyon's contribution was doubtless in the domain of versification. John Keats was younger at his death than Lyon was at the time of completing his work in the Bay Colony.

What happened to the man after his return to England? Historians have pursued the doings of William Mildmay, who, one learns, married the daughter of John Brewster of Essex and died in 1682. They have not been interested in Richard Lyon.

The *Alumni Cantabrigienses* has a surprising suggestion. The entry under Richard Lions, quoted above, goes on to say: ". . . One of these names chaplain of the Navy, 1653. On the *Resolution* at the defeat of the Dutch."

This is a cue indeed! The *Resolution* was the flagship of the generals in the decisive battle of the Dutch-English War—the Battle of the Gabbard (forty miles east of Harwich), fought on June 2 and 3, 1653. Besides being the victory which established England's supremacy over the seas for centuries to come, the Battle of the Gabbard is famous because in it were employed for the first time the new tactics of the Royal Navy—the line-formation of the ships. And the first intimation of these tactics was con-

Who Was Richard Lyon?

tained in an account of the battle sent by Richard Lyons, "minister" of the *Resolution*, to Admiral Sir William Penn on June 4. In it occurs the passage:

> ... And then the enemy endeavoured to keep all as close together as he could, that he might make the best of his way without loss, dreading our great ships. His design was, our frigates would leave them astern, and then he would deal the better with them. But our fleet did work together in better order than heretofore, and seconded one another; which I am persuaded, by God's providence, was a terror to our enemies, otherwise, for number and quality of ships ... they could not but reckon themselves of an equal strength.[16]

There is only one Richard Lions listed in the *Alumni Cantabrigienses* and none in the *Alumni Oxonienses*. Is it not possible, therefore, that the Richard Lyon (lyons) of American fame and Richard Lyons, the chaplain of the *Resolution*, were one and the same person? Psalm and hymn-writing would have been a fitting preparation for his new vocation.

In searching for further data about Mildmay and Lyon (Lions), the writer submitted this whole chapter to Dr. J. A. Venn, President of Queens' College and University Archivist of Cambridge University. The records of the early admissions at Emmanuel College have been largely destroyed; Dr. Venn, however, accepts the writer's position concerning Lyon's association with Emmanuel as well as with Mildmay and Harvard as valid. He also feels certain about Lyon's role in the Battle of the Gabbard.

Unfortunately, the writer is less optimistic about

The Enigma of the Bay Psalm Book

the latter phase. Careful reading of the report to Admiral William Penn shows the hand of an expert navigator; and further search through the volumes of the Navy Records Society reveals that, soon after the Battle of the Gabbard, a Richard Lyons served as captain of the *Taunton*. Surely, a chaplain could not have become, at such a short notice, the captain of a warship; and it is unlikely that there were two men of the same name, one a chaplain and the other a captain.[16]

Mr. R. C. Anderson of Greenwich, England, to whom an inquiry addressed to the Navy Records Society was transmitted, offered at this point a brilliant conjecture. "As far as I know," he replied, "the only authority for saying that Lyons was minister of the *Resolution* is Granville Penn. Lyons was evidently on board in some capacity and it occurs to me that 'minister' may be a mistake (at some stage) for 'master.' . . ." The report to Admiral Penn is precisely one which a master—the officer intrusted with the navigation of a ship of war—would be expected to send in; and the misreading of "minister" for "master" could have easily happened, considering that "Master" was often abbreviated to "Msr."

Dr. Venn's opinion deserves high respect; the possibility that Richard Lyon of Emmanuel and Harvard was also the chaplain of the *Resolution* cannot be excluded. However, the doubts remain. The later career of the reviser of the Bay Psalm Book awaits further research.[17]

APPENDIX C
The Draft of the Preface

The draft of the Preface, described on pages 17–18 and discussed throughout the third section, is printed here. The original spelling has been followed except that the words the, that, them, which, with, our, and against, *as well as* Apostle, Christian, *and* Epistle, *contracted in the manuscript, have been expanded. There is no reason to adhere to such halting abbreviations—the Bay Psalm Book itself did not.*

The Singing of Psalmes in setting forth the praises of the Lord, though it breath forth nothing but holy Harmony and melody: yet such is the subtilty of the enemy, and the enmity of our Nature against the Lord and his wayes, that our hearts can finde matter of discord even in this Harmony, and Crotchetts of division in this holy melody. For there be (even amongst the Godly) who scruple three Notes in the singing of Psalmes. 1. What Psalmes are to be sung in Christian Churches, whether the Psalmes of David, and of other holy Prophets left us in scripture: or the Psalmes invented by the Gifts of Godly men in every Age of the Church. 2. If the Psalmes of David and other scripture-Psalmes be to be sung, whether in their owne words, or in such meeter, as English Poëtry is wont to runne in. 3. By whom are these Psalmes to be sung, whether by the whole Church all of them Joyning with their voyces (as well as with their hearts) together: Or by one man alone, and the rest Joyning in silence, and in the close saying Amen.

To speake a word to each particular: Touching the first, Certaine it is, that the singing of the Psalmes of David was

The Enigma of the Bay Psalm Book

sometimes an acceptable worship of God, not onely in his owne time, but after that he slept with his Fathers. For his 136 Psalme was sung in the dayes of Solomon 2 Chro: 5. 13 and in the dayes of Jehoshaphat 2 Chron: 20. 21, yea and the Text is evident, that in Hezekiahs time they were commaunded to sing Praise to the Lord, with the words of David, and of Asaph, the seer; 2 Chron. 29. 30. Stay here a while and you see if this Place may not suffice to [right] two of the Questions (the first and last) at once. This Commaundement and Practise, was it Ceremoniall, or morall? Something in it indeede was Ceremoniall, as that the Levites were the cheife singers, and that they played with Instruments to the song, v 25 and 30. But what Ceremony was there in singing Praise with the wordes of David and Asaph? What if David was a type of Christ, was Asaph also? And though David was a type of Christ, yet was every thing of David Typicall also? Are his wordes which are of morall (that is, of universall and perpetuall) Authority in all Nations, in all Ages, are they Typicall? or what Type can be imagined in making use of his holy Songs to Praise the Lord? Besides, that which was Typicall in his Songs as they were sung with Instruments, and by the Levites, they must have their morall, and spirituall Accomplishment in the New Testament. Let the Instruments Type out our hearts and lippes keeping holy harmony and Concent, with the Lord and his people? but who are now in stead of the Levites, and their twenty foure orders spoken of 1 Chron. 25. 9 to 32? Are they any other than the 24 Elders, who supply the place of all the members of the Church (as the 4 Beasts decypher the officers:) Rev. 4. 4: wee being all made by Christ Kings and Preists to our heavenly Father, Rev. 1. 6 and all the children of the New Testament being now growne up as Elders or as hejres come to ripe Age, in comparison of the Saints of the Old Testament, who were counted as children under Age. Gal. 4. 1, 2, 3. And therefore it is, that the Apostle speaketh to the whole Church, and to all the members of it, That

The Draft of the Preface

they should all of them Teach and Admonish one another in Psalmes, and Hymnes, and Spirituall songs, singing with grace in their hearts to the Lord. Col. 3. Eph. 5. 19 to which Psalmes, and Hymnes, and spirituall songs doe conteyne all the severall sorts of Davids Psalmes: Some being called by David himself מזמורים, that is Psalmes, others תהדים that is Hymnes, others שירום that is, spirituall songs. Is it to be said, the Saints in the Primitive Churches did compjle spirituall Songs of their enditing, and sing them before the Church. 1 Cor. 14. 15, 26.

The Answer is ready: That those Saints compjled those spirituall Songs by the Extraordinary Gifts of the spirit, whereby they were enabled to sett forth the Prayse of God even in strange Tongues. If the like Extraordinary Gifts of the spirit were still found in the Church, wee should not refuse to allow them the like liberty in Composing Psalmes for the Churches use upon present Occasion.

If it be replyed, wee allow ministers to Pray conceived Prayers endited by the ordinary Gift of the spirit: and why not to sing Conceived Psalmes by the like Gifts? Our Answer is, there is the like Proportion indeede between Prayer and Thanksgiving: and therefore if a minister may Pray a Prayer conceived by the Ordinary Gifts of the spirit, He may in like sort Praise God with a Thanksgiving conceived by the Ordinary Gifts of the spirit. But to Compjle a Psalme requireth a further Gift, even spirituall Poëtry, as well as spirituall Grace, which is not found in every good minister. And were it found, yet seeing Psalmes are to be sung with the ioynt Concent and Harmony of all the Church, not in heart onely, but in voyce (as God helping wee shall shew anon) This cannot be done unlesse He that Composeth the Psalme, doe bring into the Church sett formes of Psalmes of his owne Invention: for which wee finde noe warrant, nor Precedent in any ordinary officers of the Church throughout the Scriptures.

If it be replyed againe, why may not one man alone who Composeth a Psalme sing it with a loude voyce before the

The Enigma of the Bay Psalm Book

Church, and all the rest of the members ioyne with him in silence, and in the end say Amen?

We Answer, It should seeme, such a Practise was indeede sometime used in the Church of Corinth, when any man had a Psalme suggested to him by the Extraordinary Gift of the spirit: But in singing Ordinary Psalmes, It may appeare to be otherwise. The whole Church ioyned together with one accord as in heart, so in voyce to Sing the Praise of the Lord.

For first, as it hath bene shewed above, The Preists and Levites to whom (as choyce choristers) the Psalmes of David were committed to be sung in the Temple, they have noe successors in the Churches of the New Testament, but the 24 elders, who represent all the members of every Christian Church. If God had ordeyned, choristers in the New Testament, as He did in the old, distinct from the Body of the People, He would doubtelesse have given Order and direction in the Gospell for their qualification, election, maintenance etc as he did for the musicians of the Temple. But evident it is, the Gospell speaketh nothing at all hereof, but on the Contrary bringeth in all the Saints (all the members of his Church) as performing the like worke of Praising and serving God day and night in his Temple, Rev. 7. 15: and in the same number of twenty foure, which were appointed for the musicians of the Temple Rev. 4. 4 and Cap. 5, vs. 8, 9, 10: compared with 1 Chron. 25. 31. And therefore if Davids Psalmes were committed to the 24 orders of the musicians of the Temple to be sung with voyces and Instruments to the Praise of God, then it is now committed to the 24 elders, that is, to all the members of the Christian Churches, to sing holy Psalmes of Praise with hearts and voyces unto the Lord.

Whence also it is, that all the twenty-four Elders are said to have had each one of them an harpe in his hand (Rev. 5. 8) as being all alike employed in the same Churchmusick with the same Instruments before the Lord. For the Harpes represented not onely their hearts but their

The Draft of the Preface

tongues also: as when David awakened his Glory to sing to Gods Praise, He awakened his Tongue as well as his heart, and both of them together in awakening his Harpe, Psa: 57. 8 whence likewise it is, that Protestant Churches and the members thereof who have gotten victory over the beast, are described with Harpes in their hands, to sing the song of Moses, and of the Lamb, Rev. 15. 3. Now the song of Moses (whether that in Exod 15: or Deut. 32:) were both of them sung not by one voyce alone, but by a Consort and Harmony as well of voyces as hearts. For in Exodus, not onely Moses but the children of Israel are said to Sing this Song, and as the word is in the Originall *They Spake Saying*, not Moses alone, but they spake &c. Exod. 15. 1. And Miriam and all the women are said to come out with Timbrells and daunces, and Answer was returned to the men in other wordes, though to the same purpose vˢ. 20, 21. And as for the song in Deut. 32: (whereto some think John in Rev. 15. 3: had reference, as well as to the other) Moses is commaunded not onely to teach it to the children of Israel, and to putt it into their hearts, but into their mouths also. Deut. 31. 19 which to what end were it, if they were not with their mouths to sing it together, as well as with their hearts? And the song of the Lambe was wont to be sung by many together crying with a loud voyce, Rev. 7. 9, 10. And Isay foretelleth of the dayes of the New Testament, That the watchmen shall lift up the voyce and with the voyce together they shall sing, and the wast places of Hierusalem (desolate and lost soules) shall break forth into ioy, and sing together with them. Isay 52. 8, 9. And the Apostle Paul (as hath bene touched above) expressly commaundeth the singing of Psalmes, Hymnes, and spirituall songs, not to any select Christian, or to any transcendently gifted man, but to the whole Church. Eph. 5. 19. Col. 3. 16. And if Paul and Silas may sing Psalmes together (so as the Prisoners could heare them) in private (Act. 16. 25:) why should the duety be restrayned to one alone in publick?

The Enigma of the Bay Psalm Book

And such was the practise of the Primative Churches after the Apostles, who cannot probably be conceived to swerve in their publique frame of worship from what they received from the Apostolick Churches. The Testimony of antient and holy Basil is in stead of many, who in his 63 Epistle speaking of the maner of their publique worship in singing of Psalmes: "wee, saith He, giving way to one to begin the song, the rest of us sett in to sing with Him, and all of us in Common as with one voyce, and one heart, doe sing a Psalme of Praise unto the Lord." And this doth Basill declare to be the Common Practise of the Churches in Aegipt, Lybia, Thebes, Palastina, Syria, and those that dwell upon the Euphrates, and generally every where, where singing of Psalmes is of any account. The like doth Eusebius record (out of Philo) in his Ecclesiasticall History. L. 2. c. 17.

The Obiections, that are alledged against the ioynt Consent of the Church in lifting up their voyces together to sing forth Gods praise, doe most of them plead aswell against ioyning in heart as in voyce. For if one be the mouth of all the rest in singing, and the rest ioyne onely in heart, others that are not in Church-fellowship may aswell ioyne with the Church, as themselves. And may not they in the close of the Psalme, as well ioyne in saying Amen, as the members of the Church doe? Moreover if wee may not in voyce ioyne in the song, because wee are not allwayes in a suitable estate to the matter sung: if that Reason were good, then neither might wee ioyne in heart therewith. But the truth is, where the matter of the Psalmes doeth not suite with our estates, yet even there wee may sing them as Psalmes for Instruction to ourselves, or others, though not as expressing our own Petitions or Thanksgivings. It is true David may sometimes Justify himself against his Adversarye, which wee allwayes cannot doe; but Davids example Instructeth us what wee ought to doe. That there be not Records in scripture, that the Saints have sung together, is utterly untrue, as hath bene allready declared.

The Draft of the Preface

The Instances alledged, do not hold. Of Moses and Miriam wee spake above. The Israelites spake and uttered that song as well as he. Exod. 15. 1. And if Miriam answered the men alone, the women Answered with her in Timbrells and daunces; but the New Testament alloweth not Timbrells and daunces nor any such outward expresses of Concent, but voyces onely. If their women may Joyne in Instrumentall musick, why not ours in vocall? Deborah sang not alone, but Barak with her. Judg. 5. 1. And as they did sing together for their private solace; why may not Publique songes of Praise be sung together by the Publique Congregation in way of Publique Thanksgiving? As Hezekiah might sing the song of Thanksgiving composed by himself for his recovery out of a daungerous sickness: So the whole Church receiving a Publique Blessing in his recovery, and finding the same song endited by the spirit of God, they might ioyne with him, as himself saith, He will Joyne with them, in singing his songs all the dayes of his life, Isay. 38. 20. What if all cannot sing with understanding? (which is another obiection) noe more can they all with understanding say Amen. Shall not therefore such as have understanding ioyne together in heart and voyce, because others are not able to doe it with understanding? Are not all the Creatures in Heaven, Earth, and Seas, men and Beasts, fishes and foules &c, all of them commaunded to Praise the Lord? Psa. 148. And yet none of all these save men, and godly men too can doe it with understanding. As for the other obiections which are taken from the difficulty of Mr. Answorths Tunes (wherein all cannot Joyne) or from the Corruptions found in the Translations of the Common Psalm Booke (wherein many dare not Joyne) wee hope they are all remooved in this new Edition of the Psalmes which wee here present unto the Lord and his Churches.

And as for the Scruple which some take at the Translation of Davids Psalmes into meeter, (because the Church of Israel sang Davids Psalmes in his owne words without

The Enigma of the Bay Psalm Book

meeter) They may please themselves to understand, That Davids Psalmes are penned by David in such verses, as are suitable to the poetry of the Hebrew Language, and not in the common style of such other Books of the Old Testament, as are not Poeticall. Now noe Protestant doubteth, That it is an Ordinance of God, That all the Bookes of Holy scripture should be extant in the mother tongue of each Nation. Else how could the Common people reade the scripture with understanding? If then Davids Psalmes ought to be Translated as into other Languages, so into our English tongue, and if in our English tongue wee are to sing them as songs of Praise to the Lord, then as all our English songs (according to the course of our English poetry) doe runne in meeter, so ought Davids Psalmes to be Translated into meeter, that so wee might sing the Lords songs as in our owne English Tongue, so in such verses as are familiar to an English eare, which are commonly metricall.

Doe but then take these two propositions for graunted (which no man iustly or reasonably can deny) 1: That Davids Psalmes are given by God to be for songs of Praise to God in each Christian Church and Countrey: 2. That Davids Psalmes being Poeticall verses are to be Translated into our English Tongue, and into such verses, as all our English songs runne in (according to the Poëtry of our Countrey) Then it will be noe offence to any good Conscience as to sing Davids Hebrew songs in English wordes, so to sing Davids Poeticall verses in English poeticall meeters, which are our verses. Men might as Justly stumble at singing Davids Psalmes in our English Tunes (and not in the Tunes used by the musicians of Israel in their Temple worship) as well as stumble at singing Davids Psalmes in our English meeters (which are our verses) and not in such verses used by David according to the Poetry of the Hebrew language. But the truth is, as God hath hid from us the Hebrew Temple Tunes, least wee should think ourselves bound to Imitate them: So hath he hid from us the

The Draft of the Preface

course and frame of their Hebrew Poetry, that wee need not thinke ourselves bound to Imitate that: But that every nation without scruple might follow, as the graver sort of Tunes of their owne Countrey songs, so the graver sort of verses of their owne Countrey Poetry. Neither let any man thinke, That wee have therefore for the meeters sake taken that liberty (or Poëticall license) to depart from the true and proper sense of Davids words in his Hebrew verses. Noe, it hath bene a speciall part of our Religious care, and faithfull endeavor to keepe close to the Originall Text, both for wordes and sence, insomuch that wee have not presumed so much as to Paraphrase upon the words of David, to give the sence of his meaning in other words.

[And so goe on in shewing what other things have bene attended to in this Translation according to the Letter which was read at Dortchester.]

Notes

Notes

I

THE PURITANS' NEED FOR A NEW TRANSLATION

1. In his poem "Aux dames de France," written in 1543, Marot, after beseeching the ladies of France to forget their worldly songs, stated, "Happy is he who will live to see the time when the farmer at his plough, the carter through the street, and the artisan in his shop solaces himself with a psalm...." Four years earlier Coverdale, in the preface to his *Goostly Psalmes*, similarly wrote: "Would God that our carters and ploughmen [had none] other thing to whistle save psalms... and if women had none other songs to pass their time withal.... They should be better occupied than with *hey nony nony, hey troly loly*, and such like phantasies." The hope, common with the early translators, came true. (O. Douen, *Clément Marot et le Psautier Huguenot* [Paris, 1878–79], I, 396; *Remains of Miles Coverdale* [Cambridge: Parker Society, 1846], p. 537.)

2. Thomas Warton, *The History of English Poetry* (London, 1840), III, 155. (The third volume was first published in 1778.) Warton (1728–90) was professor of poetry, and later of history, at Oxford. A writer of light verse, he was made poet laureate in 1785.

3. Preface to the Bay Psalm Book.

4. *Ibid.*

5. Cotton Mather, *Magnalia Christi Americana* (London, 1702), Book III, 74.

"Separatism" was the extreme form of Puritanism. It meant withdrawal from the Established Church and the organization of the congregation as an independent unit free from higher ecclesiastical government. The first such church was founded by Robert Browne, a kinsman of Lord Burghley, at Norwich in 1581. Hence the Separatists have often been called "Brownists," although Browne himself renounced his views a few years later.

Notes to Pages 8–11

The movement, however, spread and found new leaders in John Greenwood, Henry Barrow, Francis Johnson, Henry Ainsworth, and others. To escape persecution under Archbishops Whitgift and Bancroft, some of the Separatists in 1607 and 1608 fled to Holland where, at Amsterdam and Leyden, they set up their own churches. The Pilgrims, whose original home was in Nottinghamshire, Lincolnshire, and Yorkshire—"wher they border nearest togeather," as Bradford wrote—belonged to the Leyden church.

6. "I truly affirm," Dudley wrote to the Countess of Lincoln, "that I know no one person who came over with us the last year, to be altered in judgment, either in ecclesiastical or civil respects, since our coming hither" (Alexander Young, *Chronicles of Massachusetts Bay* [Boston, 1846], p. 272).

7. John White, *The Planters Plea* (London, 1630), pp. 59–66. White (1575–1648), a moderate Puritan, was Rector of Holy Trinity at Dorchester, Dorset. Already in 1624 he thought of sending out a colony of Dorset men to America. The forming of the Massachusetts Company and the obtaining of the patent from the Council of New England, with its confirmation by the royal charter (March 4, 1629), were to a large extent the result of his exertions. He continued to have great interest in the colony.

8. *The Humble Request . . . to the rest of their Brethren, in and of the Church of England* (London, 1630), in Young, *Chronicles*, p. 296.

9. *Church-Government and Church-Covenant Discussed* (London, 1643), p. 82.

10. *An Apologie of the Churches in New England for Church-Covenant* (London, 1643), p. 41. It should be noted that both this and the above treatise were composed in 1639.

11. The treatise, written in 1643, was published only in 1645. The quotation is from p. 67.

12. Cotton's *Keyes of the Kingdom of Heaven* (London, 1644) embodied (like Winthrop's "Arbitrary Government Described" of the same year) a closely reasoned political theory. "It is an usuall tenet in many of our best Divines," it affirmed, "that the government of the Church is mixt of a Monarchy, an Aristocracie, and a Democracie"—a statement which, had he known it, would have delighted John Adams.

13. John Cotton, *The Way of Congregational Churches Cleared* (London, 1648), pp. 9–10, 20. The chapter on "Touching the Line

of the Pedegree of the Independents in New-England" (pp. 12–17) is especially pertinent. Although denying that there was "any common consultation" with the Plymouth Church, Cotton admitted that the Puritans set up "the same modell of Churches, one like to another," without knowing that they imitated "Robinson's pattern." He also conceded it as "very likely" that "some of the first commers might helpe their Theory by hearing and discerning their practice at Plymouth."

Historians of Congregationalism, notably Henry C. Dexter, made much of this influence. Champlin Burrage was the first modern scholar to show, through Cotton's writings, the Puritans' independence of Plymouth and their affiliation with Ames and his school. "The early settlers of New England," he contended, "were Puritans, not separatists" (*The Early English Dissenters* [Cambridge, England, 1912], I, 356–68). The idea of Non-Separatist Congregationalism was brilliantly developed by Perry Miller in his *Orthodoxy in Massachusetts, 1630–50* (Harvard University Press, 1933).

II

THE JINGLE OF THOMAS SHEPARD

1. Book III, 100.
2. Professor Harold S. Jantz has found at the Historical Society of Pennsylvania a scrap of paper containing Shepard's quatrain in Increase Mather's handwriting. This version, undoubtedly more authentic than Cotton Mather's, reads:

> You Roxborough poets take this in Time
> see that you make very good Rythme
> And eeke of Dorchester when you the verses lengthen
> see that you them with the words of the text doe strengthen.

("The First Century of New England Verse," in *Proceedings of the American Antiquarian Society* for 1944, p. 237.)

3. None of the ministers ever mentioned his contribution. Welde, like John Cotton (see p. 128), referred to the new psalm book only in the name of the colony: "Because we desire to sing (as well as to reade) the pure Word of God, it being an Ordinance of God, as sacred as the other, wee have endeavoured, according to our light and time, to retranslate the Psalmes as neer the originall as wee could, into meeter, because the former

Notes to Pages 13–17

translation was very defective, and sing them in the Churches according thereunto" (*The Practices of the Churches in New-England* [London, 1645], p. 7).

4. With few exceptions, this has been the rule. George Parker Winship dogmatically declares: "There can be [no] doubt that the principal divines of the colony failed to collaborate . . ." Why? ". . . presumably because they were occupied with more immediate duties" (*The Cambridge Press, 1638–92* [University of Pennsylvania Press, 1948], p. 28).

5. The respect that his fellow ministers showed toward Cotton is reflected in their letters. They invariably addressed him—as did Shepard, and even Bulkeley, Stone, and others of the older generation—as "Deare Sir" or "Reverend and worthie Sir." The same men usually called each other "Deare Brother" or "Beloved Brother."

6. John Cotton, *Gods Promise to His Plantation* (London, 1630), p. 18.

7. The earliest meetings of the Boston congregation were held under a tree. The first meeting house was built, on the south side of the present State Street, in the fall of 1632. A new, larger church was erected seven years later.

8. John Norton, *The Life and Death of John Cotton* (London, 1858), pp. 29–30.

9. Foreword to the 1680 Boston edition of Wilson's *A Song of Deliverance*, first issued in London in 1626. The work was reprinted by Kenneth B. Murdock in *Handkerchiefs from Paul* (Harvard University Press, 1927), pp. 23–68.

10. *Magnalia*, Book III, 41.

11. "The Ministers," Neal wrote, "resolved on a New Version, and committed the Care of it to some of the chief Divines in the Country, among whom were the Reverend Mr. Eliot of Roxbury, Mr. Mather of Dorchester, and Mr. Welds; who have compared their several Performances together, printed the whole at Cambridge in the Year 1640" (*The History of New-England* [London, 1720], I, 188). Neal even spelled Welde's name in the same way as Cotton Mather!

12. John Josselyn, *An Account of Two Voyages to New England* (London, 1674), p. 20.

13. It was first published in the June, 1929, issue of *More Books*, bulletin of the Boston Public Library.

14. George Parker Winship's speculations about the relationship of the Preface to the draft (*The Cambridge Press*, pp. 26–27) are erroneous. The reviser adopted not only "an occasional sentence" but, with the exception of a few passages, the whole draft. He was able to use not only "about a third" of what was sent to him but nearly four-fifths. The draft covers not "about half" but three-fifths of the Preface, that is, its entire theological portion. In support of his calculations, Mr. Winship offers "parallel" passages from the draft and the Preface, showing that seventeen lines out of twenty-two (as they run in his book) are original with the Preface. However, the passages are not parallel at all. Those seventeen lines, too, are in the manuscript—only at a different place.

15. Joseph Otis Williams (1819–75) practiced law in Boston until the Civil War. Later he served as an assistant librarian at the Boston Public Library.

16. *Catalogue of the Prince Library* (Boston, 1870), p. xvi; *The Memorial History of Boston* (Boston, 1881), I, 458.

III

JOHN COTTON—NOT RICHARD MATHER

1. However, Barrow was not against "that most comfortable and heavenly harmony of singing Psalms"; he protested only against "the rhyming and paraphrasing of the Psalms" (*Observations of Mr. Gifford's Last Reply*, Art. xi).

2. One may note the spelling of "Dortchester." In a signed letter by Richard Mather, a letter now in the Boston Public Library, the word appears as "Dorthester."

3. John Cotton, *Singing of Psalmes, a Gospel Ordinance* (London, 1647), pp. 60–61.

4. The spelling of the Hebrew words, which appear in Hebrew characters in all three documents, adds its own story. The first, *mizmorim*, appears correctly in the draft and the Preface; the treatise, however, has a "typographical variant," for it uses a "final" *mem* for the third letter instead of the ordinary *mem*. The second word, *tehilim*, is right in the draft; the treatise adds an extra *l* (*lamed*), and the Preface uses both an extra *l* and a *yod* before the *l*. And finally in the case of the third word, *shirim*, the spelling is correct in all three places, but the draft and the treatise

Notes to Pages 26–27

have also the upper right-hand dot over the first letter, *shin*, indicating that it should be pronounced *sh* instead of *s*. Paradoxical though it may sound, this tiny dot alone might be significant in deciding the authorship of the draft. It was not absolutely necessary; Cotton's use of it in the treatise shows his meticulousness, and its presence in the draft displays the same spirit.

5. The largest store of Richard Mather manuscripts, described by William Sandford Piper in Thomas James Holmes's bibliography *The Minor Mathers* (Harvard University Press, 1940), is in the American Antiquarian Society, while some of the letters are in the Boston Public Library.

6. Shepard was greatly interested in the subject. Cotton's copy of the *Singing of Psalmes*, now in the Harvard College Library, has a note, on the back of the title-page, in the writing of the younger Thomas Shepard: "Mr. Edward Bulkley pastor of the Ch[urch] of X[ris]t in Concord told me Sept. 20, 1674 that when he boarded at Mr. Cotton's house at the 1st coming forth of this book of singing of psalmes, Mr. Cotton told him that my Father Shepard had the chief hand in the composing of it, and therefore, Mr. Cotton said, I am troubled that my bro: Shepard's name is not praefixed to it." The lines are at the bottom of the page, the rest of which is covered with a list of "Faults in the Printing corrected" written in Cotton's hand.

The note calls for comment. Edward Bulkeley, born in 1610, was pastor at Marshfield in 1647; thus he may have visited Cotton but could not have "boarded" at his house. He certainly could not have regarded the information as urgent, considering that he waited twenty-seven years before communicating it to his fellow minister. And, finally, if Cotton had really believed that the elder Shepard's name belonged on the title-page, he himself could have noted the omission while listing the far less important errors in the printing.

Filial piety and well-meaning friendship seem to have attached, after so long a time, too great a weight to a generous remark—such as authors often make, even in writing, without actually meaning it. Cotton may have had also Shepard's work on the Preface to the Bay Psalm Book in mind. In any case, the long treatise of the *Singing of Psalmes* would have had enough room for Shepard's contribution too.

IV
THE NEW ENGLAND PSALM BOOK

1. *Magnalia*, Book III, 100. John Cotton's statement (see note 3 on p. 123) seems to imply that the revision was already under way in 1647.

2. Winship maintains that the first edition of the New England Psalm Book was published in Cambridge, England, in 1648, making the claim solely because three undated copies with the imprint "Cambridge, Printed for Hezekiah Usher, of Boston" were bound up with a Bible of that date. However, Wilberforce Eames thought that those three copies were printed in 1658, 1669, and 1682 (*The Cambridge Press*, pp. 94–98).

3. *The Minor Mathers* lists twenty-five American, seventeen English, and nine Scotch editions of the New England Psalm Book. There is only a single copy of the first edition, in the New York Public Library.

4. The identity of Richard Lyon, a hitherto entirely obscure figure, is discussed in Appendix B.

5. This may explain the meagerness of his information about both the Bay Psalm Book and the New England Psalm Book. Cotton Mather was only six years old when Richard Mather, his grandfather, died; Thomas Welde went to England in 1641 and never returned; but he could have easily obtained the story from John Eliot, who survived till 1691.

6. Cotton Mather, *Psalterium Americanum* (Boston, 1718), pp. vii, x–xi, ix.

7. Louis F. Benson, *The English Hymn* (New York, 1915), pp. 165–66.

V
PROBLEMS FOR THE SCHOLAR

1. *A History of American Literature* (New York, 1880), I, 276.

2. Thomas Warton, *The History of English Poetry* (London, 1840), III, 155.

3. Thomas Campbell, *Specimens of the British Poets* (London, 1819), I, 116–17.

4. Harold S. Jantz, "The First Century of New England Verse," in *Proc. of Am. An. Soc.* for 1944, pp. 222–23.

5. *Ibid.*, p. 236.

6. William Tyndale, *The Obedience of a Christian Man* [1527] (Parker Society, 1848), p. 304.

7. *Treatise of the Christian Religion* (London, 1616), p. 78.

8. Vladimir Nabokov, "Problems of Translation," in *Partisan Review* (fall, 1955), p. 496.

9. *Psalterium Americanum*, p. ix.

10. The writer has gone through Mather's *A Farewel Exhortation* (Cambridge, 1657), Eliot's *Christian Commonwealth* (London, 1659), Shepard's *Indians in New England* (London, 1648), Norton's *Divinity of Christ* (London, 1653), and a number of other treatises. Welde's *Answer to W. R.* (London, 1644) has some lines from the Geneva Bible. Slightly older than Mather and Eliot, he entered Trinity College, Cambridge, before 1611.

11. *The Gospel Covenant* (London, 1646), p. 1. The quotations on the title-page are from the Geneva Bible.

12. In his *Singing of Psalmes* Cotton's quotations from Psalms 3, 9, 33, 64, and 100 are from the King James Version; those from Psalm 95 from the King James Version and the Bishops Bible; and finally the lines from Psalm 111 are from the Geneva Bible. For his *Exposition of the Book of Canticles* (London, 1642), *Exposition of Ecclesiastes* (London, 1654), and *Exposition of the Thirteenth Chapter of the Revelation* (London, 1655), he used exclusively the King James Version.

13. There were two copies of Ainsworth's Psalter among the books donated by William Backhouse to the Puritans before they sailed from Southampton ("The Library of the Mathers," by Julius Herbert Tuttle, in *Proc. of Am. An. Soc.* for 1910, pp. 271–73, 297). The libraries of John Harvard, Peter Bulkeley, and the Mathers also included copies (Thomas Goddard Wright, *Literary Culture in Early New England, 1620–1730* [Yale University Press, 1920], pp. 30, 31).

14. Wright, *op. cit.*, pp. 26, 31, 36, 137.

15. Samuel Sewall had a copy, but it is not known when it was brought to America.

16. P. 56.

17. A. Z. Idelsohn, *Jewish Music* (New York, 1929) and *Thesaurus of Hebrew Oriental Melodies* (Berlin, 1922–28), and A. M. Rothmüller, *The Music of the Jews* (London, 1953) all have pertinent chapters on the biblical accents and their nota-

tions. See also the articles on "synagogal music," "accents in Hebrew," and "cantillation" in the *Jewish Encyclopedia* (New York, 1916).

18. Alfred C. Potter, "Catalogue of John Harvard's Library," in *Publications of the Colonial Society of Massachusetts*, XXI (Boston, 1920), 190–230; Tuttle, *op. cit.*

19. "Jehovah" is a derivation of the tetragrammaton *YHWH* ("Yahweh" or "Yahaweh"), and its meaning is "He is" or "He lives." It was the highest name of God, the pronunciation of which was prohibited. The "Name" or "The Ineffable Name" was used instead by the priests. "Adonai" ("The Lord") was another substitution. "Elohim," the plural of "Eloah," meaning "He who is the object of fear," was of later origin.

VI
EXPERIMENTS IN TEXTUAL ANALYSIS

1. Of the large number of modern commentaries, the writer has found W. E. Barnes's two-volume *The Psalms* (New York, 1932) especially useful. He has consulted the similar works of T. K. Cheyne (London, 1888) and Charles A. Briggs (New York, 1907). C. H. Spurgeon's *Treasury of David* (London, 1871–85), in seven large volumes, contains extracts from the whole range of psalmodic literature. *The Hexaplar Psalter*, ed. William Aldis Wright (Cambridge, 1911), was of course a great convenience.

2. *The Holy Scriptures According to the Masoretic Text* (Jewish Publication Society of America, 1917).

3. The line occurs in the stanza:

'Twas of Geneva's Worthies said, with wonder
(Those Worthies Three:) Farell was wont to Thunder;
Viret, like Rain, on tender grass to shower;
But Calvin, lively Oracles to pour.

(In Nathaniel Morton, *New Englands Memoriall* [Cambridge, 1669], pp. 125–26.)

Pierre Viret (Viretus), 1511–71, French reformer and author of numerous theological and polemical works, was for years Calvin's coadjutor at Geneva. About 1560 he returned to France and, under constant persecution, preached at Nîmes, Montpelier, Lyons, and other places.

Notes to Pages 55–60

4. *The Complete Works of Francis Quarles* (London, 1880–81), I, lxix–lxxii.

5. See p. 17 and note.

6. Even the translators of the Bay Psalm Book were criticized for having "framed their words and sentences more to the Meeter, than the Prose"! In his *Singing of Psalmes*, John Cotton replied: "The meeter and verse of the late Translators, cometh as neare to the words and sence of the Originall, as doth the Prose; especially considering they doe withall expresse the holy Art of the Originall Hebrew Poetry, which the Prose doth not attend unto." Cotton admitted that "for the verse sake" they sometimes "put Jah for Jehovah"; however, this did not "breake the Attributes of God." Then he added: "To prevent all stumbling . . . I suppose they will helpe it in the next Edition of the Psalmes" (pp. 60–61).

VII

THE SEARCH FOR AUTHORSHIP

1. Here are some of Mr. Winship's *dicta:* "It has not been possible to find a verse anywhere that justifies a suspicion that it was not written by the person who did the rest"; "Words that can be used as a test of an individual vocabulary are almost completely lacking"; and, "With rare exceptions the simple, direct phrasing of the Bible texts then available is avoided . . ." (*The Cambridge Press*, p. 29).

2. See p. 36 and notes.

3. *American Broadside Verse*, ed. by Ola Elizabeth Winslow (Yale University Press, 1930), p. 5.

4. Thomas Shepard, *The Church-Membership of Children* (Cambridge, 1663).

5. Morton, *New Englands Memoriall*, pp. 127–29.

6. No real attempt has been made so far to compare the two psalm books and to examine the new alternate versions of sixteen psalms included in the second. Winship merely printed side by side parts of the first three and last three psalms, and the additional renderings of certain passages of psalms and spiritual songs offered by the revisers (*The Cambridge Press*, pp. 363–73, 101).

VIII
THE PSALM-SINGING OF THE PURITANS

1. *A History of Music in New England* (Boston, 1846), p. 9.
2. *Music in America* (New York, 1883), pp. 3, 4.
3. Percy A. Scholes, *The Puritans and Music in England and New England* (London, 1934), pp. 7–11, gives examples from more than twenty books.
4. Hood, *op. cit.*, pp. 50–51. Professor Samuel E. Morison notes that "twice every Sabbath, Harvard students had an opportunity to exercise their voices in singing psalms at Cambridge meeting," and finds it "probable" that Dunster and Lyon, in working on their revision, tested the singing qualities of their verses on their pupils. However, he knows of no musical instruction or musical theses at Harvard during these years (*Harvard College in the Seventeenth Century* [Harvard University Press, 1936], I, 116–17).
5. The title of S. Lothrop Thorndike's "The Psalmodies of Plymouth and Massachusetts Bay," *Pub. of Col. Soc. of Mass.* for 1894, pp. 228–38, is a misnomer. Thorndike tells only of psalm-singing in England, stopping short at the point where the music reached the colonies.
6. *History of English Music* (London, 1895), pp. 264–305.
7. Scholes, *op. cit.*, p. 269.
8. *The Flowering of New England* (New York, 1936), p. 47.
9. Phillips Barry found sixty-six versions of fourteen such ballads ("Traditional Ballads in New England," *Journal of American Folklore* [April, July, and October, 1905]). Professor George L. Kittredge and others discovered many more (July, 1917, issue of the same magazine).
10. *Singing of Psalmes*, p. 32. The taverns sold a great variety of alcoholic liquors, but the amount of drinks allowed to a person was limited. The General Court enacted severe laws against the "swinish sinne of drunkennes," and excessive drinking was closely watched by both magistrates and ministers.
11. *Faithful Warnings* (Boston, 1722), p. 7. See also Edward K. Trefz, "Satan in Puritan Preaching" in the April and July, 1956, issues of *The Boston Public Library Quarterly*.
12. *Wo to Drunkards* (Boston, 1712), pp. 50–51. Mather saw the past in rosy colors when he made his famous statement:

Notes to Pages 65–70

"There was a time when a Man might live Seven Years in New-England, and not see a Drunken Man."

13. Waldo Selden Pratt, *The Music of the Pilgrims* (Boston, 1921) is a valuable monograph. Hamilton C. MacDougall, *Early New England Psalmody* (Brattleboro, 1940) is comprehensive but sketchy.

14. *Hypocrisie Unmasked* (London, 1646), p. 90.

15. *The Reasonableness of Regular Singing, or Singing by Note* (Boston, 1720), p. 6.

16. References are given to the respective tunes to be found in the English psalm books.

17. Hood already stated that one or more editions with music had preceded the 1698 edition (*op. cit.*, p. 57); and Ritter discovered that all thirteen tunes had been selected from John Playford's *A Brief Introduction to the Skill of Musick*, first published in 1654 in London (*op. cit.*, p. 31). By comparing various editions of Playford's essay, Irving Lowens has recently shown that the original of the Boston edition of 1698 must have been compiled in England ("The Bay Psalm Book in 17th-Century New England," *Journal of the American Musicological Society* [spring, 1955]).

18. Most of the tunes received their names from the towns in which they were found in use, although they did not necessarily originate there.

19. *Diary of Samuel Sewall* (Boston, 1873–82), I, 506. Half a century before, John Cotton, conceding that new spiritual songs might be sung privately, wrote, "nor doe we forbid the private use of an Instrument of Musick therwithall." The casualness of his remark seems to indicate that musical instruments were not such rarities even among the first settlers as is commonly thought (*Singing of Psalmes*, pp. 32, 15).

20. *Diary of Samuel Sewall*, II, 151, 391; III, 171, 173, 297. Sewall owned a copy of Playford's *Introduction* in the 1679 edition, which includes Thomas Campion's *The Art of Descant*, a discussion of the several keys and of composing four parts in counterpoint. He also had a copy of the 1698 edition of Playford's psalm book, "with all the Ancient and Proper Tunes . . . Composed in Three Parts, Cantus, Medius, and Bassus." (Both volumes are in the Prince Library.)

21. One may note that the Salem church in its meeting on "the 4th of the 5th month 1667" merely resolved that "the Bay Psalm

Book should be used together with Ainsworth's to supply the defects of it"; and that the Plymouth church, on August 7, 1692, voted, "when the tunes are difficult in the translation we use, we will sing the psalms now used in our neighbor churches in the Bay" (Hood, *op. cit.*, pp. 53–54). In other words, they did not give up formally the Ainsworth Psalter, although in practice the decision amounted to the same thing. (The "difficulty" of the Ainsworth tunes, as noted before, was first mentioned in the Preface to the Bay Psalm Book. Most of the Puritans found the tunes beyond their capacity even in 1640!)

22. Symmes, *op. cit.*, p. 8.

23. Thomas Walter, *The Grounds and Rules of Musick* (Boston, 1721), pp. 2–5. The author also notes: "At present we are confined to eight or ten Tunes, and in some Congregations to little more than half that Number."

24. None of these tracts are quoted, or even mentioned, in Scholes's work. Walter alone is given a few lines. Criticizing the wrong timing of the notes, the Roxbury pastor related that he himself had to pause twice in one note to take a breath; and Scholes wittily remarks that the Reverend Thomas Walter "may have been a wheezy asthmatic" (Scholes, *op. cit.*, p. 269).

IX
THE PRINTING OF THE BAY PSALM BOOK

1. Glover's name is variously spelled as "Joos," "Joas," "Jose," "Josse," and "Jesse," a dialect form of Joseph. The son of Roger Glover, merchant of London, he studied at Oxford, where he received his bachelor's degree in 1612 and his master's in 1615. He became rector of Sutton, in Surrey, in 1624, and resigned his benefice in 1636.

2. In England, Day sometimes spelled his name with an *e*, which, however, he dropped in America.

3. The bond, which was signed on June 7, 1638, and the document explaining its "condition" are in the Archives of Harvard University. They are printed in Samuel Abbott Green, "Stephen Daye, the Earliest Printer in this Country," in *Ten Facsimile Reproductions Relating to New England* (Boston, 1902), pp. 1–3.

4. Winship interprets the sentence as if it referred to a trade that Day had been practicing in New England, instead of merely

stating that he would continue his trade in New England. He assumes that previous to their agreement Day and Glover had already visited Massachusetts and possibly returned on the same ship to England (*Cambridge Press*, pp. 5-7). However, he admits that "there is not a particle of proof" for his theory; and Professor Morison, very properly, calls it "a myth" (*The Founding of Harvard College* [Harvard University Press, 1935], p. 255).

5. Green, *op. cit.*, p. 5.

6. Edward Johnson, *A History of New England* (London, 1654), p. 129.

7. "Cambridge around 1638," a map drawn by Erwin Raisz from data compiled by Albert P. Norris, in Morison, *The Founding of Harvard College*, facing p. 192.

8. *Collections of the Massachusetts Historical Society* (Fourth Series, Vol. VI [Boston, 1863]), p. 99. Captain Peirce, born about 1590, had many friends among the leaders of the colonies. Carrying immigrants and goods, he was constantly voyaging between New England, Virginia, and England. He was also a notable figure in the commerce with the West Indies, bringing in cotton, tobacco, sugar—and on February 16, 1638, a group of Negroes, the first Negro slaves in New England. He was killed by a Spanish bullet in 1641, while taking a number of families from the Bay Colony to New Providence, one of the Bahama Islands.

9. Edward Johnson's record is too vague to throw any light upon the date of the opening of the press. "This yeare," he wrote under 1638, "the reverend and judicious Mr. Jos. Glover undertook this long voyage, being able both in person and estate for the work he provided, for further compleating the Colonies in Church and Common-wealth-work, a Printer which hath been very usefull in many respects..." (*op. cit.*, p. 129).

10. The entries were supposed to have been copied by Treasurer Danforth after 1656, "from miscellaneous documents, the originals of which no longer exist." *Pub. of Col. Soc. of Mass.* (Boston, 1925), XV, 174-75, lxxi.

11. *The Founding of Harvard College*, pp. 345-46.

12. Daniel Neal's explanation is worth quoting: "To make the College as compleat as possible," he wrote, "... they set up a Printing-Press, which was absolutely necessary for the dispersing small practical Treatises up and down the Country; for it can't be imagin'd, that they could carry off an Edition of any very

considerable Work while the Colony was so small, and there were so few Men of Letters in it" (*The History of New-England* [London, 1720], I, 187).

13. *Records of Massachusetts Bay*, I, 344. On May 29, 1655, the General Court confirmed the grant of land, given by Day in 1641 "for recompense of his care and charg in furthering the worke of printing" (Vol. IV, Part I, 236). A further entry—for May 15, 1657—states: "Steven Day, of Cambridge, having often complained that he hath suffered much dammage by erecting the printing press at Cambridge, at the request of the magistrates and elders, for which he never had yett any considerable satisfaction, this Court doe graunt him three hundred acres of land in any place not formerly graunted by this Court" (Vol. IV, Part I, 306). One should note that the interest of the magistrates and elders in the press is not mentioned elsewhere.

14. Andrew McF. Davis, "The Cambridge Press," in *Proc. of Am. Antiq. Soc.* for April, 1888, p. 296.

15. *Ibid.*, pp. 297–302.

16. Winship, *op. cit.*, pp. 144–45. In a letter to the writer, Professor Allan Stevenson points out that the number of reams needed for 37 sheets works out at 130 reams, counting 483.6 effective sheets to the ream, with allowance for cassies and waste.

17. *Middlesex Records*, I, 77–87, as quoted in Isaiah Thomas, *The History of Printing in America* (3d ed., 1874), I, 383–90. The first edition of the *History* was published in 1810.

18. Rush C. Hawkins, "The Daye Press," in *The Literary Collector* for December, 1903, and March, 1904.

19. The text, however, is known from the *Records* of the colony, and from the tract, *New England's Jonas Cast Up at London* (London, 1847).

20. Thomas, *op. cit.*, I, 44–46. Thomas—a great printer!—erroneously called the volume "a crown 8vo."

21. As noted before, Thomas Shepard may have acted as proofreader. He lived close by; Crooked Lane, where the press was located, led directly to the parsonage. Further, Shepard's friendship with Matthew Day appears clearly from the latter's will which, with Matthew's mother, he witnessed. The young printer left to the pastor twenty shillings (to be collected from the College), as also his "diaper table cloath and napkins which were not yet made up" (Green, *op. cit.*, pp. 9–10).

X
THE EXTANT COPIES

1. A man of delicate health, Crowninshield (1817–59) devoted his life to the pleasures of book collecting. His library, a friend remembered, "contained some of the most beautiful and desirable books we have ever seen, books such as it was difficult to look at without breaking the tenth commandment." An expert on the subject, Crowninshield was often consulted about the price of rare books (Memoir by Charles Deane, in *Proceedings of the Massachusetts Historical Society* for 1880, pp. 356–59).

2. Livermore (1809–65) was a wool merchant, whose real vocation, however, was biblical history and bibliography. A sweet and generous man, he was always ready to help people in bookish matters. Robert Winthrop, Oliver Wendell Holmes, Edward Everett Hale, and others paid affectionate tributes to his memory. (His biography, also by Charles Deane, fills fifty-four pages in the *P.M.H.S.* for 1869, pp. 415–68.)

3. Dr. Shurtleff (1810–74) was responsible for publishing, in thirteen volumes, the Records of the Bay and Plymouth Colonies. (His memoir by Charles S. Smith is in the *P.M.H.S.* for 1875, pp. 389–95.)

4. Armstrong (1784–1850) was a printer and bookseller who published a missionary magazine and other religious literature. In 1833–35 he was lieutenant-governor of Massachusetts, serving for the last ten months also as acting governor. Upon his retirement, he was elected mayor of Boston.

5. The reference is to the first catalogue of the Prince Library printed in 1846, and entry No. 259 consists of one line: "The Whole Book of Psalms, translated into English metre. 1640. (Perfect copy.)"

6. Henry Stevens, *Recollections of James Lenox* (London, 1886), revised by Victor Hugo Paltsits (New York, 1951), p. 48.

7. The letter copybooks of Henry Stevens, preserved in the Clements Library at Ann Arbor, Michigan, help to fill out the picture. On May 17, 1855, Stevens billed his copy of the Bay Psalm Book to Lenox for 80 pounds and on June 4 informed him: "This morning I received a long letter from Mr. Livermore inclosing the leaves to complete the Bay Psalm Book. So now the copy is perfect and genuine. Livermore does not know that I

have sold it to you, but says I might put *a very high price* upon it, as it is worth as much [as] a Coverdale and is much rarer." The Coverdale Bible of 1535—the first complete English translation—was then, as it is today, one of the great prizes in book collecting.

8. Beriah Botfield, *Cathedral Libraries of England* (London, 1849), pp. 272-79.

9. Bibliographers still have a lively interest in Dibdin's dealings at Lincoln, making minute inquiries about his booty of Caxtons, the sums he received for them, and where the books now are.

10. Archives of the Harvard Alumni Association for 1859.

11. Lothrop (1817-78) was for several years a member of the Boston School Committee.

12. Justin Winsor did not seem happy about the transactions. However, he confined his emotions to a memorandum. Visiting the American Antiquarian Society in August, 1871, he recorded, at the request of the librarian, that the three copies of the Bay Psalm Book were transferred to the three gentlemen by Lieutenant-Governor Armstrong. "He surrendered the copies to these private hands," he wrote, "in consideration of certain modern books given to said Library and of the modern binding bestowed on one or more of the copies now remaining in said Prince Library." The statement was erroneous in part, although Winsor had evidently seen Armstrong's note.

13. Six days before the auction—on November 24, 1875—the *Boston Daily Advertiser* published an editorial denying the legality of the "exchanges" by which the three copies of the Bay Psalm Book had been acquired and warning the buyer that he might have to restore Dr. Shurtleff's copy to the Old South Church.

14. Most people believed that the injunction was issued for the benefit of the Boston Public Library (*Daily Evening Traveler*, December 2, 1875; *Boston Morning Journal*, December 3, 1875).

15. Supreme Judicial Court of Suffolk County, No. 1031 Eq. *Laches* is a legal term meaning "neglect to do a thing at the proper time." A copy of Dr. Shurtleff's telltale letter is included in Sarah E. Shurtleff's answer, filed on January 13, 1876.

16. Dr. Shurtleff had three more copies of Winthrop's *New England;* they were sold at the auction of his library for $1.00, $1.25, and $1.75. He had two copies of Belknap's *American*

Notes to Page 89

Biography, which realized $1.25 and $2.12. Even copies of the reprint of the Bay Psalm Book, issued by Dr. Shurtleff in 1862, sold on the occasion for nearly ten times the combined price of the two books.

17. Sec. 1 of the statute limited the period for taking action to six years. The deacons' only chance by 1875 would have been the invoking of sec. 12 which, if "the cause of action was fraudulently concealed," extended the limit for another six years from the time of the discovery of the deceit—and this the deacons could not show. Evidently in anticipation of such a charge did the defendant emphasize that Dr. Shurtleff had been in "the open, notorious and exclusive possession" of the book.

18. Winsor returned to the subject once more, this time publicly. He stated that Richard Mather's copy "passed by an understanding" into the hands of Dr. Shurtleff, as had two others into those of Crowninshield and Livermore. He did not refer to Dr. Shurtleff's letter but mentioned that the suit for the recovery of the Mather copy was lost on account of the Statute of Limitations (*The Memorial History of Boston* [Boston, 1881], I, 459). The error of his memorandum at the American Antiquarian Society, which he wrote in 1871, shows that he had not learned about the circumstances of the transfer of this copy until the trial of 1876. He evidently did not read Dr. Shurtleff's letter even then.

Wilberforce Eames (in the Introduction of the 1903 Facsimile Reprint of the Bay Psalm Book) printed Winsor's record from the archives of the American Antiquarian Society, and also told briefly of the lawsuit. However, he did not know of Armstrong's note or of Dr. Shurtleff's letter. Men of uncompromising honesty, neither Winsor nor Eames would have slurred over Dr. Shurtleff's letter for reasons of "tact." The same is true, since their time, of other historians and bibliographers loyal to their profession.

The present writer seems to have been the first to examine the court files. The story of the three copies has been related by Robert Wallace (*Life*, November 22, 1954, pp. 95–106).

Notes to Pages 93–101

APPENDIX A
A TRANSCRIPT BY COTTON

1. Williston Walker, *Ten New England Leaders* (Boston, 1901), p. 115.

2. *A Reply to Mr. Williams his Examination*. Printed in 1647, reprinted in *Publications of the Narragansett Club* (1867), II, 103.

3. *A Disputation Concerning Church-Members and their Children* (London, 1659), A4. Nathaniel Mather's name is not signed, but the introduction is unquestionably by him.

4. Increase Mather, *The Order of the Gospel* (Boston, 1700), p. 73. Cotton Mather repeated his father's statement in *Magnalia*, Book III, 128.

5. *Prince Catalogue*, p. 158 (MSS. H. 1. 4. 4 and 6).

6. *Ibid.*, p. 151 (MSS. H. 1. 6; II, 6; III, Appendix 6; III, 10).

APPENDIX B
WHO WAS RICHARD LYON?

1. *Magnalia*, Book III, 100. See p. 12.

2. *The British Empire in America* (London, 1741), I, 215. (The first edition, published in 1708, does not contain the note about Lyon.) Oldmixon (1673–1742) was a historian and a pamphleteer.

3. *Alumni Cantabrigienses* (Cambridge, England, 1924), III, 123.

4. John Langdon Sibley, *Graduates of Harvard University* (Cambridge, Mass., 1873), I, 164–65.

5. Sir Henry Mildmay had a spectacular career: he started life as a King's favorite, became a regicide, and died in the Tower.

6. *Publications of the Colonial Society of Massachusetts* (Boston, 1925), XV, 26.

7. Morison, *Harvard College in the Seventeenth Century*, I, 78.

8. Sir Henry Mildmay was one of the hostages left with the Scots in December, 1646, after Parliament had agreed to pay them an indemnity of £400,000 if they withdrew from the country. Half of the sum was paid by February, 1647, whereupon the Scots handed over the King to the English Commissioners and departed.

9. *Pub. of Col. Soc. of Mass.*, XV, cxxxvii.

10. It was while reading about the rules of "placing" that this explanation occurred to the writer. He was happy to see his opinion confirmed—although somewhat tentatively—by an unpublished letter of the late Albert Matthews, preserved in the Harvard archives. On April 17, 1919, Matthews wrote to George P. Winship:

"As the eldest son of a Knight, W.M. was entitled to certain privileges, and no one has ever been able to explain why he was 'placed' at the bottom of his class. I have two guesses to make on this point. First, and this seems to me the more probable explanation, he may have entered as a Junior or even Senior (as the course was then three years, there were no Sophomores), and in that case would probably have been placed at the foot. I say 'probably' because we have no definite information on that point at so early a period. But it is certain that in the 18th century a student entering an upper class was placed at the foot; though later this rule was changed, and a student so entering was accorded the place that would have been his had he entered it a Freshman. It seems a fair inference that the old rule was in force in the early days, and if it was then Mildmay's 'place' is easily accounted for. My second guess is that Mildmay may have picked up some college pranks and have been degraded. This is perfectly possible, but in most cases of degradation a student regained his original position—if not before graduation, then at least before taking his A.M. . . ."

But Matthews's suggestion remained unheeded. Winship presents Mildmay as a retarded child: "One may wonder whether William Mildmay sat in a corner of the President's study, dozing over his assigned lesson, while the two scholars conned the ancient Hebrew tunes . . ." (*The Cambridge Press*, p. 98).

11. The entry in the *Alumni Cantabrigienses* also informs us that Lions came from Lancashire. The name was common in that county; the parish register of the township of Prescot, for instance, is filled with Lyons, from Abel to William. A Richard Lyon who may come nearest to our hero was christened there on August 20, 1620. This would make the student matriculating at Emmanuel in 1645 twenty-five; but during the Civil War (as during and after World War II) students went to college at irregular ages. This is, of course, mere conjecture. One should look through the records of all the townships of Lancashire, many

Notes to Pages 103–6

of which have already been published by the Lancashire Parish Register Society.

12. *Pub. of Col. Soc. of Mass.* (Boston, 1945), XXXI.

13. *Ibid.*, p. 12.

14. John Cotton's statement in *Singing of Psalmes*, pp. 60–61.

15. Granville Penn, *Life and Times of Sir William Penn* (London, 1833), I, 496–98. The address of the letter, which has been found among the papers of Sir William, is wanting. The account was reprinted in *The Letters and Papers Relating to the First Dutch War*, ed. C. T. Atkinson (The Navy Records Society, 1912), V, 82–85.

16. The name occurs on the list of "the winter guard" for December 1653. Lyons was relieved of his post in August 1654 but reappointed in the winter of 1655/56, resigning his commission for "political reasons" before March 4. No trace of the man can be found in the Archives of the Royal Naval College either before or after 1653–56.

17. Concerning Lyon's future career, the writer made an inquiry also at The Admiralty, which was forwarded to the Public Record Office where the Admiralty records for the period are now kept. The reply of the Secretary was, unfortunately, negative.

One may note that Lyon, who had produced so much verse in his youth, does not seem to have published anything afterward. At least, *The Short-Title Catalogue* does not list any book under his name.

Index of Names

Adams, John, 120
Ainsworth, Henry, 6, 7, 39, 44, 45, 65, 70, 120, 131
Alexander, William, Earl of Stirling, 37
Allen, Frederick D., 88
Ames, William, 9, 10, 121
Anderson, R. C., 106
Anne of Cleves, 4
Armstrong, Samuel T., 84, 134, 135
Atkinson, C. T., 139

Backhouse, William, 126
Bancroft, Richard, 120
Barnes, W. E., 127
Barrow, Henry, 19, 120, 123
Barry, Phillips, 129
Baynes, Paul, 9, 10
Bedford, Francis, 82
Benson, Louis F., 125
Beza, Theodore, 5
Böschenstein, Johann, 37
Botfield, Beriah, 135
Bourgeois, Louis, 4
Bradford, William, 120
Bradstreet, Anne, 98
Brady, Nicholas, 30
Brathwaite, Richard, 37, 48, 52
Brinley, George, 86
Brooks, Van Wyck, 63
Browne, Edmund, 73
Browne, Robert, 119
Bulkeley, Edward, 124

Bulkeley, Peter, vii, 16, 26, 33, 36, 58, 97, 122, 126
Bunyan, John, 62
Burghley, William Cecil, Lord, 119
Burrage, Champlin, 120
Buxtorf, Johann, 38

Calvin, John, 3, 4, 5, 34, 38, 39, 46
Campbell, Thomas, 32, 125
Campion, Thomas, 130
Cartwright, Thomas, 34
Chesholme, Thomas, 103
Cheyne, T. K., 127
Child, Francis James, 63
Church, E. Dwight, 82
Copeland, Patrick, 73
Cotton, John, vi, 10, 13–14, 17, 18, 19, 20–21, 25, 27, 33, 36, 37, 38, 46, 51, 56, 64, 93–97, 120, 122, 123, 124, 128, 130
Cotton, Seaborn, 63
Coverdale, Miles, 3, 4, 6, 119
Cranmer, Thomas, 4
Cromwell, Oliver, 62
Crowley, Robert, 5
Crowninshield, Edward A., 84–85, 87, 134, 136

Dane, Charles, 134
Danforth, Thomas, 132
Davenport, John, 10
Davey, Henry, 62

The Enigma of the Bay Psalm Book

Davis, Andrew McF., 133
Day, Matthew, 75, 133
Day, Stephen, 72, 76–78, 131, 133
Dexter, Henry C., 121
Dibdin, Thomas F., 86, 135
Douen, O., 119
Dowland, John, 67
Dudley, Thomas, 120
Dunster, Henry, 13, 28, 29, 43, 59, 76, 98, 129

Eames, Wilberforce, 125, 136
Eliot, John, 12, 13, 16, 36, 122, 125, 126
Elizabeth, Queen, 5
Elmerton, of Cranbrook, England, 25, 26
Elson, Louis C., 61
Endicott, John, 78

Farnaby, Giles, 67
Foster, John, 78
Francis I, 4

Glover, Mrs. Elizabeth Harris, 73
Glover, Jose, 11, 72, 77–78, 131
Goudimel, Jean, 4
Green, Samuel, 28, 77
Green, Samuel Abbott, 131, 132, 133
Greenwood, John, 120
Grindal, Edmund, 15
Grosart, Alexander B., 55
Grotius, Hugo, 40

Hale, Edward Everett, 134
Hall, John, 5
Harris, C. Fiske, 89
Harvard, John, 38, 126

Hawkins, Rush C., 133
Hawthorne, Nathaniel, 15
Henry VIII, 4
Higginson, Francis, 8
Holmes, Oliver Wendell, 134
Holmes, Thomas James, 124
Homes, Nathaniel, 19
Hood, George, 61, 129, 130, 131
Hooker, Thomas, 10, 58
Hopkins, John, 5, 50
Howard, Henry, Earl of Surrey, 5
Howard, John Tasker, 61
Huss, John, 34

Idelsohn, A. Z., 126

James I, 37
Jantz, Harold S., 32–33, 121, 125
Jerome, St., 50
Johnson, Edward, 75, 132
Johnson, Francis, 120
Johnson, Marmaduke, 78
Josselyn, John, 17, 55, 122

Kettell, Samuel, 31
Kirbye, George, 67
Kittredge, George L., 129

Lenox, James, 85, 134
Livermore, George, 84–85, 134, 136
Lothrop, Loring, 87, 88, 135
Lowens, Irving, 130
Luther, Martin, 3, 4, 34
Lyon, Richard, vii, 28, 29, 43, 59, 60, 98–106, 125, 129, 138, 139

Index of Names

MacDougall, Hamilton C., 130
Marot, Clément, 3, 4, 119
Mary, Queen, of England, 5
Mather, Cotton, vi, 12–13, 15, 16, 26, 28–30, 35, 64, 70, 83, 98, 110, 121, 125, 137
Mather, Increase, 64, 70, 93, 95, 121, 129, 137
Mather, Nathaniel, 93, 95, 137
Mather, Richard, vi, 10, 12, 16, 18, 19–20, 26, 36, 81, 93–97, 122, 123, 124, 125, 126
Matthews, Albert, 138
Matthews, W. S. B., 61
Mildmay, Sir Henry, 28, 98, 137
Mildmay, Sir Walter, 102
Mildmay, William, 28, 98–102, 138
Miller, Perry, 121
Milton, John, 62
Morison, Samuel Eliot, 63, 47, 103, 129, 132, 137
Morton, Nathaniel, 127, 128
Murdock, Kenneth B., 122
Musculus (Mosel, W.), 38

Nabokov, Vladimir, 35, 126
Neal, Daniel, 17, 122, 132
Norris, Albert P., 132
Norton, John, 33, 36, 122, 126

Oldmixon, John, 99, 137
Osiander, Andreas, 38

Paltsits, Victor Hugo, 134
Parker, Matthew, 5
Parker, Robert, 9, 10
Peirce, William, 11, 74, 79, 132
Penn, Granville, 139
Penn, Sir William, 105, 139

Perkins, Charles C., 61
Peter, Hugh, 73, 75, 93
Piper, William Sanford, 124
Playford, John, 130
Plumer, Avery, 88
Potter, Alfred C., 127
Pratt, Waldo Selden, 130
Prince, Thomas, 16, 30, 81, 83

Quarles, Francis, 20, 51, 54, 55, 128

Raisz, Erwin, 132
Ravenscroft, Thomas, 67
Reuchlin, Johann, 37
Rider, Sidney S., 89
Ritter, F. L., 61, 130
Rivetus (Rivet, André), 38
Robinson, John, 6
Rothmüller, A. M., 126

Saltonstall, Richard, 97
Sandys, George, 37
Scholes, Percy A., 62, 129, 131
Seager, Francis, 5
Sewall, Samuel, 69, 126, 130
Shepard, Thomas, 12, 13, 17, 26–27, 33, 36, 96, 121, 122, 124, 126, 128, 133
Shepard, Thomas, Jr., 124
Shurtleff, Nathaniel B., 84, 87–88, 134, 135, 136
Sibley, John L., 99, 137
Sinderin, A. Van, 83
Smith, Charles S., 134
Spurgeon, C. H., 127
Sternhold, Thomas, 4, 48, 52
Stevens, Henry, 85, 86, 134
Stevenson, Allan, 133
Stone, Samuel, 122
Symmes, Thomas, 65, 70, 131

Tanner, Thomas, 82
Tate, Nahum, 30
Thomas, Isaiah, 82, 133
Thorndike, S. Lothrop, 129
Trefz, Edward K., 129
Tuttle, Julius Herbert, 126, 127
Tyler, Moses C., v, 31, 41
Tyndale, William, 34, 126

Vanderbilt, Cornelius, 86
Venn, J. A., 100, 105
Venn, John, 100
Viret (Viretus), Pierre, 127

Wadsworth, Benjamin, 64
Walker, Williston, 137
Wallace, Robert, 136
Walter, Thomas, 70, 131
Ward, Nathaniel, 16, 33
Warton, Thomas, 5, 32, 49, 119, 125
Watts, Isaac, 30
Welde, Thomas, 12–13, 16, 121, 122, 125, 126

White, Alfred, 87
White, John, 8, 120
Whitgift, John, 120
Whiting, Samuel, 16
Whittingham, William, 46
Williams, Joseph Otis, 18, 123
Williams, Roger, 20, 32, 94
Wilson, John, vii, 13–15, 33, 36, 57, 122
Wilson, John, Jr., 15
Winship, George Parker, vi, 122, 123, 128, 131, 133, 138
Winslow, Edward, 65
Winslow, Ola Elizabeth, 128
Winsor, Justin, 18, 135, 136
Winthrop, John, 8, 11, 120
Winthrop, Robert, 134
Wither, George, 3
Wright, Thomas Goddard, 126
Wright, William Aldis, 127
Wyatt, Sir Thomas, 5
Wyclif, John, 34

Young, Alexander, 120

The
Bay Psalm Book

Contents

THE FACSIMILE

NOTES ON THE REPRODUCTION

THE
VVHOLE
BOOKE OF PSALMES
Faithfully
TRANSLATED *into* ENGLISH
Metre.

Whereunto is prefixed a difcourfe declaring not only the lawfullnes, but alfo
the necefsity of the heavenly Ordinance
of finging Scripture Pfalmes in
the Churches of
God.

Coll. III.
*Let the word of God dwell plenteoufly in
you, in all wifdome, teaching and exhorting one another in Pfalmes, Himnes, and
fpirituall Songs, finging to the Lord with
grace in your hearts.*

Iames V.
*If any be afflicted, let him pray, and if
any be merry let hius fing pfalmes.*

Imprinted
1 6 4 0

The Preface.

THe singing of Psalmes, though it breath forth nothing but holy harmony, and melody: yet such is the subtilty of the enemie, and the enmity of our nature against the Lord, & his wayes, that our hearts can finde matter of discord in this harmony, and crotchets of division in this holy melody.-for- There have been three questiōs especially stirrīg cōcerning singing. First, what psalmes are to be sung in churches? whether Davids and other scripture psalmes, or the psalmes invented by the gifts of godly men in every age of the church. Secondly, if scripture psalmes, whether in their owne words, or in such meter as english poetry is wont to run in? Thirdly, by whom are they to be sung? whether by the whole churches together with their voices? or by one man singing alōe and the rest joynīg in silēce, & in the close sayīg amen.

Touching the first, certainly the singing of Davids psalmes was an acceptable worship of God, not only in his owne, but in succeeding times. as in Solomons time 2 *Chron.* 5. 13. in Iehosaphats time 2 *chron.* 20. 21. in Ezra his time *Ezra* 3. 10, 11. and the text is evident in Hezekiahs time they are commanded to sing praise in the words of David and Asaph, 2 *chron.* 29, 30. which one place may serve to resolve two of the questions (the first and the last) at once. for this commandement was it ceri-

* 2   moniall

moniall or morall? some things in it indeed were cerimoniall, as their musicall inftruments &c but what cerimony was there in finging prayfe with the words of David and Afaph? what if David was a type of Chrift, was Afaph alfo? was every thing of David typicall? are his words (which are of morall, univerfall, and perpetuall authority in all nations and ages) are they typicall? what type can be imagined in making ufe of his fongs to prayfe the Lord? If they were typicall becaufe the cerimony of muficall inftruments was joyned with them, then their prayers were alfo typicall, becaufe they had that ceremony of incenfe admixt with them: but wee know that prayer then was a morall duty, notwithftanding the incenfe; and foe finging thofe pfalmes notwithftanding their muficall inftruments. Befide, that which was typicall (as that they were fung with muficall inftruments, by the twenty-foure orders of Priefts and Levites. *1 chron* 2 5. 9.) muft have the morall and fpirituall accomplifhment in the new Teftament, in all the Churches of the Saints principally, who are made kings & priefts *Rev.* 1. 6. and are the firft fruits unto God. *Rev.* 14 4. as the Levites were *Num.* 3. 45. with hearts & lippes, in ftead of muficall inftruments, to prayfe the Lord; who are fet forth (as fome iudicioufly thinke) *Rev.* 4. 4. by twenty foure Elders, in the ripe age of the Church, *Gal.* 4. 1, 2, 3. anfwering to the twenty foure orders of Priefts and Levites *1 chron.* 25. 9. Therefore not fome felect members

Preface.

members, but the whole Church is commaunded to teach one another in all the severall sorts of Davids psalmes, some being called by himselfe מִזְמוֹרִים: psalms, some תְּהִלִּים: Hymns some שִׁירִים: spirituall songs. soe that if the singing Davids psalmes be a morall duty & therfore perpetuall; then wee under the new Testamēt are bound to sing them as well as they under the old: and if wee are expresly commanded to sing Psalmes, Hymnes, and spirituall songs, then either wee must sing Davids psalmes, or else may affirm they are not spirituall songs: which being penned by an extraordīary gift of the Spirit, for the sake especially of Gods spirituall Israell; not to be read and preached only (as other parts of holy writ) but to be sung also, they are therefore most spirituall, and still to be sung of all the Israell of God: and verily as their sin is exceeding great, who will allow Davids psalmes (as other scriptures) to be read in churches (which is one end) but not to be preached also, (which is another end soe their sin is crying before God, who will allow them to be read and preached, but seeke to deprive the Lord of the glory of the third end of them, which is to sing them in christian churches.

obj. 1 If it be sayd that the Saints in the primitive Church did compile spirituall songs of their owne inditing, and sing them before the Church. 1 Cor. 14, 15, 16.

Ans. We answer first, that those Saints compiled these spirituall songs by the extraordinary gifts of

the

the spirit (common in those dayes) whereby they were inabled to praise the Lord in strange tongues, wherin learned *Pareus* proves those psalmes were uttered, in his Commēt on that place *vers* 14 which extraordinary gifts, if they were still in the Churches, wee should allow them the like liberty now. Secondly, suppose those psalmes were sung by an ordinary gift (which wee suppose cannot be evicted) doth it therefore follow that they did not, & that we ought not to sing Davids psalmes? must the ordinary gifts of a private man quench the spirit still speaking to us by the extraordinary gifts of his servant David? there is not the least foot-step of example, or precept, or colour reason for such a bold practise.

obj. 2. Ministers are allowed to pray conceived prayers, and why not to sing conceived psalmes? must wee not sing in the spirit as well as pray in the spirit?

Ans. First because every good minister hath not a gift of spirituall poetry to compose extemporary psalmes as he hath of prayer. Secondly. Suppose he had, yet seeing psalmes are to be sung by a joynt consent and harmony of all the Church in heart and voyce (as wee shall prove) this cannot be done except he that composeth a psalme, bringeth into the Church set formes of psalmes of his owne invētion; for which wee finde no warrant or president in any ordinary officers of the Church throughout the sciptures. Thirdly. Because the booke of psalmes is so compleat a System of psalmes

Preface.

pſalmes, which the Holy-Ghoſt himſelfe in infinite wiſdome hath made to ſuit all the conditions, neceſſityes, temptations, affections, &c. of men in all ages; (as moſt of all our interpreters on the pſalmes have fully and perticularly cleared) therefore by this the Lord ſeemeth to ſtoppe all mens mouths and mindes ordinarily to compile or ſing any other pſalmes (under colour that the ocaſions and conditions of the Church are new) &c. for the publick uſe of the Church, ſeing, let our condition be what it will, the Lord himſelfe hath ſupplyed us with farre better; and therefore in Hezekiahs time, though doubtleſſe there were among them thoſe which had extraoridnary gifts to compile new ſongs on thoſe new ocaſions, as Iſaiah and Micah &c. yet wee read that they are commanded to ſing in the words of David and Aſaph, which were ordinarily to be uſed in the publick worſhip of God: and wee doubt not but thoſe that are wiſe will eaſily ſee; that thoſe ſet formes of pſalmes of Gods owne appoyntment not of mans conceived gift or humane impoſition were ſung in the Spirit by thoſe holy Levites, as well as their prayers were in the ſpirit which themſelves conceived, the Lord not then binding them therin to any ſet formes; and ſhall ſet formes of pſalmes appoynted of God not be ſung in the ſpirit now, which others did then?

Queſton. But why may not one cōpoſe a pſalme & ſing it alone with a loud voice & the reſt joyne

with

with him in silence and in the end say **Amen**?

Ans. If such a practise was found in the Church of Corinth, when any had a psalme suggested by an extraordinary gift; yet in singing ordinary psalmes the whole Church is to ioyne together in heart and voyce to prayse the Lord. -for-

First. Davids psalmes as hath beene shewed, were sung in heart and voyce together by the twenty foure orders of the musicians of the Temple, who typed out the twenty foure Elders all the members especially of christian Churches *Rev* 5. 8. who are made Kings and Priests to God to prayse him as they did: for if there were any other order of singing Choristers beside the body of the people to succeed those, the Lord would doubtlesse have given direction in the gospell for their quallification, election, maintainance &c. as he did for the musicians of the Temple, and as his faithfullnes hath done for all other church officers in the new Testament.

Secondly. Others beside the Levites (the chiefe Singers) in the Iewish Church did also sing the Lords songs; else why are they commanded frequently to sing: as in pſ. 100, 1,2,3. pſ. 95, 1,2,3. pſ. 102. title. with vers 18. & *Ex.* 15. 1. not only Moses but all Israell sang that song, they spake saying (as it is in the *orig.*) all as well as Moses, the women also as well as the men. v. 20 21. and *deut.* 32. (whereto some thinke, Iohn had reference as well as to *Ex.* 15. 1. when he brings in the protestant Churches getting the victory over the

Beast

Preface.

Beast with harps in their hands and singing the song of Moses. *Reu.* 15. 3.) this song Moses is commanded not only to put it into their hearts but into their mouths also: *deut.* 31. 19. which argues, they were with their mouths to sing it together as well as with their hearts.

Thirdly. Isaiah foretells in the dayes of the new-Testament that Gods watchmen and desolate lost soules, (signified by wast places) should with their voices sing together, *Isa.* 52. 8, 9. and *Reu.* 7. 9, 10. the song of the Lamb was by many together, and the Apostle expresly commands the singing of Psalmes, Himnes, &c. not to any select christians, but to the whole Church *Eph.* 5. 19 *coll.* 3. 16. Paule & Silas sang together in private *Acts.* 16. 25. and must the publick heare oly one man sing? to all these wee may adde the practise of the primitive Churches; the testimony of ancient and holy *Basil* is in stead of many *Epist.* 63 When one of us (saith he) hath begun a psalme, the rest of us set in to sing with him, all of us with one heart and one voyce; and this saith he is the common practise of the Churches in Egypt, Lybia, Thebes, Palestina, Syria and those that dwell on Euphrates, and generally every where, where singing of psalmes is of any account. To the same putpose also *Eusebius* gives witnes, *Ecclef. Hist. lib.* 2. *cap.* 17. The objections made against this doe most of them plead against joyning to sing in heart as well as in voyce, as that by this meanes others out of the Church will sing as alſo that wee are not alway in a ſutable eſtate to the matter ſung, & likewiſe that all cannot ſing with underſtanding; ſhall not therefore all that have underſtanding ioyne in heart and voyce together? are not all the creatures in heaven, earth, ſeas: men, beaſts, fiſhes, foules &c. commanded to praiſe the Lord, and yet none of theſe but men, and godly men too, can doe it with ſpirituall underſtanding?

As for the ſcruple that ſome take at the tranſlatiō of the book of pſalmes into meeter, becauſe Davids pſalmes were ſung in his owne words without meeter: wee anſwer. Firſt. There are many verſes together in ſeveral pſalmes of David which run in rithmes (as thoſe that know the hebrew and as Buxtorf ſhews *Theſau.* pa. 629.) which ſhews at leaſt the lawfullnes of ſinging pſalmes in engliſh rithmes.

Secondly. The pſalmes are penned in ſuch verſes as are ſutable to the poetry of the hebrew language, and not in the common ſtyle of ſuch other bookes of the old Teſtament as are not poeticall; now no proteſtant doubteth but that all the bookes of the ſcripture ſhould by Gods ordinance be extant in the mother tongue of each nation, that they may be underſtood of all, hence the pſalmes are to be tranſlated into our engliſh tongue; and if in our engliſh tongue wee are to ſing them, then as all our engliſh ſongs (according to the courſe of our engliſh poetry) do run in metre, ſoe ought Davids pſalmes to be tranſlated

into

Preface.

into meeter, that foe wee may fing the Lords fongs, as in our english tongue foe in fuch verfes as are familar to an englifh eare which are commonly metricall: and as it can be no juft offence to any good confcience to fing Davids hebrew fongs in englifh words, foe neither to fing his poeticall verfes in englifh poeticall metre: men might as well ftumble at finging the hebrew pfalmes in our englifh tunes (and not in the hebrew tunes) as at finging them in englifh meeter, (which are our verfes) and not in fuch verfes as are generally ufed by David according to the poetry of the hebrew language: but the truth is, as the Lord hath hid from us the hebrew tunes, left wee fhould think our felves bound to imitate them; foe alfo the courfe and frame (for the moft part) of their hebrew poetry, that wee might not think our felves bound to imitate that, but that every nation without fcruple might follow as the graver fort of tunes of their owne country fongs, foe the graver fort of verfes of their owne country poetry.

Neither let any think, that for the meetre fake wee have taken liberty or poeticall licence to depart from the true and proper fence of Davids words in the hebrew verfes, noe; but it hath beene one part of our religious care and faithfull indeavour, to keepe clofe to the originall text.

As for other obiections taken from the difficulty of *Ainfworths* tunes, and the corruptions in

** 2 our

our common psalme books, wee hope they are answered in this new edition of psalmes which wee here present to God and his Churches. For although wee have cause to blesse God in many respects for the religious indeavours of the translaters of the psalmes into meetre usually annexed to our Bibles, yet it is not unknowne to the godly learned that they have rather presented a paraphrase then the words of David translated according to the rule 2 *chron.* 29. 30. and that their addition to the words, detractions from the words are not seldome and rare, but very frequent and many times needles, (which we suppose would not be approved of if the psalmes were so translated into prose) and that their variations of the sense, and alterations of the sacred text too frequently, may iustly minister matter of offence to them that are able to compare the translation with the text; of which failings, some iudicious have oft complained, others have been grieved, wherupon it hath bin generally desired, that as wee doe inioye other, soe (if it were the Lords will) wee might inioye this ordinance also in its native purity: wee have therefore done our indeavour to make a plaine and familiar translation of the psalmes and words of David into english metre, and have not soe much as presumed to paraphrase to give the sense of his meaning in other words; we have therefore attended heerin as our chief guide the originall, shunning all additions, except such as even the best
translators

Preface.

translators of them in prose supply, avoiding all materiall detractions from words or sence. The word ו׃ which wee translate *and* as it is redundant sometime in the Hebrew, soe somtime (though not very often) it hath been left out, and yet not then, if the sence were not faire without it.

As for our translations, wee have with our english Bibles (to which next to the Originall wee have had respect) used the Idioms of our owne tongue in stead of Hebraismes, lest they might seeme english barbarismes.

Synonimaes wee use indifferently: as *folk* for *people*, and *Lord* for *Iehovah*, and somtime (though seldome) *God* for *Iehovah*; for which (as for some other interpretations of places cited in the new Testament) we have the scriptures authority ps. 14. with 53. Heb. 1. 6. with psalme 97. 7. Where a phrase is doubtfull wee have followed that which (in our owne apprehensiō) is most genuine & edifying:

Somtime wee have contracted, somtime dilated the same hebrew word, both for the sence and the verse sake: which dilatation wee conceive to be no paraphrasticall addition no more then the contraction of a true and full translation to be any unfaithfull detraction or diminution: as when wee dilate *who healeth* and say *he it is who healeth*; soe when wee contract, *those that stand in awe of God* and say *Gods fearers*.

Lastly. Because some hebrew words have a

** 3   more

The.

more full and emphaticall signification then any one english word can or doth somtime expresse, hence wee have done that somtime which faithfull translators may doe, *viz.* not only to translate the word but the emphasis of it; as אל *mighty God*, for God. ברך *humbly blesse* for *blesse*; *rise to stand*, psalm 1. for *stand; truth and faithfullnes* for *truth*. Howbeit, for the verse sake wee doe not alway thus, yet wee render the word truly though not fully; as when wee somtime say *reioyce* for *shout for ioye.*

As for all other changes of numbers, tenses, and characters of speech, they are such as either the hebrew will unforcedly beare, or our english forceably calls for, or they no way change the sence; and such are printed usually in an other character.

If therefore the verses are not alwayes so smooth and elegant as some may desire or expect; let them consider that Gods Altar needs not our pollishings: Ex. 20. for wee have respected rather a plaine translation, then to smooth our verses with the sweetnes of any paraphrase, and soe have attended Conscience rather then Elegance, fidelity rather then poetry, in translating the hebrew words into english language, and Davids poetry into english meetre;
that

Preface.

that soe wee may sing in Sion the Lords
songs of prayse according to his owne
will; untill hee take us from hence,
and wipe away all our teares, &
bid us enter into our masters
ioye to sing eternall
Halleluiahs.

THE PSALMES

In Metre

PSALME I

O Blessed man, that in th'advice
    of wicked doeth not walk:
nor stand in sinners way, nor sit
    in chayre of scornfull folk.
2 But in the law of Iehovah,
    is his longing delight:
and in his law doth meditate,
    by day and eke by night.
3 And he shall be like to a tree
    planted by water-rivers:
that in his season yeilds his fruit,
    and his leafe never withers.
4 And all he doth, shall prosper well,
    the wicked are not so:
but they are like vnto the chaffe,
    which winde drives to and fro.
5 Therefore shall not ungodly men,
    rise to stand in the doome,
nor shall the sinners with the just,
    in their assemblie *come*.
6 For of the righteous men, the Lord
    acknowledgeth the way:
but the way of vngodly men,
    shall vtterly decay.

PSALM II

WHy rage the *Heathen* furiously?
    muse vaine things people do;
2 Kings of the earth doe set themselves,
    Princes consult also:
with one consent against the Lord,
    and his anoynted one.
3 Let us asunder break their bands,
    their cords bee from us throwne.
4 Who sits in heav'n shall laugh; the lord
    will mock them; then will he
5 Speak to them in his ire, and wrath:
    and vex them suddenlie.
6 But I annoynted have my King
    upon my holy hill
7 of Zion: The established
    counsell declare I will.
God spake to me, thou art my Son:
    this day I thee begot.
8 Aske thou of me, and I will give
    the Heathen for thy lot:
and of the earth thou shalt possesse
    the utmost coasts abroad.
9 thou shalt them break as Potters sherds
    and crush with yron rod.
10 And now yee Kings be wise, be learn'd
    yee Iudges of th'earth(*Heare.*)
11 Serve yee the lord with reverence,
    rejoyce in him with feare.
12 Kisse yee the Sonne, lest he be wroth,
    and yee fall in the way.
when his wrath quickly burnes, oh blest

are

PSALME III, IV.

are all that on him stay.

Psalme 3

1 A psalme of David when he fled from the face of Absalom his Sonne.

O Lord, how many are my foes?
 how many up against me stand?
2 Many say to my soule noe helpe
 in God for him at any hand.
3 But thou Lord art my shield, my glory
 and the-uplifter of my head,
4 with voyce to God I cal'd, who from
 his holy hill me answered.
5 I layd me downe, I slept, I wakt,
 for Iehovah did me up beare:
6 People that set against me round,
 ten thousand of them I'le not feare.
7 Arise o Lord, save me my God,
 for all mine enimies thou hast stroke
 upon the cheek-bone : & the teeth
 of the ungodly thou hast broke.
8 This, and all such salvation,
 belongeth vnto Iehovah;
 thy blessing is, and let it be
 upon thine owne people. Selah.

Psalme 4

To the cheife Musician on *Neginoth*,
 a psalme of David.

GOD of my justice, when *I* call
 answer me: when distrest
thou hast inlarg'd me, sh ew me grace,
and heare thou my request.

A 2   2 yee

PSALM IV

2 Ye Sonnes of men, my glory turne
 to shame how long will you?
how long will ye love vanity,
 and still deceit pursue?
3 But know, the Lord doth for himselfe
 set by his gracious saint:
the Lord will heare when I to him
 doe poure out my complaint.
4 Be stirred up, but doe not sinne,
 consider seriouslie:
within your heart upon your bed,
 and wholly silent be
5 Let sacrifices of justice,
 for sacrifices be,
and confidently put your trust
 on Iehovah doe ye.
6 Many there be that say o who,
 will cause us good to see:
the light, Lord, of thy countenance
 let on us lifted be.
7 Thou hast put gladnesse in my heart,
 more then the time wherein
their corne, and also their new wine,
 have much increased bin.
8 In peace with him I will lye downe,
 and take my sleepe will I:
For thou Lord mak'st me dwell alone
 in confident safety.

Psalme 5
1 To the cheife Musitian upon *Nehiloth*,
 a psalme of David.

psalm

PSALME V

Heare thou my words and understand
  my meditation, Iehovah.
2 My King, my God, attend the voyce
  of my cry: for to thee I pray.
3 At morn Iehovah, thou shalt heare
  my voyce: to thee I will addresse
4 at morn, I will looke up. For thou
  art not a God lov'st wickednesse
  neither shall evil with thee dwell.
5 Vaine glorious fooles before thine eyes
  shall never stand: for thou hatest
  all them that worke iniquities.
6 Thou wilt bring to distruction
  the speakers of lying-falshood,
  the lord will make to be abhor'd
  the man deceitfull, and of blood.
7 But I will come into thine house
  in multitude of thy mercy:
  and will in feare of thee bow downe,
  in temple of thy sanctity.
8 Lead me forth in thy rightousnes,
  because of mine observing spies,
  O Iehovah doe thou thy wayes
  make straight, and plaine, before mine eyes
9 For there no truth is in his mouth,
  their inward part iniquities;
  their throat an open sepulchre,
  their tongue is bent to flatteries.
10 O God make thou them desolate
  from their owne plots let them fall far,
  cast them out in their heapes of sinnes,

PSALM V VI

    for they against thee Rebells are.
11 *And* all that trust in thee shall joy,
    and shout for joy eternallie,
    and thou shalt them protect: & they
    that love thy name shall joy in thee.
12 For thou Iehovah, wilt bestow
    a blessing on the rightous one:
    and wilt him crowne as with a sheild,
    with gracious acceptation.

Psalme 6

To the chief Musician on *Neginoth* upon
    Sheminith, a psalme of David

LORD in thy wrath rebuke me not,
    nor in thy hot wrath chasten me.
2 Pitty me Lord, for I am weak,
    Lord heale me, for my bones vext be.
3 Also my soule is troubled sore:
    how long Lord wilt thou me forsake?
4 Returne o Lord, my soule release:
    o save me for thy mercy sake.
5 In death no mem'ry is of thee
    and who shall prayse thee in the grave?
6 I faint with groanes, all night my bed
    swims, I with tears my couch washt have.
7 mine eye with grief is dimme and old:
    because of all mine enimies.
8 But now depart away fom me,
    all yee that work iniquities:
    for Iehovah ev'n now hath heard
    the voyce of these my weeping teares.
9 Iehovah heare my humble suit,

                                      Iehovah

PSALME VI VII

Iehovah doth receive my prayers.
10 Let all mine enimies be asham'd
 and greatly troubled let them be:
 yea let them be returned back,
 and be ashamed suddenlie.

Psalme 7

Shiggajon of David which he sãg to Iehovah
 upõ the words of Cush the Benjamite.

O LORD my God in thee
 I doe my trust repose,
save and deliver me from all
 my persecuting foes.
2 Lest like a Lion hee
 my soule in peeces teare:
rending asunder, while there is
 not one deliverer.
3 Iehovah o my God
 if this thing done have I:
if so there be within my hands
 wrongfull iniquity
4 If I requited ill
 the man with me at peace,
(yea I have him delivered
 that was my foe causlesse:)
5 Let foe pursue my soule,
 and take, and tread to clay
my life: and honor in the dust
 there let him wholly lay
6 Arise Lord in thy wrath
 for th' enimies fiercentesse:
be thou lift up, & wake to me,

A 4   judgemẽt

PSALM VII

 judgement thou did'st expresse.
7 So thee encompasse round
 shall peoples assembly;
and for the same doe thou returne,
 vnto the place on high.
8 The Lord shall judge the folke;
 Iehovah judge thou me.
according to my righteousnesse,
 and mine integritie.
9 Let ill mens malice cease,
 but doe the just cousirme,
for thou who art the righteous God:
 dost hearts and reins discerne.
10 For God my sheild, the right
 in heart he saved hath.
11 The God that doth the rightous judge,
 yet daily kindleth wrath.
12 If he doe not returne,
 his sword he sharp will whet:
his bow he bended hath, and he
 the same hath ready set.
13 For him he hath prepar'd
 the instruments of death,
for them that hotly persecute,
 his arrows he sharpneth.
14 Behold he travelleth
 of vaine iniquity:
a toylesome mischeife he conceiv'd,
 but shall bring forth a lye.
15 A pit he digged hath,
 and delved deepe the same:

         but

PSALME VII, VIII.

But fall'n he is into the ditch,
   that he himselfe did frame.
16 His mischeivous labour
   shall on his head turn downe:
and his injurious violence
   shall fall upon his crowne.
17 Iehovah I will prayse
   for his just equity;
and I will sing unto the name
   of Iehovah most high.

Psalme 8
To the chiefe Musician upon *Gittith*,
a psalme of David.

O LORD our God in all the earth
   how's thy name wondrous great:
who hast thy glorious majesty
   above the heavens set.
2 out of the mouth of sucking babes.
   thy strength thou didst ordeine,
that thou mightst still the enemy,
   and them that thee disdaine.
3 when I thy fingers work, thy Heav'ns,
   the moone and starres consider
4 which thou hast set. What's wretched man
   that thou dost him remember?
or what's the Son of man, that thus
   him visited thou hast?
5 For next to Angells, thou hast him
   a litle lower plac't
and hast with glory crowned him,
   and comely majesty:

PSALM VIII, IX.

6 And on thy works haſt given him,
    lordly authoriy.
7 All haſt thou put under his feet;
    all ſheep and oxen, yea
8 and beaſts of field. Foules of the ayre,
    and fiſhes of the ſea,
    and all that paſſe through paths of ſeas.
9   O Iehovah our Lord,
  how wondrouſly-magnificent
    is thy name through the world?

Pſalme 9

To the chiefe Muſician upon *Muth-Labben*
    a pſalme of David

LORD I'le the prayſe, with all my heart;
    thy wonders all proclaime.
2 I will be glad and joy in thee;
    moſt high, I'le ſing thy name.
3 In turning back my foes, they'le fall
    and periſh at thy ſight.
4 For thou maintaines my right, & cauſe:
    In throne ſits judging right.
5 Thou t' heathen checkſt, & th'wicked ſtroyd;
    their names raz'd ever aye.
6 Thy ruines, foe, for aye are done;
    thou madſt their townes decaye;
  their memory with them is loſt.
7 Yet ever ſits the Lord:
  his throne to judgement he prepares.
8 With right he'l judge the world:
  he to the folke ſhall miniſter
    judgement in uprightneſſe.

9 The

PSALME iX

9 The Lord is for th'opreſt a fort:
   a fort in times of ſtreſſe.
10 Who knowes thy name, will truſt in thee:
   nor doſt thou, Lord forſake,
11 them that thee ſeek. Pſalmes, to the Lord
   that dwells in Sion, make:
   declare among the folk his works.
12 For blood when he doth ſeeke,
   he them remembers: nor forgets
   the crying of the meeke.

(2)

13 Iehovah, mercy on me have,
   from them that doe me hate
   marke mine afflictions that ariſe,
   thou lift'ſt me from deaths-gate.
14 That I may tell in the gates of
   the Daughter of Sion,
   thy prayſes all; and may rejoyce
   in thy ſalvation.
15 The heathen are ſunk downe into
   the pit that they had made:
   their owne foot taken is ith'net
   which privily they layd.
16 By judgement which he executes
   Iehovah is made knowne:
   the wicked's ſnar'd in's owne hand work.
   deepe meditation.
17 The wicked ſhall be turn'd to hell,
   all lands that God forget,
18 Forgot the needy ſhall ne're be:
   poores hope ne're faild him yet.

PSALM IX, X.

19 Arise, o Lord, left men prevaile,
    judge t' heathen in thy fight.
20 That they may know they be but men,
    the nations Lord affright.   Selah

Psalme 10

WHy standst thou Lord a far? why hyd'st thy selfe in times of streight?
2 In pride the wicked persecutes
    the poore afflicted wight:
snare them in their contrived plots.
3   For of his hearts desire
the wicked boasts, and covetous
    blesseth, stirring Gods ire.
4 The wicked one by reason of
    his countenances pride
will not seek *after God*: not God
    so all his thoughts abide.
5 his wayes doe alwayes bring forth griefe,
    on high thy judgements bee
above his sight: his pressing foes
    puffe at them all will hee.
6 Within his heart he thus hath sayd,
    I moved shall not bee:
from aye to aye because I *am*
    not in adversitie.
7 His mouth with cursing filled *is*,
    deceits, and fallacy:
under his tongue perversnes *is*,
    also iniquity.
8 In the close places of the townes
    he sits, in secret dens

he

PSALME X.

he slays the harmlesse: 'gainst the poore
   slyly his eyes downe bends.
9 He closely lurks as lion lurks
   in den, the poore to catch
he lurks, & trapping them in 's net
   th' afflicted poore doth snatch.
10 Downe doth he crowtch,& to the dust
   humbly he bowes *with-all*:
that so a multitude of poore
   in his strong pawes may fall.
11 He saith in heart, God hath forgot:
   he hides his face away,
so that he will not see this thing
   unto eternall aye.

(2)

12 Iehovah rise thou up, o God
   lift thou thine hand on hy,
let not the meek afflicted one
   be out of memory.
13 Wherefore doth the ungodly man
   contemne th' almighty one?
he in his heart saith, **thou** wilt not
   make inquisition.
14 Thou seest, for thou markst wrong,& spight,
   with thy hand to repay:
the poore leavs it to thee, thou art
   of fatherlesse the stay.
15 Break thou the arme of the wicked,
   and of the evil one.
search thou out his impiety,
   untill thou findest none.

PSALM X, XI.

16 Iehovah king for ever is,
    and to eternall aye:
out of his land the heathen folke
    are perished away.
17 The meeke afflicted-mans desire
    Iehovah, thou dost heare:
thou firmly dost prepare their heart,
    thou makst attent thine eare.
18 To judge the fatherlesse & poore:
    that adde no more he may
sorrowfull man out of the land
    with terror to dismay.

Psalme 11
To the chiefe Musician a psalme of David.

1 In the Lord do trust; how then
    to my soule doe ye say,
as doth a litle bird unto
    your mountaine flye away?
2 For loe, the wicked bend their bow,
    their arrows they prepare
on string; to shoot in dark at them
    in heart that upright are.
3 If that the firme foundationes,
    utterly ruin'd bee:
as for the man that righteous is,
    what then performe can hee?
4 The Lord in's holy temple is,
    the Lords throne in heaven:
his eyes will view, and his eye lids
    will prove the Sonnes of men.

PSALME XI, XII.

5 The man that truly-righteous is
    ev'n him the Lord will prove;
his soule the wicked hates, & him
    that violence doth love.
6 Snares, fire, & brimstone he will raine,
    ungodly men upon:
and burning tempest; of their cup
    shall-be their portion.
7 For Iehovah that righteous is,
    all righteousnesse doth love:
his countenane the upright one
    beholding, doth approve.

Psalme 12
To the chiefe Musician upon *Sheminith*
a psalme of David.

Helpe Lord: for godly men doe cease:
    faithfull faile men among.
2 Each to his freind speaks vanity;
    with flattring lips, *and tongue*
and with a double heart they speake.
3 All flatt'ring lips the Lord
shall cut them of, with every tongue
    that speaketh boasting word.
4 Thus have they sayd, we with our tongue,
    prevailing pow're shall get:
are not our lips our owne. for Lord
    who over us is set?
5 Thus saith the Lord, for sighs of them
    that want, for poor opprest,
I'le now arise, from such as puffe,
    will set him safe at rest.

PSALM XII, XIII.

6 Pure are the words the Lord doth speak:
   as silver that is tryde
in earthen furnace, seven times
   that hath been purifyde.
7 Thou shalt them keep, o Lord, thou shalt
   preserve them ev'ry one,
For evermore in safety from
   this generation.
8 The wicked men on evry side
   doe walk presumptuously,
when as the vilest sons of men
   exalted are on hye.

Psalme 13
To the chiefe Musician: a psalme of David.

O IEHOVAH, how long
   wilt thou forget me aye?
how long wilt thou thy countenance
   hide from me farre away?
2 How long shall I counsell,
   in my soule take, sorrow
in my heart dayly? o're me set
   how long shall be my foe?
3 Iehovah, o my God,
   behold me answer make,
Illuminate mine eyes, lest I
   the sleepe of death doe take.
4 Lest my foe say, I have.
   prevaild 'gainst him: & me
those who doe trouble, doe rejoyce,
   when I shall moved bee.

5 But

PSALME XIII, XIIII.

5 But I asured trust
   have put in thy mercy;
my heart in thy salvation
   shall joy exceedingly.
6 Vnto Iehovah I
   will sing, because that hee,
for evil bountifully hath
   rewarded good to mee.

Psalme 14
To the chiefe Musician a psalme of Dauid.

THe foole in's heart saith ther's no **God**;
   they are corrupt, have done
abominable-practises,
   that doth good there is none.
2 The Lord from heaven looked downe
   on Sonnes of men: to see,
if any that doth understand,
   that seeketh God there bee.
3 All are gone back, together they
   ev'n filthy are become:
and there is none that doeth good,
   noe not so much as one.
4 The workers of iniquityes,
   have they no knowledge all?
that eate my people: they eate bread,
   and on God doe not call.
5 There with a very grievous feare
   affrighted sore they were,
for God in generation is
   of such as righteous are.

C   the

PSALM XIV, XV.

6 The counsell yee would make of him
    that poore afflicted is,
  to be asham'd & that because
    the Lord his refuge is.
7 Who Israels health from Syon gives?
    his folks captivitie
  when God shall turne: Iacob shall joye
    glad Israel shall be.

Psalme 15
A psalme of David.

IEHOVAH, who shall in thy tent
  so ourne, and who is hee
shall dwell within thy holy mount?
2 He that walks uprightlie,
  And worketh justice, and speaks truth
3 in s heart, And with his tongue
he doth not slander, neither doth
    unto his neighbour wrong,
  And 'gainst his neighbour that doth not
    take up reproachfull lyes.
4 Hee that an abject person is
    contemn'd is in his eyes;
  But he will highly honour them
    that doe Iehovah feare:
  and changeth not, though to his losse,
    it that he once doe sweare.
5 Nor gives his coyne to usury,
    and bribe he doth not take
  against the harmelesse. he that doth
    these things shall never shake.

PSALME XVI.

Psalme 16
Michtam of David

O Mighty God, preserve thou mee,
   for on thee doe I rest.
2 Thou art my God, vnto the Lord
   my soule thou hast profest:
My goodnes reacheth not to thee.
3 But to the Saints upon
   the earth & to the excellent,
   whome all my joye is on.
4 They who give gifts to a strange God,
   their sorrowes multiplye:
their drink oblations of blood
   offer up will not I.
Neither will I into my lips
   the names of them take up.
5 Iehovah is the portion
   of my part, & my cup:
Thou art maintainer of my lot.
6 To me the lines fal'n bee
in pleasant places: yea, faire is
   the heritage for mee.
7 I will Iehovah humbly-blesse,
   who hath mee counselled:
yea in the nights my reines have mee,
   chastising nurtured.
8 Iehovah I have alwayes set
   as present before mee:
because he is at my right hand
   I shall not moved bee.
9 Wherefore my heart rejoyced hath,

                    and

PSALM XVI, XVII.

and glad is my glory:
moreover also my flesh shall
in hope lodge securely.
10 Because thou wilt not leave my soule
within the grave to bee,
nor wilt thou give thine holy one,
corruption for to see.
11 Thou wilt shew me the path of life,
of joyes abundant-store
before thy face, at thy right hand
are pleasures evermore.

Psalme 17
A Prayer of David.

Harken, o Lord, unto the right,
attend vnto my crye,
give eare vnto my pray'r, that goes
from lips that doe not lye.
2 From thy face let my judgement come:
thine eyes the right let see.
3 Thou provſt mine heart, thou visitest
by night, and tryeſt mee.
yet nothing find'ſt, I have resolvd
my mouth shall not offend.
4. From mens works: by word of thy lips
I spoylers paths attend.
5 Stay my feet in thy paths, lest my
6 steps slip. I cal'd on thee,
for thou wilt heare, God, heare my speech,
incline thine eare to mee.
7 O thou that sav'ſt by thy right hand,
thy merveilous-mercyes,

shew

PSALME XVII.

shew vnto them that trust in thee,
   from such as 'gainst them rise.
(2)

8 As apple of thine eye mee keepe.
   In thy wings shade mee hide.
9 From wicked who mee wast: my foes
   in heart are on each side.
10 Clos'd in their fat they are: & they
   speak with their mouth proudly.
11 They round us in our stepps: they set
   on earth their bow'd downe eye.
12 His likenes as a lion is,
   that greedy is to teare,
 in secret places lurking as
   hee a young lion were.
13 Him, in his sight, rise, disappoynt
   make him bow downe o Lord,
 doe thou my soule deliver from
   the wicked one, thy sword,
14 From mortall men thine hand, o Lord
   from men that mortall are,
 and of this passing-world, who have
   within this life their share,
 with thy hid treasure furthermore
   whose belly thou fillest:
 their sonnes are fil'd, & to their babes
   of wealth they leave the rest.
15 In righteousnes, thy favour I
   shall very clearely see,
 and waking with thine image, I
   shall satisfied bee.

PSALM XVIII

Pſalme 18

To the chiefe Muſician, a *pſalme* of Dauid, the ſervant of
the Lord, who ſpake the words of this Song, in the day that
the Lord deliuered him from the hands of all his enemies,
& from the hand of Saule, and hee Sayde,

I'Le dearely love thee, Lord, my ſtrength.
 The Lord is my rock, and my towre
 and my deliverer, my God,
 I'le truſt in him *who is* my powre,
 My ſhield, & my ſalvationes-horne,
3 my high-fort; Who is prayſe worthy:
 I on the Lord will call, ſo ſhall
 I bee kept from mine enemye.
4 Deaths ſorrowes mee encompaſſed,
 mee fear'd the floods of ungodlie,
5 Hells pangs beſet me round about,
 the ſnares of death prevented mee.
6 I in my ſtreights, cal'd on the Lord,
 and to my God cry'd: he did heare
 from his temple my voyce, my crye,
 before him came, unto his eare.
7 Then th' earth ſhooke, & quak't, & moūtaines
 roots moov'd, & were ſtird at his ire,
8 Vp from his noſtrils went a ſmoak,
 and from his mouth devouring fire:
 By it the coales inkindled were.
9 Likewiſe the heavens he downe-bow'd,
 and he deſcended, & there was
 under his feet a gloomy cloud.
10 And he on cherub rode, and flew;
 yea he flew on the wings of winde.
11 His ſecret place hee darknes made

his

PSALME XVIII.

his covert that him round confinde,
Dark waters, & thick clouds of skies.
12 From brightnes, that before him was,
his thickned clouds did passe away,
hayl-stones and coales of fire did passe.
13 Also Iehovah thundered,
within the heavens, the most high
likewise his angry-voyce did give,
hayl-stones, and coales of fire *did fly*.
14 Yea he did out his arrows send,
and bruising he them scattered,
and lightnings hee did multiply,
likewise he them discomfited.
15 The waters channels then were seene,
and the foundationes of the world
appear'd; at thy rebuke, at blast,
of the breath of thy nostrils Lord.

(2)

16 Hee from above sent hee me took:
me out of waters-great he drew.
17 Hee from mine enemies-strong, & from
them which me hated did rescue:
For they were mightyer then I.
18 They mee prevented in the day
of my cloudy calamity;
but for me was the Lord a stay.
19 And hee me to large place brought forth:
hee sav'd mee, for he did delight
20 in mee. The Lord rewarded me
according as I did aright,
According to the cleannesse of

my

PSALM XVIII.

my hands, he recompenced mee.
21 For the wayes of the Lord I kept:
  nor from my God went wickedlie.
22 For all his judgements mee before:
  nor from me put I his decree.
23 With him I upright was, and kept
  my selfe from mine iniquitie.
24 The Lord hath recompenced mee,
  after my righteousnes therefore:
  according to the cleannesse of
  my hands that was his eyes before.
25 With mercifull, thou mercifull,
  with upright thou deales uprightly.
26 With pure thou pure, thou also wilt
  with froward turne thy selfe awry.
27 For thou wilt save th'afflicted folke:
  but wilt the lofty looks suppresse.
28 For thou wilt light my lampe: the Lord,
  my God will lighten my darknesse.
29 For by the I rann through a troupe,
  and by my God leapt o're a wall.
30 Gods way is perfect: Gods word tryde:
  that trust in him hee's shield to all.
31 For who is God except the Lord?
  or who a rock, our God except?
32 Its God that girdeth me with strength,
  and hee doth make my way perfect.
33 Like to the hyndes he makes my feet:
  and on my high place maks me stand.
34 Mine armes doe break a bow of brasse;
  so well to warre he learnes my hand.

35 the

PSALME XVIII.

35 The shield of thy salvation
    thou furthermore hast given mee:
    and thy right-hand hath mee upheld,
    thy meeknes made mee great to bee.
36 Vnder mee thou makst large my steps,
    so that mine anckles did not slyde
37 My foes pursu'de I, & them caught:
    nor turn'd I till they were destroyd.
38 I wounded them & they could not
    rise up: under my feet they fell.
39 Becaufe that thou hast girded mee
    with fortitude to the battel:
    Thou hast subdued under mee,
    those that did up against me rise.
40 And my foes necks thou gavest mee,
    that I might wast mine enemyes.
41 They cryde but there was none to save,
    to God, yet with no answer meet.
42 I beat them then as dust i'th winde
    and cast them out as dirt i'th street.

(4)

43 And thou from the contentions
    hast of the people mee set free;
    thou of the heathen mad'st me head:
    people I knew not shall serve mee.
44 They'le at first hearing me obey:
    strangers shall yield themselvs to mee.
45 The strangers shall consume away,
    and from their closets frighted bee.
46 The Lord lives, and blest be my Rock,
    let my healths God exalted bee.

D   47 Its

PSALM XVIII, XIX.

47 It's God for mee that vengeance works,
and brings downe people under mee.
48 Mee from mine enemies he doth save:
and above those that 'gainst me went,
thou lift'st me up; and thou hast freed
mee from the man that's violent.
49 I with confession will therefore
unto thee render thanksgiving,
o Lord, among the heathen-folk;
and to thy name I'le prayses sing;
50 He giveth great deliverance
to his King, and doth shew mercy
to his annoynted, to David,
and to his seed eternally.

Psalme 19
To the chiefe musician a psalme of David.

THe heavens doe declare
the majesty of God:
also the firmament shews forth
his handy-work abroad.
2 Day speaks to day, knowledge
night hath to night declar'd.
3 There neither speach nor language is,
where their voyce is not heard.
4 Through all the earth their line
is gone forth, & unto
the utmost end of all the world,
their speaches reach also:
A Tabernacle hee
in them pitcht for the Sun.
5 Who Bridegroom like from's chamber goes
glad

PSALME xix.

glad Giants-race to run.
6 From heavens utmost end,
    his course and compassing;
to ends of it, & from the heat
    thereof is hid nothing.

(2)

7 The Lords law perfect is,
    the soule converting back:
Gods testimony faithfull is,
    makes wise who-wisdome-lack.
8 The statutes of the Lord,
    are right, & glad the heart:
the Lords commandement is pure,
    light doth to eyes impart.
9 Iehovahs feare is cleane,
    and doth indure for ever:
the judgements of the Lord are true,
    and righteous altogether.
10 Then gold, then much fine gold,
    more to be prized are,
then hony, & the hony-comb,
    sweeter they are by farre.
11 Also thy servant is
    admonished from hence:
and in the keeping of the same
    is a full recompence.
12 Who can his errors know?
    from secret faults cleanse mee.
13 And from presumptuous-sins, let thou
    kept back thy servant bee:
Let them not beare the rule

PSALM XIX, XX.

   in me, & then shall I
be perfect, and shall cleansed bee
   from much iniquity.
14 Let the words of my mouth,
   and the thoughts of my heart,
be pleasing with thee, Lord, my Rock
   who my redeemer art.

Psalme 20

To the chiefe Musician, a psalme of David.

IEHOVAH heare thee in the day
   of sore calamity,
the name of the God of Iacob
   defend thee mightily.
2 Send thee help from his holy place:
   from Sion strengthen thee.
3 Minde all thy gifts, thy sacrifice
   accepted let it bee.   Selah.
4 Grant thee according to thy heart,
   all thy counsell fulfill.
5 In thy perfect salvation
   with singing joy we will:
And we in the name of our God
   our banners will erect:
when as all thy petitions
   Iehovah shall effect.
6 Now I know, that Iehovah doth
   save his annoynted-*Deare:*
with saving strength of his right hand
   from his pure heav'n will heare.
7 In charrets some their confidence,
   and some in horses set:

PSALME xx, xxi.

    but we the name of Iehovah
      our God will not forget.
8 They are brought downe & fal'n: but we,
      rise and stand stedfastly.
9 Save Lord,& let the King us heare
      when as to him we cry.

Psalme 21

    To the chiefe Musician a psalme
      of David.

IEHOVAH, in thy strength
    the King shall joyfull bee;
and joy in thy salvation
    how vehemently shall hee?
2 Thou of his heart to him
    hast granted the desire:
and thou hast not witholden back,
    what his lips did require.   Selah.
3 For thou dost with blessings
    of goodnes prevent him:
thou on his head of finest gold
    hast set a Diadem.
4 Of thee hee asked life,
    to him thou gav'st it free,
even length of days for evermore
    unto eternitie.
5 In thy salvation
    his glory hath bene great:
honour, and comely dignity
    thou hast upon him set.
6 For thou him blessings setst
    to perpetuitie;

PSALM XXI.

Thou makſt him with thy countenance
   exceeding glad to bee.
7 Becauſe that in the Lord
   the King doth truſt, & hee
through mercy of the higheſt one,
   ſhall not removed bee.
8 The Lord ſhall finde out all
   that are thine enemies:
thy right hand alſo ſhall finde out
   thoſe that doe thee deſpiſe.
9 Thou ſetſt as fiery oven
   them in times of thine ire:
the Lord will ſwallow them in's wrath
   and them conſume with fire.
10 Thou wilt deſtroy the fruit,
   that doth proceed of them,
out of the earth: & their ſeed from
   among the Sonnes of men.
11 Becauſe they evill have
   intended againſt thee:
a wicked plot they have deviſ'd,
   but ſhall not able bee.
12 For thou wilt as a butt
   them ſet; & thou wilt place
thine arrows ready on thy ſtring,
   full right againſt their face.
13 Lord, in thy fortitude
   exalted bee on high:
and wee will ſing; yea prayſe with pſalmes
   thy mighty powr will wee.

PSAL,

PSALME XXII.

Psalme 22
To the chiefe musician upon *Aijeleth Shahar*
a psalme of David.

MY God, my God, wherefore hast thou
 forsaken mee? & why,
art thou so farre from helping mee,
 from the words of my cry?
2 O my God, I doe cry by day,
 but mee thou dost not heare;
and eke by night, & unto mee
 no quiet rest is there.
3 Neverthelesse thou holy art,
 who constantly dost dwell,
within the thankfull prayses of
 thy people Israell.
4 Our fore-fathers in thee have put
 assured confidence:
they trusted have, & thou to them
 didst give deliverance.
5 Vnto thee they did cry aloud,
 and were delivered:
in thee they put their confidence,
 and were not confounded.
6 But I a worme, & not a man;
 of men an opprobrie,
and also of the people am
 despis'd contempruouslie.
7 All they that doe upon mee look,
 a scoffe at mee doe make:
they with the lip doe make a mow,
 the head in scorne they shake,

upō

PSALM XXII.

8 Vpon the Lord he rold himfelfe,
   let him now rid him quite:
let him deliver him, becaufe
   in him he doth delight.
9 But thou art hee that me out of
   the belly forth didft take:
when I was on my mothers breafts,
   to hope thou didft mee make.
10 Vnto thee from the tender-womb
   committed been have I:
yea thou haft been my mighty-God
   from my mothers belly.

(2)

11 Be thou not farre away from mee,
   for tribulation
exceeding great is neere at hand,
   for helper there is none.
12 Mee many buls on every fide
   about have compaffed:
the mighty- buls of Bafhan have
   mee round invironed.
13 They have with their wide-opened-mouths
   fo gaped mee upon;
like as it were a ravening
   and a roaring Lion.
14 As water I am poured-out,
   and all my bones fundred:
my heart in midft of my bowels,
   is like to wax melted.
15 My ftrength like a potfherd is dryde;
   and my tongue faft cleaveth

unto

PSALME XXII.

unto my jawes,& thou haft brought
   me to the duft of death.
16 For dogs have compaſt me abour;
   th' affembly me befet
of the wicked; they pierced through
   my hands, alfo my feet.
17 My bones I may them number all:
   they lookt, they did me view.
18 My cloths among them they did part:
   and lot for my coat threw.
19 But thou Lord be not far, my ftrength,
   to help me haften thou.
20 My foule from fword, my darling from
   the powre of dogs refcue.
21 And from the mouth of the Lion
   give me falvation free:
for thou from hornes of Vnicornes
   anfwer haft given mee.
22 Thy name, I will declare to them
   that Brethren are to mee:
in midft of congregation
   I will give prayfe to thee.

(3)

23 Yee that doe feare the Lord prayfe him,
   all Iacobs feed prayfe yee,
him glorify, & dread him all
   yee Ifraels feed that bee.
24 For he the poors affliction
   loaths not, nor doth defpife;
nor hides his face from him, but heats
   when unto him hee cryes.

         E   25 concern-

PSALM XXII, XXIII.

25 Concerning thee shall be my prayse
    in the great assembly:
before them that him reverence
    performe my vowes will I.
26 The meek shall eat & be suffic'd:
    Iehovah prayse shall they
that doe him seek: your heart shall live
    unto perpetuall aye.
27 All ends of th'earth remember shall
    and turne unto the Lord:
and thee all heathen-families
    to worship shall *accord*.
28 Because unto Iehovah doth
    the kingdome appertaine:
and he among the nations
    is ruler Soveraigne.
29 Earths-fat-ones, eat & worship shall:
    all who to dust descend,
(though none can make alive his soule)
    before his face shall bend.
30 With service a posterity
    him shall attend upon:
to God it shall accounted bee
    a generation.
31 Come shall they, & his righteousnes
    by them declar'd shall bee,
unto a people yet unborne,
    that done this thing hath hee.

    23   *A Psalme of David.*

THe Lord to mee a shepheard is,
    want therefore shall not I.

Hee

PSALME XXIII, XXIIII.

2 Hee in the folds of tender-grasse,
    doth cause mee downe to lie:
To waters calme me gently leads
3 Restore my soule doth hee:
he doth in paths of righteousnes:
    for his names sake leade mee.
4 Yea though in valley of deaths shade
    I walk, none ill I'le feare:
because thou art with mee, thy rod,
    and staffe my comfort are.
5 For mee a table thou hast spread,
    in presence of my foes:
thou dost annoynt my head with oyle,
    my cup it over-flowes.
6 Goodnes & mercy surely shall
    all my dayes follow mee:
and in the Lords house I shall dwell
    so long as dayes shall bee.

Psalme 24
A psalme of david.

THe earth Iehovahs is,
    and the fulnesse of it:
the habitable world, & they
    that there upon doe sit.
2 Because upon the seas,
    hee hath it firmly layd:
and it upon the water-floods
    most sollidly hath stayd.
3 The mountaine of the Lord,
    who shall thereto ascend?
and in his place of holynes,

PSALM XXIIII.

    who is it that shall stand?
4 The cleane in hands, & pure
      in heart;to vanity
    who hath not lifted up his soule,
      nor sworne deceitfully.
5 From God he shall receive
      a benediction,
    and righteousnes from the strong-God
      of his salvation.
6 This is the progenie
      of them that seek thy face:
    of them that doe inquire for him:
      of Iacob 'tis the race.   Selah.
7 Yee gates lift-up your heads,
      and doors everlasting,
    be yee lift up: & there into
      shall come the glorious-King.
8 Who is this glorious King?
      Iehovah, puissant,
    and valiant, Iehovah is
      in battel valiant.
9 Yee gates lift-up your heads,
      and doors everlasting,
    doe yee lift-up: & there into
      shall come the glorious-King.
10 Who is this glorious-King?
      loe, it is Iehovah
    of warlike armies, hee the King
      of glory is; Selah.

        Psalme 25
     A psalme of David.

PSALME XXV.

1 I Lift my soule to thee o Lord.
   My God I trust in thee,
   let mee not be asham'd: nor let
   my foes joy over mee.
3 Yea, all that wait on thee shall not,
   be fill'd with shamefulnes:
   but they shall be ashamed all,
   who without cause transgresse.
4 Thy wayes, Iehovah, make mee know,
   thy paths make me discerne.
5 Cause mee my steps to order well,
   in thy truth, & mee learne,
   For thou God of my saving health,
   on thee I wait all day.
6 Thy bowels, Lord, & thy mercyes
   minde; for they are for aye.
7 Sinnes of my youth remember not,
   neither my trespasses:
   after thy mercy minde thou mee
   o Lord for thy goodnes.
8 Good and upright God is, therefore
   will sinners teach the way.
9 The meek he'le guide in judgement: &
   will teach the meek his way.
10 Iehovahs paths they mercy are,
    all of them truth also;
    to them that keep his covenant,
    and testimonies do.
          (2)
11 For thy names sake o Iehovah,
    freely doe thou remitt

mine

PSALM xxv.

mine owne perverse iniquitie:
   because that great is it.
12 Who fears the Lord, him hee will teach
   the way that he shall chuse.
13 his soule shall dwell at ease, his seed
   as heirs the earth shall vse.
14 The secret of God is with those
   that doe him reverence:
and of his covenant he them
   will give intelligence.
15 Mine eyes continually are
   upon Iehovah set:
for it is hee that will bring forth
   my feet out of the net.
16 Vnto me-wards turne thou thy face,
   and on mee mercy show:
because I solitary am
   afflicted poore also.
17 My hearts troubles inlarged are;
   from my distresse me bring.
18 See mine affliction, & my paine;
   and pardon all my sin.
19 Mark my foes; for they many are,
   and cruelly mee hate,
20 My soule keep, free mee; nor let mee
   be sham'd, who on thee wait.
21 Let soundnes, & uprightnesse keep
   mee: for I trust in thee.
22 Israel from his troubles all,
   o God, doe thou set free.
   25 A *psalme* of david.

PSALME xxvi, xxvii.

Ivdge mee, o Lord, for I have walkt
  in mine integrity:
and I have trusted in the Lord,
  therefore slyde shall not I.
2 Examine mee, Lord, & mee prove;
  my reins, & my heart try.
3 For thy grace is before mine eyes;
  and in thy truth walk I.
4 I sat not with vaine men, nor goe
  with men themselves that hide.
5 Evill mens company I hate:
  nor will with vile abide.
6 In cleannesse, Lord, I'le wash mine hands,
  so I'le thine altar round:
7 That I may preach with thankfull-voyce,
  and all thy prayses sound.
8 The habitation of thy house,
  Lord, dearly love doe I,
  the place and tabernacle of
  thy glorious majesty.
9 My soule with sinners gather not,
  with men of blood my life.
10 In whose hand 's guile, in whose right hand
  bribery is full rife.
11 Redeeme, & pitty mee; for I'le
  walk in mine uprightnesse.
12 My foot stands right: in th'assembly
  I will Iehovah blesse.

27 *A Psalme of David.*

THe Lord my light, & my health is,
  what shall make me dismaid?

the

PSALM XXVII.

The Lord is my lifes-strength, of whom
  should I *then* be afrayd?
2 When wicked men, mine enemies,
  and my foes in battel;
  against mee come, to eate my flesh,
  themselves stumbled & fell.
3 If that an hoast against mee camp,
  my heart undaunted is:
  if war against mee should arise,
  I am secure in this.
4 One thing of God I asked have,
  which I will still request:
  that I may in the house of God,
  all dayes of my life rest:
  To see the beauty of the Lord,
  and in his Temple seeke.
5 For in his tent in th'evill-day,
  hidden hee will mee keepe:
  Hee will me hide in secrecy
  of his pavillion:
  and will me highly lift upon
  the rocks-munition.
6 Moreover at this-time my head
  lifted on high shall bee,
  above mine enemies, who doe
  about encompasse mee.
  Therefore in's tent I'le sacrifice,
  of joye an offering,
  unto Iehovah, sing will I,
  yea, I will prayses sing.

PSALME XXVII.
(2)

7 When as I with my voyce doe cry,
   mee, o Iehovah, heare,
have mercy also upon mee,
   and unto mee answer.
8 *When thou didst say*, seek yee my face,
   my heart sayd unto thee,
thy countenance, o Iehovah,
   it shall be sought by mee.
9 Hide not thy face from mee, nor off
   in wrath thy servant cast:
God of my health, leave, leave not mee,
   my helper been thou hast.
10 My father & my mother both
   though they doe mee forsake,
yet will Iehovah gathering
   unto himselfe me take.
11 Iehovah, teach thou mee the way,
   and be a guide to mee
in righteous path, because of them
   that mine observers bee.
12 Give mee not up unto the will
   of my streight-enemies:
for witnesse false against me stand,
   and breath out cruelties.
13 *I should have fainted*, had not I
   believed for to see,
Iehovahs goodnes in the land
   of them that living bee.
14 Doe thou upon Iehovah waite:
   bee stablished, & let

              thine

PSALM XXVII, XXVIII.

thine heart be strengthened, & thine hope
upon Iehovah set.

Psalme 28.
A psalme of David.

IEHOVAH, unto thee I cry,
my Rock, be thou not deafe me fro:
left thou be dumb from mee & I
be like them downe to pit that go.

2 Heare thou the voyce of my requeſt
for grace, when unto thee I cry:
when I lift up mine hands unto
thine Oracle of Sanctity.

3 With ill men draw me not away,
with workers of unrighteouſnes,
that with their neighbours peace doe ſpeak,
but in their hands is wickednes.

4 Give thou to them like to their works
and like the evill of their deeds:
give them like to their handy-works,
and render unto them their meeds.

5 Becauſe unto Iehovahs work
they did not wiſe-attention yeild,
neither unto his handy work,
them he will waſt, but not up-build.

6 The Lord be bleſt, for he hath heard
the voyce of my requeſts for grace.

7 God is my ſtrength, my ſhield, in him
my heart did truſt, & helpt I was:
Therefore my heart will gladnes ſhew,
and with my ſong I'le him confeſſe.

8 The Lord of his annoynted ones

their

PSALME XXVIII, XXIX.

their strength, & towre of safety is.
9 Salvation to thy people give,
 and blesse thou thine inheritance,
 and ev'n unto eternity
 doe thou them feed & them advance.

This. After the common tunes.

Save *Lord*, thy people, & doe thou
 blesse thine inheritance:
and unto all eternity
 them feed & them advance.

Psalme 29
A psalme of David.
Vnto the Lord doe yee ascribe
 (o **Sonnes** of the mighty)
unto the Lord doe yee ascribe
 glory & potency.
2 Vnto the Lord doe yee ascribe
 his names glorious renowne,
in beauty of his holynes
 unto the Lord bow downe.
3 The mighty voyce of Iehovah
 upon the waters is:
the God of glory thundereth,
 God on great waters is.
4 Iehovahs voyce is powerfull,
 Gods voyce is glorious,
5 Gods voyce breaks Cedars: yea God breaks
 Cedars of Lebanus.
6 He makes them like a calfe to skip:

PSALM XXIX, XXX.

the mountaine Lebanon,
and like to a young Vnicorne
the hill of Syrion.
7 Gods voyce divides the flames of fire.
8 Iehovahs voyce doth make
the desart shake: the Lord doth cause
the Cadesh-desart shake.
9 The Lords voyce makes the hindes to calve,
and makes the forrest bare:
and in his temple every one
his glory doth declare.
10 The Lord sate on the flouds: the Lord
for ever sits as King.
11 God to his folk gives strength: the Lord
his folk with peace blessing.

Psalme 30
A Psalme & Song, *at* the dedication
of the house of David.

IEHOVAH, I will thee extoll,
  for thou hast lift up mee;
and over mee thou hast not made
  my foes joyfull to bee.
2 O Lord my God, to thee I cry'de
  and thou hast made mee whole.
3 Out of the grave, o Iehovah,
  thou hast brought up my soule:
Thou mad'st mee live, I went not downe
4 to pit. Sing to the Lord,
  (yee his Saints) & give thanks when yee
  his holynes record.
5 For but a moment in his wrath;

life

PSALME xxx.

life in his love doth stay:
weeping may lodge with us a night
but joye at break of day.
6 I sayd in my prosperity,
I shall be moved never.
7 Lord by thy favour thou hast made
my mountaine stand fast ever:
Thou hidst thy face, I troubled was.
8 I unto thee did cry,
o Lord: also my humble suit
unto the Lord made I.
9 What gaine is in my blood; when I
into the pit goe downe?
shall dust give glory unto thee?
shall it thy truth make knowne?
10 Doe thou mee o Iehovah, heare,
and on mee mercy have:
Iehovah, o bee thou to mee
an helper me to save.
11 Thou into dancing for my sake
converted hast my sadnes:
my sackcloth thou unloosed hast,
and girded me with gladnes:
12 That sing to thee my glory may,
and may not silent bee:
o Lord my God, I will give thanks
for evermore to thee.

Psalme 31
To the chief Musician, a psalme
of David.

PSALM xxxi.

IN thee, o Lord, I put my trust,
　　let me be shamed never:
according to thy righteousnes
　　o doe thou mee deliver.
2 Bow downe to mee thine eare, with speed
　　let mee deliverance have:
be thou my strong rock, for an house
　　of defence mee to save.
3 Because thou unto mee a rock
　　and my fortresse wilt bee:
therefore for thy names sake doe thou,
　　leade mee & guide thou mee.
4 Doe thou mee pull out of the net,
　　which they have for mee layd
so privily: because that thou
　　art to mee a sure ayd.
5 Into thy hands my spirit I
　　reposing doe commit:
Iehovah God of verity,
　　thou hast redeemed it.
6 I hated them that have regard
　　to lying vanity:
7 but I in God trust. I'le be glad,
　　and joy in thy mercy:
Because thou hast considered
　　my afflicting distresse;
thou hast my soule acknowledged
　　in painfull anguishes;
8 And thou hast not inclosed mee
　　within the enemies hand:
thou mad'st my feet within the place

　　　　　　　　　　　　　　of

PSALME xxxi.

of liberty to stand.
(2)
9 Have mercy upon mee, o Lord,
for in distresse am I,
with grief mine eye consumed is,
my soule & my belly.
10 For my life with grief & my years
with sighs are consumed:
because of my sin, my strength failes,
and my bones are wasted.
11 To all my foes I was a scorne,
chiefly my neighbours to;
a feare to freinds: they that saw mee
without, did flye me fro.
12 I am forgot as a dead man
that's out of memory:
and like a vessel that is broke
ev'n such a one am I.
13 Because that I of many men
the slandering did heare,
round about me on every side
there was exceeding feare:
While as that they did against mee
counsell together take,
they craftily have purposed
my life away to make.
14 But o Iehovah, I in thee
my confidence have put
15 I sayd thou art my God. My times
within thy hand *are shut*:
From the hands of mine enemies

PSALM xxxi.

doe thou deliver mee,
  and from the men who meeagainst
    my persecuters bee.
        (3)
16 Thy countenance for to shine forth
  upon thy servant make:
o give to me salvation
  even for thy mercy sake.
17 Let me not be asham'd, o Lord,
  for cal'd on thee I have:
let wicked men be sham'd, let them
  be silent in the grave.
18 Let lying lips be silenced,
  that against men upright
doe speak such things as greivous are,
  in pride, & in despight.
19 How great 's thy goodnes, thou for the
  that feare thee hast hidden:
which thou work'st for them that thee trust,
  before the Sonnes of men.
20 Thou in the secret of thy face,
  shalt hide them from mans pride:
in a pavillion, from the strife
  of tongues, thou wilt them hide.
21 O let Iehovah blessed be;
  for he hath shewed mee
his loving kindnes wonderfull
  in a fenced-cittie.
22 For I in hast sayd, I am cast
  from the sight of thine eyes:
yet thou heard'st the voyce of my suit,
                when

PSALME xxxi, xxxii.
when to thee were my cryes.
23 O love the Lord all ye his Saints:
    because the Lord doth guard
the faithfull, but the proud doer
    doth plenteously reward.
24 See that yee be encouraged,
    and let your heart wax strong:
all whosoever hopefully
    doe for Iehovah long.

    32 A *psalme* of David, Maschil.

O Blessed is the man who hath
    his trespasse pardoned,
and he *whose* aberration
    is wholly covered,
2 O blessed is the man to whom
    the Lord imputes not sin:
and he who such a spirit hath
    that guile is not therein.
3 When I kept silence then my bones,
    began to weare away,
with age; by meanes of my roaring
    continuing all the day.
4 For day & night thy hand on mee,
    heavily did indure:
into the drought of Summer time
    turned is my moisture.   Selah.
5 Mine aberration unto thee
    I have acknowledged,
and mine iniquity I have
    not closely covered:
Against my selfe my sin, sayd I,
        G   I will

PSALM xxxii, xxxiii.

I will to God confesse,
  and thou didst the iniquitie
    forgive of my trespasse.   Selah.
6 For this each godly one to thee
  in finding time shall pray.
  surely in floods of waters great,
    come nigh him shall not they.
7 Thou art my hyding-place, thou shalt
  from trouble save me out:
  thou with songs of deliverance
    shalt compasse me about.
8 I will instruct thee, also teach
  thee in the way will I
  which thou shalt goe: I will to thee
    give counsell with mine eye.
9 Like to the horse & mule, which have
  noe knowledge be not yee:
  whose mouths are held with bridle-bit,
    that come not neere to thee.
10 To those men that ungodly are,
  their sorrows doe abound:
  but him that trusteth in the Lord,
    mercy shall compasse round.
11 Be in Iehovah joyfull yee,
  yee righteous ones rejoyce;
  and all that are upright in heart
    shout yee with joyfull voyce.

psalme 33

Ye just in God rejoyce,
  prayse well th'upright doth sute:
2 Prayse God with Harp, with psaltry sing

PSALME xxxiii.

to him, on ten string'd lute.
3 Sing to him a new song,
   aloud play skilfully.
4 For the Lords word is right: and all
   his works in verity.
5 He loveth righteousnes,
   and also equity:
the earth replenished is with
   the Lords benignity.
6 By the word of the Lord
   the heavens had their frame,
and by the spirit of his mouth,
   all the host of the same.
7 The waters of the seas,
   he gathers as an heape;
together as in store-houses
   he layeth up the deepe.
8 Be all the earth in feare,
   because of Iehovah:
let all the dwellers of the world
   before him stand in awe.
9 Because he did but speak
   the word, & it was made:
he gave out the commandement,
   and it was firmly stay'd.
10 The Lord to nought doth bring
   the nations counsell; hee
devises of the people makes
   of none effect to bee.
11 The counsell of the Lord
   abide for ever shall,

PSALM XXXIII.

the cogitations of his heart
to generations all.
(2)
12 O blessed nation,
    whose God Iehovah is:
and people whom for heritage
    chosen hee hath for his.
13 The Lord from heaven looks,
    all Sonnes of men views well.
14 From his firme dwelling hee looks forth,
    on all that on earth dwell.
15 The hearts of all of them
    alike he fashioneth:
and all their operations
    he well considereth.
16 By multitude of hoast
    there is no King saved:
nor is by multitude of strength
    the strong delivered.
17 A horse a vaine thing is
    to be a saviour:
nor shall he work deliverance
    by greatnes of his power.
18 On them that doe him feare
    loe, is Iehovahs eye:
upon them that doe place their hope
    on his benignity.
19 To save alive in dearth,
    and their soule from death free.
20 Our soule doth for Iehovah wayt,
    our help, & shield is hee.

21 For our heart joyes in him:
　　for in's pure name trust wee.
22 Let thy mercy (Lord) be on us:
　　like as we trust in thee.

Psalme 34

A psalme of David, whē he changed his behaviour
　before Abimelech, who drove him away
　　　& he departed.

I Le blesse God alwayes, his prayse shall
　still in my mouth be had.
2 My soule shall boast in God: the meeke
　shall heare *this* & bee glad.
3 Exalt the Lord with mee, his name
　let us together advance.
4 I sought, God heard, who gave from all
　my fears deliverance.
5 Him they beheld, & light'ned were,
　nor sham'd were their faces.
6 This poore man cry'd, the Lord him heard,
　and freed from all distresse.
7 His camp about them round doth pitch
　the Angell of the Lord;
who doe him feare; and to them doth
　deliverance afford.
8 O tast, also consider yee,
　that God is good: o blest,
that man is ever whose hope doth
　for safety in him rest.
9 O stand in feare of Iehovah,
　his holy ones who bee.
because that such as doe him feare

PSALME xxxIIII.

not any want shall see.
10 The Lions young doe suffer lack,
    and suffer hungering:
but they that seek Iehovah, shall
    not want any good thing.
(2)
11 I will you teach to feare the Lord:
    come children hark to mee.
12 Who is the man that willeth life:
    and loves good dayes to see?
13 Thy tongue from evill, & thy lips
    from speaking guile keep thou.
14 Depart from evill & doe good:
    seek peace, and it follow.
15 Vpon the men that righteous are
    the Lord doth set his eye:
and likewise he doth bow his eare
    when unto him they cry.
16 Iehovahs face is set against
    them that doe wickedly:
that he of them from off the earth
    may cut the memory.
17 They cry'd, God heard, & set them free,
    from their distresses all.
18 To broken hearts the Lord is neere,
    and contrite save he shall.
19 The just mans sorrows many are,
    from all God sets him free.
20 Hee kepeth all his bones, that none
    of them shall broken bee.
21 Evill shall certainly bring death
    the wicked man upon: and

PSALM xxxv.

and those that hate the just shall come
   to desolation.
22 The soules of them that doe him serve,
   Iehovah doth redeeme:
nor any shall be desolate,
   that put their trust in him.

35 *A psalme* of David.

Plead, Lord, with them that with me plead:
   fight against them that fight with mee.
2 Of shield & buckler take thou hold,
   stand up my helper for to bee.
3 Draw out the speare & stop the way
   'gainst them that my pursuers bee:
   and doe thou say unto my soule
   I am salvation unto thee.
4 Let them confounded be, & sham'd,
   that seek my soule how they may spill:
   let them be turned back & sham'd
   that in their thoughts devise mine ill.
5 As chaffe before the winde, let them
   be, & Gods Angell them driving.
6 Let their way dark & slippery bee,
   and the Lords Angell them chasing.
7 For in a pit without a cause,
   they hidden have for me a net:
   which they without a cause have digg'd
   that they there in my soule may get.
8 Let unknowne ruin come on him,
   and let his net that he doth hide,
   himselfe insnare: let him into
   the very same destruction slyde.

6 My

PSALM xxxv.

9 My soule shall in the Lord be glad:
in his salvation joyfull bee
10 And all my bones shall also say,
o Lord, who is like unto thee?
Who from the stronger then himselfe
the poore afflicted settest free:
the poore afflicted & needy,
from such as spoylers of him bee.

(2)

11 False witnesses did up arise:
what I knew not they charg'd on mee.
12 Evill for good they mee repay'd,
whereby my soule might spoyled bee,
13 But I, when they were sick, was cloath'd
with sackcloath, & I afflicted
my soule with fasting, & my pray'r
into my bosom returned.
14 I walked as if he had been
my neere freind or mine owne brother:
I heavily bow'd downe as one
that mourneth for his owne mother.
15 But they in mine adversity
rejoyced, & they gathered
themselves together: yea abjects
themselves against mee gathered;
And I was ignorant *hereof*,
and they unceasantly mee teare,
16 With hypocrites, mockers in feasts;
at me their teeth they gnashing were.
17 How long o Lord wilt thou look on?
my soule from their destructions,

o doe

PSALME xxx v.

o doe thou set at liberty,
mine only one from the Lions.

18 I freely will give thanks to thee
within the congregation great:
and I thy prayses will set forth
where there be many people met.

19 Those that are wrongfully my foes,
let them not rejoyce over mee:
neither let them wink with the eye,
that are my haters causlesly.

20 Because that they doe not speak peace:
but in their thoughts they doe invent
deceitfull matters against them
that in the land for peace are bent.

21 Gainst me they op'ned their mouths wide,
& sayd, ah, ah our eye it saw.

22 Thou saw'st it (Lord) hold not thy peace:
Lord, from me be not far away.

23 Stirre up & wake to my judgement,
my God & my Lord, to my plea.

24 After thy justice, judge me, Lord
my God, lest or'e me joy should they.

25 Let them not say within their hearts,
aha, our soules desire have wee:
we now have swallowed him up,
o let them never say of mee.

25 Sham'd let them be & confounded
joyntly, who at my hurt are glad:
let them that 'gainst me magnify,
with shame & dishonour be clad.

27 Let them for joy shout, & be glad

H

that

PSALM xxxv, xxxvi.

that favour doe my righteous cause:
yea, let them say continually,
extolled be the Lord with prayse,
  Who doth in the prosperity
of his servants his pleasure stay
28 And my tongue of thy justice shall,
and of thy prayse speake all the day.

Psalme 36.
To the chief Musician a psalme of David,
the servant of the Lord.

THe trespasse of the wicked one
  saith in assured-wise:
within my heart, the feare of God
is not before his eyes.
2 For in his eyes he sooths himselfe:
his sin is found meane while
3 hatefull. The words of his mouth are
iniquity & guile:
He to be wise, to doe good leaves.
4   He mischief plotts on's bed,
he sets himselfe in way not good:
he hath not ill hated.

(2)
5 Thy mercy (Lord) in heaven is,
to clouds thy faithfullnes.
6 Thy judgements a great deep, like great
mountains thy righteousnes:
Thou savest man & beast, o Lord.
7   How pretious is thy grace,
therefore in shadow of thy wings
mens sonnes their trust doe place.

They

8 They of the fatnes of thy house
    unto the full shall take:
  and of the river of thy joyes
    to drink thou shalt them make.
9 For with thee is the spring of life:
    in thy light wee'll see light.
10 To them that know thee stretch thy grace;
    to right in heart thy right.
11 Let no proud foot against me come,
    nor wicked hand move mee.
12 Wrong doers there are fal'n:cast downe,
    and rays'd they cannot bee.

37 A Psalme of David.

Fret not thy selfe because of those
    that evill workers bee,
  nor envious bee against the men
    that work iniquitie.
2 For like unto the grasse they shall
    be cut downe, suddenly:
  and like unto the tender herb
    they withering shall dye.
3 Vpon the Lord put thou thy trust,
    and bee thou doing good,
  so shalt thou dwell within the land,
    and sure thou shalt have food.
4 See that thou set thy hearts delight
    also upon the Lord,
  and the desyers of thy heart
    to thee he will afford.
5 Trust in the Lord: & hee'l it work,
    to him commit thy way.

PSALM XXX VII.

6 As light thy justice hee'l bring forth,
    thy judgement as noone day.
7 Rest in Iehovah, & for him
    with patience doe thou stay:
fret not thy selfe because of him
    who prospers in his way,
Nor at the man, who brings to passe
    the crafts he doth devise.
8 Cease ire, & wrath leave: to doe ill
    thy selfe fret in no wise.
9 For evil doers shall be made
    by cutting downe to fall:
but those that wayt upon the Lord,
    the land inherit shall.

(2)

10 For yet a litle while, & then
    the wicked shall not *bee*:
yea, thou shalt diligently mark
    his place, & it not see.
11 But meek ones the inheritance
    shall of the earth possesse:
also they shall themselves delight
    in multitude of peace.
12 The wicked plotts against the just,
    gnashing at him his teeth.
13 The Lord shall laugh at him: because
    his day coming he seeth.
14 The wicked have drawne out their sword,
    & bent their bowe have they,
to cast the poor & needy downe,
    to kill th'upright in way.

PSALME XXXVII.

15 Their sword shall enter their owne heart,
    their bowes shall broken bee.
16 The just mans little, better *is*
    then wickeds treasurie.
17 For th'armes of wicked shall be broke:
    the Lord the just doth stay.
18 The Lord doth know upright mens dayes:
    and their lot is for aye.
19 Neither shall they ashamed bee
    in any time of ill:
and when the dayes of famine come,
    they then shall have their fill.
20 But wicked,& foes of the Lord
    as lambs fat shall decay:
they shall consume: yea into smoake
    they shall consume away.

(3)

21 The man ungodly borroweth,
    but he doth not repay:
but he that righteous is doth shew
    mercy,& gives away.
22 For such as of him blessed bee,
    the earth inherit shall,
and they that of him cursed are,
    by cutting downe shall fall.
23 The foot-steps of a godly man
    they are by Iehovah
establisned: & also hee
    delighteth in his way.
24 Although he fall, yet shall he not
    be utterly downe cast:

PSALM XXXVII.

because Iehovah with his hand
    doth underprop him fast.
25 I have been young & now am old;
    yet have I never seen
the just man left, nor that his seed
    for bread have beggars been.
26 But every day hee's mercifull,
    and lends: his seed is blest.
27 Depart from evill, & doe good:
    and ever dwell at rest.
28 Because the Lord doth judgement love,
    his Saints forsakes not hee;
kept ever are they: but cut off
    the sinners seed shall bee.
29 The just inherit shall the land,
    and therein ever dwell.
30 The just mans mouth wisdome doth speak,
    his tongue doth judgement tell.
31 The law of his God is in's heart:
    none of his steps slideth.
32 The wicked watcheth for the just,
    and him to slay seeketh.
33 Iehovah will not such a one
    relinquish in his hand,
neither will he condemne him when
    adjudged he doth stand.

(4)

34 Wayt on the Lord, & keep his way,
    and hee shall thee exalt
th'earth to inherit: when cut off
    the wicked see thou shalt,

PSALME xxxvii, xxxviii.

35 The wicked men I have beheld
   in mighty pow'r to bee:
 also himsefe spreading abroad
   like to a green-bay-tree.
36 Neverthelesse he past away,
   and loe, then was not hee;
 moreover I did seek for him,
   but found hee could not bee.
37 Take notice of the perfect man,
   and the upright attend:
 because that unto such a man
   peace is his latter end.
38 But such men that transgressors are
   together perish shall:
 the latter end shall be cut off
   of the ungodly all,
39 But the salvation of the just
   doth of Iehovah come:
 he is their strength to them in times
   that are most troublesome.
40 Yea, help & free them will the Lord:
   he shall deliver them
 from wiced men, because that they
   doe put their trust in him.

Psalme 38
A psalme of David,
  to bring to remembrance.

LORD, in thy wrath rebuke me not:
   nor in thy hot rage chasten mee.
2 Because thine hand doth presse me sore:
   and in me thy shafts fastened bee.

       3 There

PSALM XXXVIII.

3 *There is* no soundnes in my flesh,
 because thine anger I am in:
 nor *is there* any rest within
 my bones, by reason of my sin.
4 Because that mine iniquityes
 ascended are above my head:
 like as an heavy burden, they
 to heavy upon me are layd.
5 My wounds stink, *and* corrupt they be:
 my foolishnes doth make it so.
6 I troubled am, & much bow'd downe,
 all the day long I mourning goe.
7 For with foule sores my loynes are fill'd:
 & in my flesh *is* no soundnes.
8 I'me weak & broken sore; I roar'd
 because of my hearts restlesnes.
9 All my desire's before thee, Lord;
 nor is my groaning hid from thee.
10 My heart doth pant, my strength me fails:
 & mine eye sight is gone from mee.

(2)

11 My freinds & lovers from my sore
 stand off: off stand my kinsmen eke.
12 And they lay snares that seek my life,
 that seek my hurt, they mischief speak,
 And all day long imagin guile,
13 But as one deafe, I did not heare,
 and as a dumb man I became
 as if his mouth not open were.
14 Thus was I as man that heares not,
 & in whose mouth reproofes none were.

15 because

PSALME XXXVIII.

15 Becauſe o Lord, in thee I hope:
o Lord my God, thou wilt mee heare.
16 For ſayd I, leſt or'e me they joy:
when my foot ſlips, they vaunt the more
17 themſelves 'gainſt me. For I to halt
am neere, my grief's ſtill mee before.
18 For my tranſgreſſion I'le declare;
I for my ſins will ſorry bee.
19 But yet my lively foes are ſtrong,
who falſly hate me, multiplie.
20 Moreover they that doe repay
evill in ſtead of good to mee,
becauſe I follow what is good,
to mee they adverſaryes bee.
21 Iehovah, doe not mee forſake:
my God o doe not farre depart
22 from mee. Make haſt unto mine ayd,
o Lord who my ſalvation art.

Pſalme 39

To the chief muſician, *even* to Ieduthun,
a Pſalme of David.

I Sayd, I will look to my wayes,
leſt I ſin with my tongue:
I'le keep my mouth with bit, while I
the wicked am among.
2 With ſilence tyed was my tongue,
my mouth I did refraine,
From ſpeaking that thing which is good,
and ſtirred was my paine.
3 Mine heart within me waxed hot,
while I was muſing long,

I   inkindled

PSALM xxxix.

inkindled in me was the fire;
 then spake I with my tongue.
4 Mine end, o Lord, & of my dayes
 let mee the measure learne;
that what a momentany thing
 I am I may discerne.
5 Behold thou mad'st my dayes a span,
 mine age as nought to thee:
surely each man at's best estate,
 is wholly vanity.   Selah.
6 Sure in a vaine show walketh man;
 sure stir'd in vaine they are:
he heaps up riches,& knows not
 who shall the same gather.

(2)

7 And now, o Lord what wayt I for?
 my hope is upon thee.
8 Free me from all my trespasses:
 the fooles scorne make not mee.
9 I was dumb nor opned my mouth,
 this done because thou hast.
10 Remove thy stroke away fom mee:
 by thy hands blow I wast.
11 When with rebukes thou dost correct
 man for iniquity;
thou blast's his beauty like a moth:
 sure each man 's vanity. Selah.
12 Heare my pray'r, Lord, hark to my cry,
 be not still at my tears:
for stranger, & pilgrim with thee,
 I 'me, as all my fathers.

13 O turne aside a while from mee,
   that I may strength recall:
before I doe depart from hence,
   and be noe more at all.

Psalme 40.
To the chief musician, a psalme
   of David.

With expectation for the Lord
   I wayted patiently,
and hee inclined unto mee,
   also he heard my cry.
2 He brought mee out of dreadfull-pit,
   out of the miery clay:
and set my feet upon a rock,
   hee stablished my way.
3 And in my mouth put a new song,
   of prayse our God unto:
many shall see, & feare, upon
   the Lord shall trust also.
4 Blest is the man that on the Lord
   maketh his trust abide:
nor doth the proud respect, nor such
   to lies as turne aside.
5 O thou Iehovah, thou my God,
   hast many a wonder wrought:
and likewise towards us thou hast
   conceived many a thought.
Their summe cannot be reck'ned up'
   in order unto thee:
would I declare & speak *of them*,
   beyond account they bee.

PSALM xl.

6 Thou sacrifice & offering
    wouldst not; thou boar'st mine eare:
  burnt offring, & sin offering
    thou neither didst requere.
7 Then sayd I: loe, I come: ith books
    rolle it is writt of mee.
8 To doe thy will, God, I delight:
    thy laws in my heart bee.
9 In the great congregation
    thy righteousnes I show:
  loe, I have not refraynd my lips,
    Iehovah, thou dost know.
10 I have not hid thy righteousnes
    within my heart alone:
  I have declar'd thy faithfullnes
    and thy salvation:
  Thy mercy nor thy truth have I
    from the great Church conceald.
11 Let not thy tender mercyes bee
    from mee o Lord with-held.
  Let both thy kindnes & thy truth
    keep me my life throughout.
12 Because innumerable ills
    have compast mee about:
  My sins have caught me so that I
    not able am to see:
  more are they then hairs of my head,
    therefore my heart fails mee

13 Be pleas'd Lord, to deliver mee

PSALME xl, xli.

to help me Lord make haſt.
14 At once abaſht & ſham'd let bee
    who ſeek my ſoule to waſte:
Let them be driven back, & ſham'd,
    that wiſh me miſery.
15 Let them be waſte, to quit their ſhame,
    that ſay to me, fy fy.
16 Let all be glad, & joy in thee,
    that ſeek thee: let them ſay
who thy ſalvation love, the Lord
    be magnifyde alway.
17 I both diſtreſt & needy am,
    the Lord *yet* thinks on mee:
my help & my deliverer thou
    my God, doe not tarry.

Pſalme 41
To the chief muſician, a pſalme
of David.

Bleſſed is hee that wiſely doth
    unto the poore attend:
the Lord will him deliverance
    in time of trouble ſend.
2 Him God will keep, & make to live,
    on earth hee bleſt ſhall be,
nor doe thou him unto the will
    give of his enemie.
3 Vpon the bed of languiſhing,
    the Lord will ſtrengthen him:
thou alſo wilt make all his bed
    within his ſicknes time.
4 I ſayd, Iehouah, o be thou

PSALM xli.

mercifull unto mee;
 heale thou my soule, because that I
  have sinned against thee.
5 Those men that be mine enemies,
  with evill mee defame:
 when will the time come hee shall dye,
  and perish shall his name?
6 And if he come to see *mee*, hee
  speaks vanity: his heart
 sin to it selfe heaps, when hee goes
  forth hee doth it impart.

(2)

7 All that me hate, against mee they
  together whisper still:
 against me they imagin doe
  to mee malicious ill.
8 T*hus doe they say* some ill disease,
  unto him cleaveth sore:
 and *seing now* he lyeth downe,
  he shall rise up noe more.
9 Moreover my familiar freind,
  on whom my trust I set,
 his heele against mee lifted up,
  who of my bread did eat.
10 But Lord me pitty, & mee rayse,
  that I may them requite.
11 By this I know assuredly,
  in mee thou dost delight:
 For o're mee triumphs not my foe.
12 And mee, thou dost mee stay,
 in mine integrity; & set'st

        mee

PSALME xlɪ, xlɪɪ.

mee thee before for aye.
13 Blest hath Iehovah Israels God
  from everlasting *been*,
also unto everlasting:
  Amen, yea and Amen.

THE
Second Booke.

PSALME 42
To the chief musician, *Maschil*, for the
  Sonnes of Korah.

Like as the Hart panting doth bray
  after the water brooks,
even in such wise o God, my soule,
  after thee panting looks.
2 For God, even for the liuing God,
  my soule it thirsteth sore:
oh when shall I come & appeare,
  the face of God before.
3 My teares have been unto mee meat,
  by night also by day,
while all the day they unto mee
  where is thy God doe say.
4 When as I doe in minde record
  these things, then me upon
I doe my soule out poure, for I
  with multitude had gone:
With them unto Gods house I went,
  with voyce of joy & prayse:

I with

PSALM xlii.

I with a multitude did goe
   that did keepe-holy-days.
5 My soule why art cast downe?& art
   stirr'd in mee: thy hope place
in God, for yet him prayse I shall
   for the help of his face.

(2)

6 My God, my soule in mee's cast downe,
   therefore thee minde I will
from Iordanes & Hermonites land,
   and from the litle hill.
7 At the noyse of thy water spouts
   deep unto deep doth call:
thy waves they are gone over mee,
   also thy billowes all.
8 His loving kindnes yet the Lord
   command will in the day:
and in the night his song with mee,
   to my lifes God I'le pray.
9 I unto God will say, my Rock
   why hast thou forgot mee?
why goe I sad, by reason of
   pressure of th' enemie.
10 As with a sword within my bones
   my foes reproach mee do:
while all the day, where is thy God?
   they doe say mee unto.
11 My soule o wherefore dost thou bowe
   thy selfe downe heavily;
and wherefore in mee makest thou
   a stirr tumultuously?

                         Hope

PSALME xlii, xliii.

Hope thou in God, becauſe I ſhall
   with prayſe him yet advance:
who is my God, alſo he is
   health of my countenance.

Pſalme 43.

IVdge me, o God, & plead my cauſe
   from nation mercyleſſe;
from the guilefull & man unjuſt,
   o ſend thou me redreſſe.

2 For of my ſtrength thou art the God,
   why caſt's thou mee thee fro:
why goe I mourning for the ſore
   oppreſſion of the foe?

3 Thy light o ſend out & thy truth,
   let them lead, & bring mee,
unto thy holy hill, & where
   thy tabernacles bee.

4 Then will I to Gods Altar goe,
   to God my joyes gladnes:
upon the Harp o God my God
   I will thy prayſe expreſſe.

5 My ſoule o wherfore doſt thou bowe
   thy ſelfe downe heavily;
and wherefore in mee makeſt thou
   a ſtirre tumultuouſly?
Hope thou in God, becauſe I ſhall
   with prayſe him yet advance:
who is my God, alſo he is
   health of my countenance.

Pſalme 44

To the chief muſician, for the ſonnes
of Korah.

PSALM xliv.

WEE with our eares have heard, o God,
   our fathers have us told,
what works thou diddest in their dayes,
   in former dayes of old.
2 *How* thy hand drave the heathen out,
   and them thou planted hast;
how thou the people didst afflict,
   and thou didst them out-cast.
3 For they got not by their owne sword
   the lands possession,
neither yet was it their owne arme
   wrought their salvation:
But thy right hand, thine arme also,
   thy countenances light;
because that of thine owne good will
   thou didst in them delight.
4 Thou art my king, o mighty God,
   thou dost the same indure:
doe thou for Iacob by command
   deliverances procure.
5 Through thee as with a horne wee will
   push downe our enemies:
through thy name will wee tread them downe
   that up against us rise.
6 Because that I will in no wise
   any affiance have,
upon my bow, neither is it
   my sword that shall mee save.
7 But from our enemies us thou sav'd,
   and put our foes to shame.
8 In God wee boast all the day long,

                    and

PSALME xliv.

and for aye prayse thy name.　　　Selah.
(2)
9 But thou hast cast us off away,
　　thou makest us also
　to be asham'd; neither dost thou
　　forth with our armies goe.
10 Vs from before the enemy
　　thou makest back recoyle:
　likewise they which our haters bee,
　　for themselves us doe spoyle.
11 Thou hast us given like to sheep
　　to slaughter *that belong*:
　also thou hast us scattered
　　the heathen folk among.
12 Thou dost thy people set to sale
　　whereby no wealth doth rise:
　neither dost thou obtaine increase
　　of riches by their price.
13 Vnto our neighbours a reproach
　　thou doest us expose,
　a scorne we are & mocking stock,
　　to them that us inclose.
14 Among the heathen people thou
　　a by word dost us make:
　also among the nations,
　　at us their heads they shake.
15 Before me my confusion
　　it is continually,
　and of my countenance the shame
　　hath over covered mee.
16 Because of his voyce that doth scorne,

PSALM xliv.

and scoffingly despight:
  by reason of the enemy,
    and selfe revenging wight.
(3)

17 All this is come on us, wee yet
    have not forgotten thee:
  neither against thy covenant
    have wee dealt faithleslie.
18 Our heart is not turn'd back, nor have
    our steps from thy way stray'd;
19 Though us thou brake in dragons place,
    and hid us in deaths shade.
20 had wee forgot Gods name, or stretcht
    to a strange God our hands:
21 Shall not God search this out? for hee
    hearts secrets understands.
22 Yea, for thee all day wee are kil'd:
    counted as sheep to slay.
23 Awake, why sleepst thou, Lord? arise,
    cast us not off for aye.
24 Thy countenance away from us
    o wherefore dost thou hide?
  of our grief & oppression
    forgetfull dost abide.
25 For our soule is bowd downe to dust:
    to earth cleaves our belly.
26 Rise for our help, & us redeeme,
    because of thy mercy.

Psalme 45
To the chief musician upon Shoshannim, for-
the sonnes of Korah, Maschil a song of loves.

PSAL-

PSALME xl, xlv.

MY heart good mater boyleth forth,
  my works touching the King
I speak: my tongue is as the pen
  of Scribe swiftly writing.
2 Fairer thou art then sonnes of men,
  grace in thy lips is shed:
 because of this the Lord hath thee
  for evermore blessed.
3 Thy wasting sword o mighty one
  gird thou upon thy thigh:
 thy glorious-magnificence,
  and comely majesty.
4 Ride forth upon the word of truth,
  meeknes & righteousnes:
 and thy right hand shall lead thee forth
  in works of dreadfulnes.
5 Within the heart of the kings foes
  thine arrows piercing bee:
 whereby the people overcome,
  shall fall downe under thee.
6 Thy throne o God, for ever is,
  the scepter of thy state
7 right scepter is. Iustice thou lov'st,
  but wickednes dost hate:
 Because of this, God ev'n thy God
  hee hath annoynted thee,
 with oyle of gladnes above them,
  that thy companions bee.
8 Myrrhs, Aloes, and Cassias *smell*,
  all of thy garments *had*:
 out of the yvory pallaces

K 3

they

PSALM xlv.

wherby they made thee glad.
9 Amongst thine honourable maids
    kings daughters present were,
the Queen is set at thy right hand
    in fine gold of Ophir.

(2)

10 Harken o daughter, & behold,
    doe thou incline thine eare:
doe thou forget thine owne people,
    and house of thy father.
11 So shall the king delighting-rest
    himselfe in thy beautie:
and bowing downe worship thou him,
    because thy Lord is hee.
12 Then shall be present with a gift
    the daughter there of Tyre:
the wealthy ones of the people
    thy favour shall desire.
13 The daughter of the king she is
    all glorious within:
and with imbroderies of gold,
    her garments wrought have been.
14 She is led in unto the king
    in robes with needle wrought:
the virgins that doe follow her
    shall unto thee be brought.
15 They shall be brought forth with gladnes,
    also with rejoycing,
so shall they entrance have into
    the Pallace of the king.
16 Thy children shall in stead of those
    that were thy fathers bee: whom

PSALME xlv xlvi.

whom thou mayst place in all the earth
 in princely diginty.
17 Thy name remembred I will make
 through generations all:
therefore for ever & for aye
 the people prayse thee shall.

Psalme 46

To the chief musician, for the sonnes of
 Korah, a song upon Alemoth.

GOD is our refuge, strength, & help
 in troubles very neere.
2 Therefore we will not be afrayd,
 though th'earth removed were.
Though mountaines move to midst of seas
3 Though waters roaring make
and troubled be, at whose swellings
 although the mountaines shake.   Selah.
4 There is a river streames whereof
 shall rejoyce Gods city:
the holy place the tent wherin
 abideth the most high.
5 God is within the midst of her,
 moved shee shall not bee:
God shall be unto her an help,
 in the morning early.
6 The nations made tumultuous noyse,
 the kingdomes moved were:
he did give forth his thundering voyce
 the earth did melt *with feare*.
7 The God of Armies is with us
 th'eternall Iehovah:

the

PSALM xlvi, xlv ii.

    the God of Iacob is for us
      a refuge high. Selah.
8 O come yee forth behold the works
      which Iehovah hath wrought,
    the fearfull desolations,
      which on the earth he brought.
9 Vnto the utmost ends of th'earth
      warres into peace hee turnes:
    the speare he cuts, the bowe he breaks,
      in fire the chariots burnes.
10 Be still, & know that I am God,
      exalted be will I
    among the heathen: through the earth
      I 'le be exalted hye.
11 The God of armyes is with us,
      th'eternall Iehovah:
    the God of Iacob is for us
      a refuge high. Selah.

Psalme 47.

To the chief musician: a psalme for the Sonnes of Korah.

CLap hands all people, shout for joy,
    to God with voyce of singing mirth:
2 For high Iehovah fearfull is,
    a great King over all the earth.
3   People to us he doth subdue,
    and nations under our feet lay.
4 For us our heritage he chose,
    his deare Iacobs glory. Selah.
5   God is ascended with a shout:
    Iehovah with the trumpets noyse.

PSALME xlvii, xlviii.

6 Sing psalmes to God, sing psalmes, sing-
unto our King with singing voyce. (psalmes
7 For God is King of all the earth,
sing yee psalmes of instruction:
8 Over the heathen God will reigne
God sits his holy throne upon.
9 To the people of Abrahams-God
Princes of peoples gathered bee,
for shields of th'earth to God belong:
he is exalted mightylie.

Psalme 48
To the chief musician, a song & psalme for
the sonnes of Korah.

GReat is Iehovah, & he is
to be praysed greatly
within the city of our God,
in his mountaine holy.
2 For situation beautifull,
the joy of the whole earth
mount Sion; the great Kings city
on the sides of the north.
3 God in her pallaces is knowne
to be a refuge high.
4 For loe, the kings assembled were:
they past together by.
5 They saw, & so they merveiled,
were troubled, fled for feare.
6 Trembling seiz'd on them there & paine
like her that childe doth beare.
7 The navies that of Tarshish are
in pieces thou breakest:

L   even

PSALM xlviii.

ev'n with a very blast of winde
    coming out of the east.
8 As we heard, so we saw within
    the Lord of hoasts citty,
in our Gods citty, God will it
    stablish eternally.   Selah.

(2)

9 O God we have had thoughts upon
    thy free benignity,
within the very midle part
    of thy temple holy,
10 According to thy name, o God
    so is thy prayse unto
the ends of earth: thy right hand 's full
    of righteousnes also.
11 Let the mountaine Sion rejoyce,
    and triumph let them make
who are the daughters of Iudah,
    ev'n for thy judgements sake.
12 About the hill of Sion walk,
    and goe about her yee,
and doe yee reckon up thereof
    the tow'rs *that therein* bee.
13 Doe yee full well her bulwarks mark,
    her Pallaces view well,
that to the generation
    to come yee may it tell.
14 For this same God he is our God
    for ever & for aye:
likewise unto the very death
    he guides us in our way.

PSALME xlix.

Pſalme 49
To the chief muſician a pſalme for the
 ſonnes of Korah.

HEare this all people, all give eare
 that dwell the world all o're.
2 Sonnes both of low, & higher men,
 joyntly both rich & poore.
3 My mouth it ſhall variety
 of wiſdome be ſpeaking:
and my hearts meditation ſhall
 be of underſtanding.
4 Vnto a ſpeech proverbiall
 I will mine eare incline;
I will alſo upon the Harp
 open my dark doctrine.
5 Why ſhould I be at all afrayd
 in dayes that evill bee:
when that my heeles iniquity
 about ſhall compaſſe mee.

(2)

6 Thoſe men that make their great eſtates
 their ſtay to truſt unto,
who in the plenty of their wealth
 themſelves doe boaſt alſo:
7 Ther 's not a man *of them* that can
 by any meanes redeeme
his brother, nor give unto God
 enough to ranſome him.
8 So deare their ſoules redemption is
 & ever ceaſeth it.

L 2   9 That

PSALM xlix.

9 That he should still for ever live
    and never see the pit.
10 For he doth see that wise man dye,
    the foole and brutish too
to perish, & their rich estate
    to others leave they doo.
11 They think their houses are for aye
    to generations all
their dwelling places, & their lands
    by their owne names they call.
12 Neverthelesse, in honour man,
    abideth not a night:
become he is just like unto
    the beasts that perish quite.
13 This their owne way their folly is;
    yet whatsoe're they say,
their successors that follow them
    doe well approve. Selah.
14 Like sheep so are they layd in grave,
    death shall them feed upon;
& th' upright over them in morn
    shall have dominion.
And from the place where they doe dwell,
    the beauty which they have,
shall utterly consume away
    in the devouring grave.

(3)

15 But surely Gods redemption
    unto my soule will give,
even from the power of the grave,
    for he will me receive.   Selah.

PSALME xlix, l.

16 Be not afrayd when as a man
    in wealth is made to grow,
  and when the glory of his house
    abundantly doth flow.
17 Becauſe he ſhall carry away
    nothing when he doth dye:
  neither ſhall after him deſcend
    ought of his dignity.
18 And albeit that he his ſoule
    in time of his life bleſt,
  and men will prayſe thee, when as thou
    much of thy ſelfe makeſt.
19 He ſhall goe to his fathers race,
    they never ſhall ſee light.
20 Man in honour, & know'th not, is
    like beaſts that periſh quite.

Pſalme 50.
A pſalme of Aſaph.

THe mighty God, the Lord hath ſpoke,
    and he the earth doth call,
  from the upriſing of the Sun,
    thereof unto the fall.
2 The mighty God hath clearely ſhyn'd
    out of the mount Sion,
  which is of beauty excellent
    the full perfection.
3 Our God ſhall come, and not be ſtill
    fire ſhall waſte in his ſight;
  and round about him ſhall be rayſ'd
    a ſtorme of vehement might.
4 His folk to judge he from above

L 3   calls

PSALM L

  calls heavens, & earth likewise,
5 Bring mee my Saints, that cov'nant make
  with mee by sacrifice.
6 And the heavens shall his righteousnes
  shew forth apparentlie:
because the mighty God himselfe
  a righteous judge will bee.   Selah.

(2)

7 Heare, o my people, & I will
  speake, I will testify
also to thee o Israell,
  I even thy God am I.
8 As for thy sacrifices I
  will finde no fault with thee,
or thy burnt offrings, *which have been*
  at all times before mee.
9 Ile take no bullocks, nor he-goates
  from house, or foldes of thine.
10 For forrest beasts, & cattell all
  on thousand hills are mine.
11 The flying foules of the mountaines
  all of them doe I know:
and every wilde beast of the field
  it is with mee also.
12 If I were hungry I would not
  it unto thee declare:
for mine the habitable world,
  and fullnes of it *are*.
13 Of bullocks eate the flesh, or drink
  the blood of goates will I ?
14 Thanks offer unto God, & pay

         thy

PSALME L.

    thy vowes to the most high.
15 And in the day of trouble sore
    doe thou unto mee cry,
and I will thee deliver, and
    thou mee shalt glorify.
        (3)
16 But to the wicked God sayth, why
    dost thou the mention make
of my statutes, why in thy mouth
    should'st thou my cov'nant take?
17 Sith thou dost hate teaching and dost
    my words behinde thee cast.
18 When thou didst see a thief, then thou
    with him consented hast;
And likewise with adulterers
    thy part hath been the same.
19 Thy mouth to evill thou dost give,
    and guile thy tongue doth frame,
Thou sittest, thou dost speake against
    the man that is thy brother:
and thou dost slaunder him that is
    the sonne of thine owne mother.
21 These things hast thou committed, and
    in silence I kept close:
that I was altogether like
    thy selfe, thou didst suppose:
I'le thee reprove, & in order
    before thine eyes them set.
22 O therefore now consider this
    yee that doe God forget:
Lest I you teare, & there be not

                      any

any deliverer.
23 He glorifieth mee that doth
  prayse unto mee offer.
24 And hee that doth order *aright*
  his conversation,
 to him will I give that hee may
  see Gods salvation.

Psalme 51.

To the chief musician, a psalme of David, when
Nathan the prophet came unto him, after he
had gone in unto Bathsheba.

HAve mercy upon mee o God,
  in thy loving kyndnes:
 in multitude of thy mercyes
  blot out my trespasses.
2 From mine iniquity doe thou
  wash mee most perfectly,
 and also from this sin of mine
  doe thou mee purify.
3 Because, of my transgressions
  my selfe doe take notice,
 and sin that I committed have
  before mee ever is.
4 Gainst thee, thee only I have sin'd
  this ill done thee before:
 when thou speakst just thou art, & cleare
  when thou dost judge therfore.
5 Behold, how in iniquity
  I did my shape receive:
 also my mother *that mee bare*
  in sin did mee conceive.

6 Behold

PSALME LI

6 Behold, thou dost desire the truth
   within the inward part:
and thou shalt make mee wisdome know
   in secret of my heart.

7 With hysope doe me purify,
   I shall be cleansed so:
doe thou mee wash, & then I shall
   be whiter then the snow.

8 Of joy & of gladnes doe thou
   make me to heare the voyce:
that so the bones which thou hast broke
   may cheerfully rejoyce.

9 From the beholding of my sin
   hide thou away thy face:
also all mine iniquityes
   doe utterly deface.

(2)

10 A cleane heart (Lord) in me create,
   also a spirit right
11 in me renew. O cast not mee
   away out of thy sight;
Nor from me take thy holy spirit.

12 Restore the joy to mee
   of thy salvation, & uphold
me with thy spirit free.

13 Then will I teach thy wayes to those
   that work iniquitie:
and by this meanes shall sinners bee
   converted unto thee.

14 O God, God of my health, set mee
   free from bloud guiltines,

M   and

PSALM LI.

and so my tongue shall joyfully
   sing of thy righteousnes.
15 O Lord-my-stay, let thou my lips
   by thee be opened,
and by my mouth thy prayses shall
   be openly shewed.
16 For thou desir'st not sacrifice,
   it would I freely bring:
neither dost thou contentment take
   in a whole burnt offring.
17 The sacrifices of the Lord
   they are a broken sprite:
God, thou wilt not despise a heart
   that's broken, & contrite.
18 In thy good pleasure o doe thou
   doe good to Sion hill:
the walles of thy Ierusalem
   o doe thou build up still.
19 The sacrifice of justice shall
   please thee, with burnt offring,
and whole burnt offring; then they shall
   calves to thine Altar bring.

Another of the same.

O GOD, have mercy upon mee,
   according to thy kindenes deare:
and as thy mercyes many bee,
quite doe thou my transgressions cleare.
2   From my perversues mee wash through,
   and from my sin mee purify.
3 For my transgressions I doe know,

                            before

PSALME LI.

before mee is my sin dayly.
4 Gainst thee, thee only sin'd have I,
& done this evill in thy sight:
that when thou speakst thee justify
men may, and judging cleare thee quite.
5 Loe, in injustice shape't I was:
in sin my mother conceav'd mee.
6 Loe, thou in th'inwards truth lov'd haz:
and made mee wise in secrecie.
7 Purge me with hyssope, & I cleare
shall be; mee wash, & then the snow
8 I shall be whiter. Make me heare
Ioy & gladnes, the bones which so
Thou broken hast joy cheerly shall.
9 Hyde from my sins thy face away
blot thou iniquityes out all
which are upon mee any way.

(2)

10 Create in mee cleane heart *at last*
God: a right spirit in me new make.
11 Nor from thy presence quite me cast,
thy holy spright nor from me take.
12 Mee thy salvations joy restore,
and stay me with thy spirit free.
13 I wil, transgressors teach thy lore,
and sinners shall be turnd to thee.
14 Deliver mee from guilt of bloud,
o God, God of my health-saving,
which if thou shalt vouchsafe, aloud
thy righteousnes my tongue shall sing.
15 My lips doe thou, o *L*ord, unclose,

PSALM Lɪ.

and thy prayſe ſhall my mouth forth ſhow.
16 For ſacrifice thou haſt not choſe,
that I ſhould it on thee beſtow:
  Thou joy'ſt not in burnt ſacrifice.
17 Gods ſacrifices are a ſp'ryte
broken; o God, thou'lt not deſpiſe,
a heart that's broken & contrite.
18 In thy good will doe thou beſtow
on Sion goodnes bounteouſlie:
Ieruſalems walles that lye ſo low
doe thou vouchſafe to edifie.
19 Then ſhalt thou pleaſe to entertaine
the ſacrifices with content
of righteouſnes, the offrings ſlaine,
which unto thee wee ſhall preſent,
  Together with the offerings
ſuch as in fire whole burned are:
and then they ſhall their bullocks bring,
offrings to be on thine altar.

Pſalme 52

To the chief muſician, *Maſchil.* a pſalme of
David: when Doeg the Edomite came and
told Saule, & ſayd unto him, Dauid is
come to the houſe of Ahimılech.

O Man of might, wherefore doſt thou
  thus boaſt thy ſelfe in ill?
the goodnes of the mighty God
  endureth ever ſtill.
2 Thy tongue preſumptuouſly doth
  miſchievous things deviſe:
it is like to a razor ſharp,

working

PSALME LII, LIII.

working deceitfull lies.
3 Thou lovest evil more then good,
   more to speak lies then right.
4 O guilefull tongue, thou dost in all
   devouring words delight.
5 God shall likewise for evermore
   destroying thee deface,
he shall take thee away, & pluck
   thee from thy dwelling place,
And also root thee out from off
   the land of the living.   Selah.
6 The righteous also shall it see
   and feare, at him laughing.
7 Loe, this the man *that* made not God
   his strength: but trusted in
his store of wealth, himselfe made strong
   in his mischievous sin.
8 But in the house of God *am* I
   like a greene Olive-tree:
I trust for ever & for aye,
   in Gods benignitie.
9 Thee will I prayse for evermore,
   because thou hast done this:
and I'le wayt on thy name, for good
   before thy Saints that is.

Psalme 53.
To the chief musician upon Mahalath,
Maschil. a *psalme* of David.

THe foole in's heart saith, *there's* no God;
   they are corrupt, have done
abominable practises;

PSALM LIII, LIV.

that doth good there is none.
2 The Lord from heaven looked downe
  on sonnes of men, to see
if any that doth understand,
  that seeketh God there bee.
3 All are gone back, together they
  ev'n filthy are become:
and there is none that doeth good,
  noe not so much as one.
4 The workers of iniquityes
  have they noe knowledge all?
who eate my people: they eate bread;
  and on God doe not call.
5 Greatly they fear'd, *where* noe feare was,
  'gainst thee in camp that lyes
his bones God scattered; & them sham'd
  for God doth *them* despise.
6 Who Israells health from Sion gives?
  his folks captivitie
when God shall turne: Iacob shall joye
  glad Israell shall bee.

Psalme 54

To the chief musician on Neginoth, Maschil, *a psalm:* of David, when the Ziphims came & sayd to Saul, doth not David hide himselfe with us?

PReserve mee, by thy name, o God,
  & by thy strength judge mee.
2 O God, my pray'r heare, give eare to
  words in my mouth that bee.
3 For strangers up against me rise,
  and who oppresse me sore,

pursue

PSALME 14ꞏꞏꞏ, 15.

 pursue my soule; neither have they
  set God themselves before.   Selah.
4 Loe, God helps mee, the Lord's with them
  that doe my soule sustaine.
5 He shall reward ill to my foes:
  them in thy truth restrayne.
6 Vnto thee sacrifice will I,
  with voluntarines;
 Lord, to thy name I will give prayse,
  because of thy goodnes.
7 For he hath mee delivered,
  out of all miseryes:
 and its desire mine eye hath seen
  upon mine enemyes.

Psalme 55

To the chief musician on Neginoth, Maschil,
  a psalme of David.

O GOD, doe thou give eare unto
  my supplication:
and doe not hide thy selfe away
  from my petition.
2 Bee thou attentive unto mee,
  and answer mee returne,
 I in my meditation
  doe make a noyse & mourne.
3 Because of th'enemies voyce, because
  the wicked haue opprest,
 for they injustice on mee cast
  and in wrath mee detest.
4 My heart in mee is payn'd, on mee
  deaths terrors fallen bee.
        5 Trembling

PSALM Lv.

5 Trembling & feare are on mee come,
    horrour hath covered mee.
6 Then did I say, o who to mee
    wings of a dove will give;
 that I might flie away & might
    in quiet dwelling live.
7 Loe, I would wander farre away,
    and in the desart rest.   Selah,
8 Soone would I scape from windy storme,
    from violent tempest.

(2)

9 Lord bring on them destruction,
    doe thou their tongues divide;
 for strife & violence I within
    the city have espy'd.
10 About it on the walles thereof,
    they doe walk night & day:
 mischief also & sorrow doe
    in middest of it stay.
11 In midst thereof there's wickednes;
    deceitfullnes also,
 and out of the broad streets thereof
    guilefullnes doth not go.
12 For t'was no foe reproacht mee, then
    could I have borne; nor did
 my foe against me lift himselfe
    from him had I me hid.
13 But thou it was, the man that wert
    my well esteemed peere,
 which wast to mee my speciall guide,
    and mine acquaintance neere.

PSALME lv.

14 Wee did together counsell take
    in sweet society:
and wee did walk into the house
    of God in company.
15 Let death seize on them, & let them
    goe downe quick into hell:
for wickednes among them is
    in places where they dwell.

(2)

16 As for mee, I will call on God;
    and mee the Lord save shall.
17 Ev'ning morn, & at noon will I
    pray, & aloud will call,
18 and he shall heare my voyce. He hath
    in peace my soule set free
from warre that was 'gainst mee, because
    there many were with mee.
19 God shall heare, & them smite, ev'n he
    that doth of old abide;   Selah.
because they have no change, therefore
    Gods feare they lay aside.
20 Gainst such as be at peace with him
    hee hath put forth his hand:
he hath also the covenant
    which he had made prophan'd.
21 His words then butter smoother were,
    but warre in's heart: his words
more then the oyle were softened
    but yet they were drawne swords.
22 Thy burden cast upon the Lord,
    and he sustaine thee shall:

nor shall he suffer righteous ones
  to be remov'd at all.
23 But thou o God, shalt downe to hell
  bring them who bloody bee,
guilefull shall not live halfe their dayes:
  but I will trust in thee.

Psalme 56.

To the chief musician upō Ionath Elem Recho-
-kim, Michtam of David, when the Philistims
    tooke him in Gath.

LORD, pitty mee, because
  man would up swallow mee:
and fighting all the day throughout,
  oppresse mee sore doth hee.
2 Mine enemies they would
  me swallow up dayly;
for they *be* many that doe fight
  against mee, o most high.
3 I'le put my trust in thee,
  what time I am afrayd.
4 In God I'le prayse his word, in God
  my confidence have stayd;
I will not be afrayd
  what flesh can doe to mee.
5 All day they wrest my words: their thoughts
  for ill against me bee.
6 They joyne themseves together;
  themselves they closely hyde;
they mark my steps when for my soule
  wayting they doe abyde.
7 Shall they make an escape

                   by

by their iniquity;
thou in thine anger downe depresse
  the folk, o God mighty.
8 My wandrings thou dost tell,
    put thou my weeping teares
into thy bottle; *are* they not
  within thy registers.
9 Then shall my foes turne back,
    when I crye unto thee:
this I doe know assuredly,
  because God is for mee.
10 In God I'le prayse his word:
    the Lords word I will prayse.
11 In God I trust: I will not feare
    what man 'gainst mee can rayse.
12 Thy vowes on me o God,
    I'le render prayse to thee.
13 Because that thou my soule from death
    delivering dost free;
Deliver wilt not thou
  my feet from downe falling?
so that I may walk before God
  ith light of the living.

Psalme 57

To the chief musician Altaschith, Michtam of
  David, when he fled from Saul in the cave.

O GOD, to me be mercifull,
    be mercifull to mee:
because my soule for shelter-safe
  betakes it selfe to thee.
Yea in the shaddow of thy wings,
  my refuge I have plac't,

PSALM LVII.

untill these sore calamities
    shall quite be over past.
2 To God most high I cry: the God
    that doth for me performe.
3 He will from heaven send, & save
    mee from the spightfull scorne
Of him that would with greedy hast,
    swallow me vtterly: Selah.
the Lord from heaven will send forth
    his grace & verity.
4 My soule's 'mongst lions, & I lye
    with men on-fier-set:
mens sonnes whose teeth are spears, & shafts,
    whose tongues as swords are whet.
5 O God, doe thou exalt thy selfe,
    above the heavens high:
up over all the earth also
    lifted be thy glory.
6 They for my steps prepar'd a net,
    my soule is bow'd; a pit
they dig'd before me, but *themselves*
    are fall'n in midst of it.   Selah.
7 My heart o God, prepared is,
    prepared is my heart,
sing will I, & sing prayse with psalmes.
8 Vp o my glorie start;
    Wake Psaltery & Harp, I will
    awake in the morning.
9 Among the folk I'le prayse thee, Lord,
    'mongst nations to thee sing.

10 For great unto the heavens is
 thy mercifull bounty:
 thy verity also doth reach
 unto the cloudy skye.
11 O God, doe thou exalt thy selfe,
 above the heavens high:
 up over all the earth also
 lifted *be* thy glory.

Psalme 58
To the chief musician, Altaschith, michtam of David.

Doe yee o congregation,
 indeed speak righteousnes?
and o yee sons of earthly men,
 doe yee judge uprightnes?
2 Yea you in heart will working be
 injurious-wickednes;
 and in the land you will weigh out
 your hands violentnes.
3 The wicked are estranged from
 the womb, they goe astray
 as soone as ever they are borne;
 uttering lyes are they.
4 Their poyson's like serpents poyson:
 they like deafe Aspe, her eare
5 that stops. Though Charmer wisely charme,
 his voice she will not heare.
6 Within their mouth doe thou their teeth
 break out, o God most strong,
 doe thou Iehovah, the great teeth
 break of the lions young.

PSALM lviii, lix.

7 As waters let them melt away,
   that run continually:
and when he bends his shafts, let them
   as cut asunder bee.
8 Like to a snayle that melts, so let
   each of them passe away;
like to a womans untimely birth
   see Sun that neuer they may.
9 Before your potts can feele the thornes,
   take them away shall hee,
as with a whirlwinde both living,
   and in his jealousee.
10 The righteous will rejoyce when as
   the vengeance he doth see:
his feet wash shall he in the blood
   of them that wicked bee.
11 So that a man shall say, surely
   for righteous there is fruit:
sure there's a God that in the earth
   judgement doth execute.

Psalme 59

To the chief musician Altaschith, Michtam of
David: when Saul sent, & they watched the
house to kill him.

O GOD from them deliver mee
   that are mine enemies:
set thou me up on high from them
   that up against me rise.
2 Deliver mee from them that work
   grievous-iniquity:
and be a saviour unto mee

                  from

PSALME lix.

from men that be bloody.
3 For loe, they for my soule lay wayt;
   the strong causlesse combine
against me, not for my crime, Lord,
   nor any sin of mine.
4 Without iniquity in me
   they run, & ready make
themselves, doe thou behold, also
   unto my help awake.
5 Lord God of hoast, thou Israels God,
   rise to visit therefore
all heathens; who sin wilfully,
   to them shew grace no more.
6 At ev'ning they returne, & like
   to dogs a noyse doe make;
and so about the city round
   a compasse they doe take.
7 Behold they belch out with their mouths,
   within their lips swords are:
for who is he (doe these men say)
   which *us* at all doth heare.
8 But thou o *L*ord, at them wilt laugh,
   and heathens all wilt mock.
9 *And for* his strength. I'le wayt on thee
   for God is my high Rock.

(2)

10 God of my mercy manyfold
   with good shall prevent mee:
and my desire upon my foes
   the Lord will let mee see.
11 Slay them not, lest my folk forget:

but

PSALM LIX.

but scatter them abroad
  by thy strong-power;& bring them downe,
who art our shield o God.
12 For their mouths sin,& their lips words,
  and in their pride them take:
and for their cursing,& lying
  which in their speech they make.
13 Consume in wrath, consume & let
  them be no more;that they
may know that God in Iacob rules,
  to th'ends of th'earth. Selah.
14 And at ev'ning let them returne,
  and like dogs a noyse make;
and so about the citty round
  a compasse let them take.
15 And let them wander up & downe
  seeking what they may eat,
and if they be not satisfiyde,
  then let them grudge thereat.
16 But I will sing thy powre;& shout
  i'th morning thy kindenesse:
for thou my towre & refuge art
  in day of my distresse.
17 Thou art my strength,& unto thee,
  sing psalmes of prayse will I:
for God is mine high towre, he is
  the God of my mercy.

Psalme 60.

To the chief musician upon Shushan Eduth
Michtam of David,to teach. when he strove with
Aram Naharaim, & with Aram Zobah when
Ioab

PSALME lx.

Ioab returned,& smote of Edom in the valley
of salt, twelve thousand.

O GOD, thou hast rejected us,
and scattered us abroad:
thou hast displeased been with us,
returne to us o God.
2 The land to tremble thou hast caus'd,
thou it asunder brake:
doe thou the breaches of it heale,
for it doth moveing shake.
3 Thou hast unto thy people shew'd
things that are hard, thou hast
also the cup of trembleing
given to them to tast.
4 But unto them that doe thee feare,
a Banner to display
thou given hast to be lift up
for thy truths sake. Selah.
5 That those who thy beloved are
delivered may bee,
o doe thou save with thy right hand,
and answer give to mee.
6 God in his holynes hath spoke,
rejoyce therein will I,
Shechem I will divide, & meete
of Succoth the valley.
7 To mee doth Gilead appertaine,
Manasseh mine besides:
Ephraim the strength is of my head,
Iudah my lawes prescribes.
8 Moab's my wash-pot, I will cast

Q over

PSALM lx, lxi

over Edom my shoo,
o Palestine, because of mee
be thou triumphant too.
9 O who is it that will mee lead
to th'citty fortifyde?
and who is he that will become
into Edom my guide?
10 Is it not thou, o God, who hadst
cast us off heretofore?
and thou o God, who with our hoasts
wouldst not goe out before?
11 O give to us help from distresse
for mans help is but vaine:
12 Through God wee'l doe great acts, he shall
our foes tread with disdaine.

Psalme 61
To the chief musician upon Neginath,
A psalme of David.

HArken o God, unto my cry,
unto my prayr attend.
2 When my heart is opprest, I'le cry
to thee from the earths end.
Doe thou mee lead unto the rock
that higher is then I.
3 For thou my hiding-place, hast been
strong Fort from th'enemy.
4 Within thy Tabernacle I
for ever will abide,
within the covert of thy wings
I'le seek my selfe to hide. Selah·
5 For thou o God, hast heard the vowes

that

PSALME lxi, lxii.

that I to thee have past:
their heritage that feare thy name
  to mee thou given hast.
6 Thou to the dayes of the Kings life
  wilt make addition:
his yeares as generation,
  and generation.
7 Before the face of the strong God
  he shall abide for aye:
doe thou mercy & truth prepare
  that him preserve they may.
8 So then I will unto thy name
  sing prayse perpetually,
that I the vowes which I have made
  may pay continually.

Psalme 62

To the chief musician, to Ieduthun,
  a psalme of David.

TRuly my soule in silence waytes
  the mighty God upon:
from him it is that there doth come
  all my salvation.
2 He only is my rock, & my
  salvation; it is hee
that my defence is, so that I
  mov'd greatly shall not bee.
3 How long will yee mischief devise
  'gainst man; be slaine yee shall,
all yee are as a tottring fence,
  & like a bowing wall.
4 Yet they consult to cast him downe

from

PSALM lxii.

from his excellency:
lyes they doe love, with mouth they blesse,
   but they curse inwardly.   Selah.
5 Yet thou my soule in silent wayt
   the mighty God upon:
because from him there doth arise
   my expectation.
6 He only is my rock, & my
   salvation; it is hee
that my defence is, so that I
   shall never mooved bee.
7 In God is my salvation,
   also is my glory:
and the rock of my fortitude,
   my hope in God doth ly.
8 Yee people, see that you on him
   doe put your trust alway,
before him poure ye out your hearts:
   God is our hopefull-stay.   Selah.
9 Surely meane men are vanity
   high mens sonnes are a lye:
in ballance laid together are
   lighter then vanity.
10 In robbery be not vaine, trust not
   yee in oppression:
if so be riches doe increase
   set not your heart *thereon*.
11 The mighty God hath spoken once:
   once & againe this word
I have it heard that *all* power
   belongs unto the Lord.

                                  12 Also

PSALME lx11, lx111

12 Also to thee benignity
　　o Lord, doth *appertaine*:
for thou according to his work
　　rendrest each man againe.

Psalme 63
A psalme of David, when he was in the wildernes of Iudah.

O GOD, thou art my God, early
　　I will for thee inquire:
my soule thirsteth for thee, my flesh
　　for thee hath strong desire,
In land whereas no water is
　　that thirsty is & dry.
2 To see, as I saw in thine house
　　thy strength & thy glory.
3 Because thy loving kindenes doth
　　abundantly excell
ev'n life it selfe: wherefore my lips
　　forth shall thy prayses tell.
4 Thus will I blessing give to thee
　　whilst that alive am I:
and in thy name I will lift up
　　these hands of mine on high.
5 My soule as with marrow & fat
　　shall satisfied bee:
my mouth also with joyfull lips
　　shall prayse give unto thee.
6 When as that I remembrance have
　　of thee my bed upon,
and on thee in the night watches
　　have meditation.

7 Because that thou hast been to me
he that to me help brings;
therefore will I sing joyfully
in shaddow of thy wings.
8 My soule out of an ardent love
doth follow after thee:
also thy right hand it is that
which hath upholden mee.
9 But as for those that seek my soule
to bring it to an end,
they shall into the lower parts
of the earth downe descend.
10 By the hand of the sword also
they shall be made to fall:
and they be for a portion
unto the Foxes shall.
11 But the King shall rejoyce in **God**,
all that by him doe sweare
shall glory, but stopped shall be
their mouths that lyars are.

Psalme 64
To the chief musician, a psalme
of David.

O GOD, when I my prayer make,
my voyce *then* doe thou heare;
also doe thou preserve my life
safe from the enemies feare.
2 And from the secret counsell of
the wicked hide thou mee:
from th' insurection of them
that work iniquitee.

PSALME lxiv.

3 Who have their tongue now sharpened
 like as it were a sword;
and bend *their bowes to shoot* their shafts
 ev'n a most bitter word:
4 That they in secrecie may shoot
 the perfect man to hitt.
suddenly doe they shoot at him,
 & never feare a whitt.
5 Them selves they in a matter ill
 encourage; how they may
lay snares in secret, thus they talk;
 who shall them see? they say.
6 They doe search out iniquity,
 a search exact they keep:
both inward thought of every man
 also the heart is deep.
7 But God shall shoot at them a shaft,
 be sudden their wound shall.
8 So that they shall make their owne tongue
 upon themeselves to fall,
All that see them shall flee away.
9   All men shall feare, & tell
the works of God, for his doeing
 they shall consider well.
10 The just shall in the Lord be glad,
 and trust in him he shall:
and they that upright are in heart
 in him shall glory all.

Psalme 65
To the chief musician, a psalme and
song of David.

PSALM

PSALM lxv.

O GOD, in Sion silently
 prayse wayteth upon thee:
and thankfully unto thee shall
 the vow performed bee.
2 O thou that harken dost unto
 the prayr that men doe make,
ev'n unto thee therefore all flesh
 themselves they shall betake.
3 Works of iniquitie they have
 prevailed against mee;
as for our trespasses they shall
 be purgde away by thee.
4 O blessed is the man of whom
 thou thy free choyce dost make;
and that he may dwell in thy courts
 him neere to thee dost take:
For with the good things of thy house
 be satisfyde shall wee;
and with the holy things likwise
 that in thy temple bee.
5 In righteousnes, thou, by the things
 that dreadfully are done,
wilt answer give to us, o God,
 of our salvation:
Vpon whom all the ends of th'earth
 do confidently stay,
& likewise they that are remov'd
 far off upon the sea.
6 He sets fast mountaines by his strength
7 girt with might. Hee doth swage
 the noyse of seas, noyse of their waves

also

PSALME lxv.

also the peoples rage.
(2)
8 They at thy tokens are afrayd
    that dwell in parts far out;
out goings of the morning thou
    and ev'ning makſt to ſhout.
9 Thou viſiteſt the earth, & doſt
    it moiſten plenteouſly,
thou with Gods ſtreame, full of water
    enricheſt it greatly:
When thou haſt ſo prepared it,
    thou doſt them corne prepare.
10 The ridges thou abundantly
    watreſt that in it are;
The furrows of it thou ſetleſt,
    with ſhowers that do fall
thou makſt it ſoft, thou doſt therof
    the ſpringing bleſſe withall.
11 Thou doſt the yeare with thy goodnes
    adorne as with a crowne,
alſo the paths where thou doſt tread,
    fatnes they doe drop downe.
12 They drop upon the paſtures that
    are in the wildernes;
and girded are the little hills
    about with joyfullnes.
13 Clothed the paſtures are with flocks,
    corne over-covering
the valleys is; ſo that for joy
    they ſhout, they alſo ſing.

P   pſalme

PSALM lxvi.

Psalme 66

To the chief musician a psalme or song.

O All yee lands, a joyfull noyse
  unto God doe yee rayse.
2 Sing forth the honour of his name:
  make glorious his prayse.
3 How dreadfull in thy works art thou?
  unto the Lord say yee:
 through thy powres greatnes thy foes shall
  submit themselves to thee.
4 All they shall bow themselves to thee
  that dwell upon the earth,
 and sing unto thee, they shall sing
  unto thy name with mirth.   Selah.
5 Come hither, also of the works
  of God take yee notice,
 he in his doing terrible
  towards mens children is.
6 He did the sea into dry land
  convert, a way they had
 on foot to passe the river through,
  there we in him were glad.
7 He ruleth by his powre for ever,
  his eyes the nations spie:
 let not those that rebellious are
  lift up themselves on high.   Selah.
8 Yee people blesse our God, & make   (2 *part*)
  his prayses voyce be heard.
9 Which holds our soule in life, our feet
  nor suffers to be stird.
10 For God thou hast us prov'd, thou hast

PSALME lxvi.

us tryde as silver's tryde.
11 Into the net brought us, thou haſt
   on our loynes ſtreightnes tyde.
12 Men o're our heads thou madſt to ride,
   through fire & water paſſe
 did wee, but us thou broughſt into
   a place that wealthy was.
13 With offrings I'le go to thine houſe:
   my vowes I'le pay to thee.
14 Which my lips uttred, & mouth ſpake,
   when trouble was on mee.
15 Burnt offrings I'le offer to thee
   that full of fatnes are,
 with the incenſe of rams, I will
   bullocks with goates prepare.   Selah.
16 Come harken unto me all yee   (*3 part*)
   of God that fearers are,
 and what he hath done for my ſoule
   to you I will declare.
17 With mouth I cryde to him, & with
   my tongue extoll'd was hee.
18 If in my heart I ſin regard
   the Lord will not heare mee.
19 But God that is moſt mighty hath
   me heard aſſuredly;
 unto the voyce of my prayr he
   liſt'ned-attentively.
20 Bleſt be the mighty God, becauſe
   neither my prayr hath hee,
 nor yet his owne benignity,
   turned away from mee.

PSALM lxvii.

Psalme 67

To the chief musician on Neginoth
a psalme *or* Song.

GOD gracious be to us, & give
his blessing us unto,
   let him upon us make to shine
      his countenance also.   Selah.
2 That there may be the knowledg of
      thy way the earth upon,
   and also of thy saving health
      in every nation.
3 O God let thee the people prayse,
      let all people prayse thee.
4 O let the nations rejoyce,
      and let them joyfull bee:
For thou shalt give judgement unto
      the people righteously,
   also the nations upon earth
      thou shalt them lead safely.   Selah.
5 O God let thee the people prayse
      let all people prayse thee.
6 *Her* fruitfull increase by the earth
      shall then forth yeilded bee:
God ev'n our owne God shall us blesse.
7   God *I say* blesse us shall,
   and of the earth the utmost coasts
      they shall him reverence all.

Psalme 68
To the chief musician, a psalme or song
of David.

PSALME lxviii.

Let God arise, his enemies
　　let them disperſed bee,
　let them alſo that doe him hate
　　away from his face flee.
2 As ſmoake is driven away, ev'n ſo
　　doe thou them drive away:
　as wax at fire melts, in Gods ſight
　　let wicked ſo decay.
3 But let the righteous ones be glad:
　　o let them joyfull bee
　before the Lord, alſo let them
　　rejoyce exceedinglie.
4 Sing to God, to his name ſing prayſe,
　　extoll him that doth ride
　on ſkies, by his name IAH, before
　　his face joyfull abide.
5 A father of the fatherleſſe,
　　and of the widdows caſe
　God is a judge, & that within
　　his holy dwelling place.
6 God ſeates the deſolate in houſe,
　　brings forth thoſe that are bound
　in chaines, but the rebellious
　　dwell in a barren ground.
(2)
7 O God when as thou didſt goe forth
　　in preſence of thy folk,
　when through the deſart wildernes
　　thou diddeſt marching walk.　　Selah.
8 The earth did at Gods preſence ſhake,
　　from heav'ns the drops downe fell:
　　　　　　P 3　　　　　　　　　　Sinai

Sinai it selfe moved before   PSAL- lxviii.
   the God of Israell.
9 O God thou on thy heritage
   didst send a plenteous raine,
whereby when as it weary was
   thou it confirm'd againe.
10 Thy congregation hath dwelt
   therin, thou dost prepare
o God of thy goodnes, for them
   that poore afflicted are.
11 The Lord the word gave, great their troup
   that it have published.
12 Kings of hoasts fled, fled, she that stayd
   at home spoyle devided.
13 Though yee have lyen among the pots,
   be like doves wings shall yee
with silver deckt, & her feathers
   like yellow gold that bee.
14 When there th'Almighty scattred Kings,
   t'was white as Salmons snow.
15 Gods hill like Bashan hill, high hill,
   like Bashan hill unto.
16 Why doe ye leap ye lofty hills?
   this is the very hill
in which God loves to dwell, the Lord
   dwell in it ever will.

(5)

17 Gods charrets twice ten thousand fold,
   thousands of Angells bee;
with them as in his holy place,
   on Sinai mount is hee.
18 Thou didst ascend on high, thou ledst
   captivity captive,

for

for men, yea, for rebells also   PSA- lxviii.
    thou diddest gifts receive;
That the Lord God might dwell with them.
19 Who dayly doth us load
    with benefits, blest be the Lord
      that's our salvations God.   Selah.
20 He is God of salvation
    that is our God most strong:
  and unto Iehovah the Lord
    issues from death belong.
21 But God shall wound the enemies head,
    the hairy scalp also
  of him that in his trespasses
    on forward still doth go.
            (4)
22 The Lord sayd I·le bring back againe,
    againe from Bashan hill:
  my people from the depths of seas
    bring back againe I will.
23 That thy foot may be dipt within
    blood of thine enemyes;
  imbrude the tongue of thy dogs may
    be in the same likewyse.
24 They have thy goings seene o God
    thy goings in progresse;
  ev'n of my God my King within
    place of his holynesse.
25 Singers went first, musicians then,
    in midst maids with Timbrel.
26 Blesse God i'th Churches, the Lord from
    the spring of Israell.
27 There litle Benjamin the chief
    with Iudahs Lords, & their   counsel

PSALM lxviii.

 counsell, with Zebulons princes,
  and Naphtalies lords were.
23 That valliant strength the which thou hast
  thy God hath commanded;
 strengthen o God, the thing which thou
  for us hast effected.

(4)

29 For thy house at Ierusalem
  Kings shall bring gifts to thee.
30 Rebuke the troups of spearmen, troups
  of bulls that mighty bee:
 With peoples calves, with him that stoops
  with peeces of silvar:
 o scatter thou the people that
  delight themselves in war.
31 Princes shall out of Egipt come,
  & Ethiopias land
 shall speedily unto the Lord
  reach her out-streched hand.
32 Earths kingdomes sing yee unto God:
  unto the Lord sing prayse. Selah.
33 To him that rides on heav'ns of heav'ns
  that were of ancient dayes:
 Loe, he his voyce, a strong voyce gives.
34 To God ascribe yee might,
 his excellence o're Israell is,
  & his strength in the height.
35 God fearfull from his holy place
  the God of Israell, hee
 gives strength & powre unto his folk,
  o let God blessed bee.

psalme

PSALME lxix.

To the chief musician upon Shoshannim,
A psalme of David.

THe waters in unto my soule
  are come, o God, me save.
2 I am in muddy deep sunk downe,
  where I no standing have:
Into deep waters I am come,
  where floods mee overflow.
3 I of my crying weary am,
  my throat is dryed so;
Mine eyes faile: I wayt for my God.
4   They that have hated mee
without a cause, then mine heads haires
  they more in number bee:
Also mine enemies wrongfully
  they are that would me slay,
mighty they are; then I restor'd
  what I took not away.
5 O God thou know'st my foolishnes;
  my sin's not hid from thee.
6 Who wayt on thee, Lord God of hoasts,
  let not be shamd for mee:
O never suffer them, who doe
  for thee inquiry make,
o God of Israell, to be
  confounded for my sake,

(2)

7 By reason that I for thy sake,
  reproach have suffered:
confusion my countenance
  hath overcovered.

PSALM lxix.

8 I as a stranger am become
    unto my bretherren;
 and am an aliant unto
    my mothers childerren.
9 For of thy house the zeale me hath
    up eaten: every one
 who thee reproach, their reproaches
    are fallen mee upon
10 In fasts, I wept & spent my soule,
    this was reproach to mee.
11 And I my garment sackcloth made:
    yet must their proverb bee.
12 They that do sit within the gate,
    against mee speak they do;
 unto the drinkers of strong drink,
    I was a song also.
13 But I in an accepted time
    to thee Lord, make my prayr:
 mee Lord, in thy salvations truth,
    in thy great mercy heare.

(3)

14 Deliver me out of the mire,
    and mee from sinking keep:
 let mee be freed mine haters from,
    and out of waters deep.
15 O'reflow mee let not water floods,
    nor mee let swallow up
 the deep, also let not the pitt
    her mouth upon mee shut.
16 Iehovah heare thou mee, for good
    is thy benignity:

                                  turne

PSALME lxix.

turne unto mee according to
  greatnes of thy mercy.
17 And hide not thou thy countenance
  from thy servant away;
because that I in trouble am;
  heare me without delay.
18 O draw thou nigh unto my soule,
  doe thou it vindicate;
give mee deliverance, because
  of them that doe mee hate.
19 Thou hast knowne my reproach, also
  my shame, & my disgrace:
mine adversaryes every one
  they are before thy face.
(4)
20 Reproach mine heart brake, I was griev'd:
  for some me to bemone
I sought, but none there was; & for
  comforters, but found none.
21 Moreover in stead of my meate
  unto mee gall they gave;
and in me thirst they vineger
  for drink made me to have.
22 Their table set before their face,
  to them become a snare:
and *that let be* a trap, *which should
  have been* for *their* welfare.
23 And let their eyes be darkened,
  that they may never see:
their loynes also with trembleing
  to shake continuallee.

Q 2   24 Poure

PSALM lxix.

24 Poure out thine ire on them, let seize
    on them thine anger fell.
25 Their Pallace let be desolate:
    none in their tents let dwell.
26 Because they *him* doe persecute
    on whom thy stroke is found:
also they talk unto the grief
    of them whom thou dost wound.
27 Thou unto their iniquity
    iniquity doe add:
into thy righteousnes for them
    let entrance none be had.
28 Out of the book of the living
    o doe thou them forth blot,
and amongst them that righteous are
    be written let them not.

(5)

29 But Lord, I'me poore & sorrowfull:
    let thy health lift me hy.
30 With song I'le prayse the name of God:
    with thanks him magnify.
31 Vnto Iehovah *this* also
    shall be more pleasing far,
then *any* oxe *or* bullock young,
    that horn'd & hoofed are.
32 This thing when as they shall behold,
    then shall be glad the meek;
also their heart shall ever live
    that after God doe seek.
33 For the Lord hears the poore, nor doth
    despise whom he hath bound.

PSALME lxix, lxx.

34 Let heav'n, earth, seas & all therin
 that moves, his prayses sound.
35 For God will Iudahs cittyes build,
 and Sion he will save:
 that they may dwell therin, & may
 it in possession have.
36 The seed also of his servants
 inherit shall the same:
 also therin inhabit shall
 they that doe love his name.

Psalme 70
To the chief musician, a psalme to bring
 to remembrance.

O GOD, to rescue mee,
 Lord, to mine help, make hast.
2 Let them that after my soule seek
 asham'd be, & abasht:
 Turnd back & shamd let them
 that in my hurt delight.
3 Turnd back let them ha, ha, that say,
 their shame for to requite.
4 Let all those that thee seek
 joy, & be glad in thee:
 let such as love thy health say still,
 magnifyde let God bee.
5 Make hast to me Lord, for
 I poore am & needy:
 thou art mine ayd, & my helper
 o Lord; doe not tarry.

Psalme 71
R 3   PSALM

PSALM lxxi.

JEHOVAH, I for safety doe
  betake my selfe to thee:
 o let me not at any time
  put to confusion bee.
2 Me rescue in thy righteousnes,
  let me deliverance have:
 to me doe thou incline thine eare,
  also doe thou me save.
3 Be thou my dwelling Rock, whereto
  I alwayes may resort:
 thou gav'st commandment me to save,
  for thou my Rock & Fort.
4 Out of the hand of the wicked
  my God, deliver mee,
 out of the hand of the unjust,
  leaven'd with crueltie.
5 For thou o God, Iehovah art
  mine expectation:
 and thou art hee whom from my youth
  my trust is set upon:
6 Thou hast upheld mee from the womb,
  thou art he that tookst mee
 out of my mothers belly; still
  my prayse shall be of thee.

(2)

7 To many I a wonder am
  but thou my refuge strong.
8 Let my mouth fill'd be with thy prayse,
  & honour all day long.
9 Within the time of elder age
  o cast me not away,

and

PSALME lxxi.

and doe not thou abandon me
   when my strength doth decay.
10 Because they that be enemyes
   to me, against me spake,
and they that for my soule lay-wayt,
   counsell together take.
11 Saying, God hath forgotten him:
   doe yee him now pursue,
and apprehend him, for *there is*
   not one him to rescue.
12 Depart not farre from mee, o God,
   my God hast to helpe mee.
13 The adversaryes of my soule,
   let them ashamed bee:
Let them consumed be, let them
   be also covered,
both with reproach & dishonour,
   that for my hurt wayted.
        (3)
14 But *I* with patience will wayt
   on thee continuallee,
and I will adde yet more & more
   to all the prayse of thee.
15 My mouth it shall thy righteousnes,
   and thy salvation show
from day to day, for *of the same*
   no number doe I know.
16 In the strong might of God the Lord
   goe on a long will I:
I'le mention make of thy justice,
   yea ev'n of thine only.

PSALM lxxi.

17 From my youth up o mighty God,
    thou hast instructed mee:
 and hitherto I have declar'd
    the wonders wrought by thee.
18 And now unto mine elder age,
    and hoary head, o God,
 doe not forsake mee: till I have
    thy power showne abroad,
Vnto this generation,
    and unto every one
that shall hereafter be to come,
    thy strong dominion.

(4)

19 Thy righteousnes o God, it doth
    reach up on high also,
 great are the things which thou hast done;
    Lord who's like thee unto?
20 Thou who hast caused mee to see
    afflictions great & sore,
 shalt mee revive, & me againe
    from depths of earth restore.
21 Thou shalt my greatnes multiply
    & comfort me alwayes.
22 Also with tuned *P*saltery
    I will shew forth thy prayse,
 O thou my God, I will sing forth
    to thee mine Harp upon,
thy verity & faithfullnes,
    o Israels Holy-one.
23 My lips with shouting shall rejoyce
    when I shall sing to thee:

PSALME lxxi, lxxii.

my soule also, which freely thou
   haft brought to liberty.
24 Likewise my tongue shall utter forth
   thy justice all day long:
for they confounded are, & brought
   to shame, that seek my wrong.

Psalme 72
A psalme for Solomon.

O GOD, thy judgements give the King,
   & thy justice to the Kings Sonne.
2 He shall thy folk with justice judge,
   & to thy poore see judgement done,
3   The mountaines shall abundantly
   unto the people bring forth peace:
the little hills shall bring the same,
   by executing righteousnes.
4   Poore of the people he shall judge,
   and children of the needy save;
& he in peeces shall break downe
   each one that them oppressed have.
5   They shall thee feare, while Sun & moon
   endure through generations all.
6 Like raine on mowne grasse he shall come:
   as showres on earth distilling-fall.
7   The just shall flourish in his dayes,
   & store of peace till no moore bee.
8 And from the sea unto the sea,
   from floud to lands end reigne shall hee.
9   They that within the wildernes
   doe dwell, before him bow they must:
and they who are his enemies

PSALM lxxii.

they verily shall lick the dust.
(2)
10 Vpon him presents shall bestow
of Tarshish, & the Iles, the Kings,
Shebahs, & Sebahs Kings also,
shall unto him give offerings.
11 Yea to him all the kings shall fall,
& serve him every nation:
12 For needy crying save he shall,
the poore, & helper that hath none.
13 The poore & needy he shall spare,
and the soules of the needy save.
14 Their soules from fraud & violence
by him shall free redemption have:
And pretious in his sight shall be
15 the bloud of them. And he shall live,
and unto him shall *every one*
of purest gold of Shebah give:
Also each one their humble prayr
in his behalfe shall make alwayes:
and every one his blessednes
shall dayly celebrate with prayse.
(3)
16 Of corne an handfull there shall be
ith land the mountains tops upon,
the fruit whereof shall moving shake
like to the trees of Lebanon:
And they that of the citty be
like grasse on earth shall flourish all.
17 His name for ever shall indure
as long as Sun continue shall:

PSALME lxxii.

So shall his name continued be,
and men in him themselves shall blesse,
and all the nations of the world
shall him the blessed one professe.

18 O let Iehovah blessed be,
the God, the God of Israell,
hee worketh by himselfe alone
such things whereat men may marvell.

19 And blessed be his glorious name
for ever, let the whole earth be
fill'd full with glory of the same,
Amen, also Amen *say wee*.

This. *After the common tunes.*

19 And aye be blest his glorious name,
  also let the earth all
be filled with his glorious fame,
  Amen, & so it shall.

---

20   The prayers of David, the
      Son of Iesse, are
        ended.

THE
THIRD BOOKE.

Psalme 73
A psalme of Asaph.

TRuly to Israell God is good;
  to men of a cleane heart.
2 But my feet almost slipt, my steps
  aside did well nigh starr.
3 For I was envious at the fooles,
  in peace to see the ill.
4 For in their death no ban's there are,
  but firme their strength is still.
5 Like other meane men they are not
  in toylesome misery,
  nor are they stricken with like plagues
  as other mortals bee.
6 Therefore doth pride like to a chaine
  encompasse them about,
  and like a garment; violence
  doth cover them throughout.
7 Within the fatnes *which they have*
  extended are their eyes:
  greater prosperity they have
  then their hearts can devise.
8 Corrupt they are, & wickedly
  speak guile: proudly they talk.
9 Against the heav'ns they set their mouth;
  their tongue through th'earth doth walk.

PSALME lxx iii.
(2)
10 Therefore his people unto them
　　have hither turned in,
　and waters out of a full cup
　　wrung out to them have been.
11 And they have sayd, how can it be
　　that God this thing should know,
　& is there in the highest one
　　knowledge hereof also?
12 Loe, these are the ungodly ones
　　who have tranquillity:
　within the world they doe increase
　　in rich ability.
13 Surely in vaine in purity
　　cleansed my heart have I.
14 And hands in innocence have washt,
　　for plagu'd am I dayly:
　And every morning chastened.
15 　If I think thus to say,
　thy childrens generation
　　loe then I should betray;
16 And when this poynt to understand
　　casting I did devise,
　the matter too laborious
　　appeared in mine eyes.
17 Vntill unto the sanctuary
　　of God I went, & then
　I prudently did understand
　　the last end of these men.
(3)
18 Surely in places slippery

these

PSALM lxxiii.

    these men thou placed hast:
and into desolations
    thou dost them downward cast.
19 As in a moment, how are they
    brought to destruction?
how are they utterly consum'd
    with sad confusion?
20 Like to a dreame when as a man
    awaking doth arise,
so thou o God, when thou awakst
    their Image shalt despise.
21 My heart thus was leaven'd with grief,
    prickt were my reins by mee:
22 So foolish was I, & knew not,
    like a beast before thee.

(4)

23 Neverthelesse continually
    before thee I doe stand:
thou hast upheld mee stedfastly
    also by my right hand.
24 Thou with thy prudent counsell shalt
    guidance unto mee give:
up afterward also thou shalt
    to glory mee receive.
25 In heavn above but thee alone
    who is it that I have?
and there is nothing upon earth
    besides thee that I crave.
25 This flesh of mine, my heart also
    doth faile me altogether:
but God the strength is of my heart,

                      and

and portion mine for ever.
27 For loe, they that are far from thee
utterly perish shall:
those who a whoring goe from thee
thou hast destroyed all.
28 But as for mee, for mee it's good
neere God for to repaire:
in God the Lord I put my trust,
all thy works to declare.

Psalme 74
Maschil of Asaph.

O GOD, why hast thou cast us off,
why doth thy rage indure?
for ever smoaking out against
the sheep of thy pasture?
2 Thy congregation call to minde
of old by thee purchast:
the rod of thine inheritance
which thou redeemed hast,
This mount Sion wherin thou dwelst.
3   Lift up thy foot on hye,
unto the desolations
of perpetuity:
Thy foe within the Sanctuary
hath done all lewd designes.
4 Amidst thy Church thy foes doe roare:
their Banners set for signes.
5 The man that axes on thick trees
did lift up had renowne:
6 But now with axe & maules at once,
her carv'd works they beat downe.

7 Thy

PSALM lxxiv.

7 Thy sanctuaryes into fire
    they cast, the dwelling place
of thy name downe unto the ground
    prophanely they did raze.
8 Let us together them destroy,
    thus in their hearts they sayd:
Gods Synagogues throughout the land
    all in the flames they layd.
        (?)
9 Our signes we see not, there's no more
    a Prophet us among:
nor with us any to be found
    that understands how long.
10 How long shall the oppressing foe
    o mighty God, defame?
thine enemy for evermore
    shall he blaspheme thy name?
11 Why dost thou thus withdraw thine hand,
    the right hand of thy strength?
out of thy bosom o doe thou
    draw it forth to the length.
12 Because the mighty God hath been
    from ancient time my King,
in middest of the earth he is
    salvation working.
13 Thou diddest by thy mighty powre
    devide the sea asunder:
the Dragons heads in peeces thou
    didst break the waters under.
14 The heads of the *Leviathan*
    thou into peeces brake:

PSALME lxxiv.

to people that in desarts dwell
    for meat thou didst him make.
15 Thou clav'st the fountain & the floud,
    thou dri'dst up flouds of might.
16 Thine is the day, & night is thine:
    thou Sun prepar'st, & light.
17 Thou all the borders of the earth
    hast constituted fast:
the summer & the winter cold
    the same thou formed hast.

(3)

18 Remember this, the enemy
    reproachfully doth blame,
o Lord, also the foolish folk
    blasphemed have thy name.
19 O doe not to the multitude
    thy turtles soule deliver:
the congregation of thy poore
    forget not thou for ever.
20 Vnto thy cov'nant have respect:
    because the dark places
of th'earth with habitations
    are full of furiousnes.
21 O let not the oppressed one
    returne away with shame:
o let the poor & needy one
    give prayse unto thy name.
22 Arise o God, plead thine owne cause:
    have thou in memorie
how day by day the foolish man
    with scorne reproacheth thee.

PSALM lxxiv, lxxv.

23 Thine enemyes voyce forget not thou:
  the loud tumult of thofe
continually on high afcends
  that rife thee to oppofe.

Pfalme 75

To the chief mufician **Altafchith**, pfalme
  or fong of Afaph.

O GOD, to thee doe we give thanks,
  thanks give we unto thee:
& that thy name is neere at hand;
  thy wonders fhew to bee.
2 When I th'affembly fhall receive
  uprightly judge I will.
2 Th'earth & its dwellers all do melt:
  I ftay its pillars ftill,
4 I did unto the foolifh fay,
  deale not fo foolifhly:
alfo unto the wicked ones,
  lift not the horne on hye.
5 Lift yee not up your horne on high:
  with ftiffned neck fpeak not,
6 For neither from Eaft, Weft, nor South,
  promotion can be got.
7 But God is judge: he fets up one,
  another downe doth tread.
8 For in the Lords hand is a cup,
  alfo the wine is red:
It's full of mixture, & thereout
  he poures: but on earth all
the wicked ones the dregs therof
  both ftrein, & drink them fhall.
9 But as for me I will declare,   for

PSALME lxxv, lxxvi.

for evermore I will
  sing prayses unto him that is
    the God of Iacob *still.*
10 Of men ungodly all the hornes
    also cut off will I:
but the hornes of the righteous,
    shall be exalted high.

Psalme 76
*To the chief musician, on Neginoth, a psalm
or song of Asaph*

IN Iudah God is knowne: his name
  is great in Israell.
2 In Salem also is his tent:
    in Sion he doth dwell,
3 There brake he th'arrows of the bow,
    the shield, sword, & battell.   Selah.
4 Illustrious thou art, thou dost
    the mounts of prey excell.
5 They that are stout of heart are spoyld,
    they slept their sleep profound:
and of the men of might there is
    none that their hands have found.
6 Of Iacob o thou mighty God,
    as thy rebuke out past,
the chariot also, & the horse
    in a dead sleepe are cast.

(2)

7 Thou ev'n thou art to be feared,
    and who is it before
thy presence that can stand, when as
    that thou art angry sore?
8 **Thou** diddest cause for to be heard   judge.

PSALM lxx vi, lxx vii.

judgement from heav'n above:
 the earth exceedingly did feare,
  also it did not move.
9 When as the mighty God arose,
  to th' execution
of judgement, to save all the meek
  that are the earth upon.   Selah.
10 Assuredly unto thy prayse,
  shall turne the wrath of man:
& the remainder of the earth
  also thou shalt restraine.
11 Vow, & pay to the Lord your God;
  that him surround all yee,
and bring ye presents unto him,
  that feared ought to bee.
12 The spirit that in Princes is,
  asunder cut he shall:
unto the Kings on earth that be,
  dreadfull he is *withall*.

Psalme 77

To the chief musician, to Ieduthun, a
psalme of Asaph.

TO GOD I cryed with my voyce:
  yea with my voyce I have
cryed unto the mighty God;
  and eare to mee he gave.
2 In my distresse I sought the Lord:
  my sore ran in the night,
& ceased not: also my soule
  refused comfort quite.
3 I did remember God, also

disqui-

PSALME lxxvii.

    disquieted was I:
I did complaine, & my spirit
    o'rewhelmd was heavily.   Selah.
4 Awaking thou dost hold mine eyes:
    I cannot speak for feares.
5 I have considered dayes of old,
    of ancient times the yeares.

(2)

6 To my remembrance I doe call
    the song in night I had:
I commun'd with my heart, also
    strict search my spirit made.
7 For ever will the Lord cast off?
    & pleasd will he not bee?
8 His tender mercy is it ceast
    to perpetuitee?
His promise doth it, faile for aye?
9   Hath God forgot likewise
gracious to be? hath he shut up
    in wrath his deare mercyes?   Selah.
10 Then did I say, within my selfe,
    tis mine infirmity:
the yeares of the right hand I will
    think on of the most high.

(3)

11 I will unto remembrance call
    the actions of the Lord:
thy wondrous works of ancient time
    surely I will record.
12 I'le muse also of all thy works,
    & of thy doings talk.

PSALM lxxvii, lxxviii.

13 Within the temple is thy way,
 o God, *where thou dost walk*.
What god so great as our God is?
 1 Works wonderfull that are
thou God hast done; among the folk
 thou dost thy strength declare.
15 Those that thy people are thou hast
 with thine owne arme set free,
of Iacob also of Ioseph
 the childeren that bee.   Selah.
(4)
16 Thee did the waters see, o God,
 thee did the waters see:
they were afraid, the deeps also
 could not but troubled bee.
17 With waters were the clouds pour'd forth,
 the skies a sound out sent:
also thine arrows on each side
 abroad dispersed went.
18 Thy thunders voyce in heaven was:
 the world illuminate
thy lightnings did, the earth also
 trembled & shook hereat.
19 Thy wayes ith sea, thy paths & steps
 unkowne, are in the deep.
20 By Moses & by Arons hand
 thou ledst thy folk like sheep.
Psalme 78
Maschil of Asaph.
GIve listning eare unto my law,
 yee people that are mine,

unto

PSALME lxxviii.

unto the sayings of my mouth
   doe yee your eare incline.
2 My mouth I'le ope in parables,
   I'le speak hid things of old:
3 Which we have heard & knowne:& which
   our fathers have us told.
4 Them from their children wee'l not hide,
   to th'after age shewing
the Lords prayses: his strength, & works
   of his wondrous doing.
5 In Iacob he a witnesse set,
   & put in Israell
a law, which he our fathers charg'd,
   they should their children tell:
6 That th'age to come & children which
   are to be borne might know;
that they might rise up & the same
   unto their children show.
7 That they upon the mighty God
   their confidence might set:
and Gods works & his commandment
   might keep & not forget,
8 And might not like their fathers be,
   a stiffe, stout race; a race
that set not right their hearts: nor firme
   with God their spirit was.

(2)

9 The armed sonnes of Ephraim,
   that went out with their bowe,
did turne their backs in the day when
   they did to battell goe.

10 Gods

PSALM lxxviii.

10 Gods cov'nant they kept not: to walk
    in his law they denyde:
11 His works, & wonders, they forgot,
    that he to them descryde.
12 Things that were mervielous he did
    within their fathers sight:
  in Egipts land, within the field
    of Zoan, *by his might*.
13 He did devide the sea, also
    he caus'd them through to passe:
  & he the waters made to stand
    that as an heap it was.
14 With cloud by day, with fire all night
15   he led them; Rocks he clave
in wildernes, as from great deeps
    drink unto them he gave.
16 Ev'n from out of the stony rock
    streames he did bring also,
  & caused water to run downe
    like as the rivers do.

(3)

17 Moreover they did adde yet more
    against him for to sin:
  by their provoaking the most high
    the wildernes within.
18 And also they within their heart
    did tempt the God of might:
  by asking earnestly for meat
    for their soules appetite:
19 Moreover they against God spake:
    they sayd can God be able

within

PSALME lxxviii.

within the desart wildernes
   to furnish us a table?
20 Loe, he the rock smote, thence gusht out
   waters, & streames did flow:
for his folk can he flesh provide,
   can he give bread also?
21 The Lord heard, he was wroth for this,
   so kindled was a fire
'gainst Iacob:&'gainst Israell
   there came up wrathfull ire.
22 For they in God believed not:
   nor in his health did hope:
23 Though from above he charg'd the clouds:
   & doores of heav'n set ope:

(4)

24 Manna to eate he raind on them;
   & gave them the heavns wheat.
25 Each man of them ate Angells food:
   to th'full he sent them meate.
26 Ith heav'ns he made the East-winde blow:
   brought South-winde by his powre.
27 He flesh on them like dust: wing'd foules
   like the seas sand did showre.
28 And in the middest of their camp
   he caused it to fall,
ev'n round about on every side
   their dwelling places *all*.
29 So they did eate, they filled were
   abundantly also:
for that which was their owne desire
   he did on them bestow;

          T   30 How-

PSALM lxxviii.

30 Howbeit they were not estrang'd
    from their lustfull desire:
but while their meat was in their mouths,
31   Vpon them came Gods ire,
And slew their fat ones: & smote downe
    of Israell the choise men.
32 Still for all this they sin'd: nor did
    believe his wonders then.

(5)

33 Therefore he did in vanity
    the dayes of their life spend,
and hastily he brought their yeares
    vnto a fearfull *end*.
34 When he them slew, then after him
    they sought with their desire:
and they return'd, early also
    did after God enquire.
35 Likewise that God was their strong rock
    they cal'd to memoree:
and that the mighty God most high,
    was their Redeemer free.
36 Yet with their mouth they flattred him:
    and to him their tongues lyde.
37 For right their heart was not in them:
    nor did in's cov'nant byde.
38 But full of mercy, he forgave
    their sin, & stroyd them not;
yea, oft he turn'd his wrath aside,
    nor rays'd all's anger hot.
39 For he, that they were but fraile flesh,
    and as it were a winde

that

PSALME lxxviii.

that passeth, & comes not againe,
  recalled unto minde.
(6)
40 How oft in desart vext they him:
  and made him there to moane?
41 Yea, they turn'd, tempted God: & did
  stint Isr'ells holy one.
42 His hand they did not, nor the day
  keep in their remembrance:
wherein he from the enemy
  gave them deliverance:
43 And how his signes miraculous
  in Egipt he had showne:
and his most fearfull prodigies
  within the field of Zoan:
44 Also how he their rivers had
  converted into bloud:
  & (that they could not drink therof)
  the waters of their floud.
45 Amongst them, which did them devoure,
  he sent forth divers flies:
  & them amongst, which them destroyd,
  he sent forth frogs likewise.
46 He gave their fruit to th'Caterpillar:
  their labour to th'Locust.
47 He did their Vines destroy with haile:
  their Sycamores with frost.
48 Also unto the haile he did
  their cattell shut up fast:
likewise their heards of cattell to
  the fiery thunder blast,

PSALM lxxviii.

49 He cast on them fierce ire, & wrath,
    & indignation,
  & sore distresse: by sending forth
    ill Angells them upon.
(7)
50 He made a way unto his wrath,
    and their soule did not save
  from death: also their life over
    to Pestilence he gave,
51 He within Egipt land also
    all the first borne did smite:
  those that within the tents of Ham
    were chiefest of their might:
52 But he made like a flock of sheep
    his owne folk forth to go:
  like to a flock ith wildernes
    he guided them also.
53 And he in safety did them lead
    so that they did not dread:
  within the sea their enemies
    he also covered.
54 And to the border he did bring
    them of his holy place:
  unto this mountaine which he did
    by his right hand purchase.
55 Fore them he cast the heathen out,
    their lot he did devide
  by line: & Isr'ells tribes he made
    in their tents to abide.
(8)
56 Yet they tempted the most high God,

PSALME lxxviii.

    & griev'd him bitterly:
also his testimonyes they
    kept not *attentively*:
57 But like their fathers back they turn'd
    and faithlesnesse did show:
they turned were aside ev'n like
    to a deceitfull bowe.
58 For they to anger did provoake
    him with their places hye:
  & with their graven Images,
    mov'd him to jealousy.
59 God hearing this, was wroth, & loath'd
    Isr'ell with hatred great:
60 So Shilohs tent he left: the tent
    which men amongst he set,
61 And he delivered his strength
    into captivity:
also into the enemies hand
    his beautifull glory.
62 To th' sword he gave his folk: & was
    wroth with his heritage.
63 Fire their young men devour'd: their maides
    none gave to marriage.
64 Their Priests fell by the sword: also
    their widdows did not weepe.
65 Then did the Lord arise as one
    awakned out of sleepe:
Like a strong man that after wine
65   doth shout. He also smote
his foes behinde: & so he gave
    them an eternall blot.

PSALM lxxviii, lxxix.

67 Then he did Iosephs tent refuse:
   nor Ephr'ims tribe approv'd.
68 But he the tribe of Iudah chose:
   mount Sion which he lov'd.
69 And he his Sanctuary built
   like unto places high:
   like to the earth which he did found
   to perpetuity.
70 Of David also his servant
   election he did make,
   and from the place of folding up
   the sheep he did him take.
71 From following the ewes with young
   he did him then advance;
   to feed Iacob his folk, also
   Isr'ell his heritance.
72 So he according to his hearts
   integrity them fed:
   and by the wise discretion
   of his hands he them led.

Psalme 79
A psalme of Asaph.

O GOD, the heathen entred have
   thine heritance, & defylde
thine holy temple: they on heaps
   Ierusalem have pylde.
2 The dead bodyes of thy servants
   they given have for meate
to th' fowles of heav'n: flesh of thy Saints
   for beasts of earth to *eate*.

2 Their

PSALME lxxix.

3 Their bloud they have forth powred round
    about Ierusalem
like unto waters: & there *was*
    none for to bury *them.*
4 To those that neere unto us dwell
    reproach become are wee:
a scoffing & a scorne to them
    that round about us bee.
5 How long, Iehovah, wilt thou still
    continue in thine ire,
for ever? shall thy jealousie
    burne like as doth the fire?
6 Vpon the heathen poure thy wrath
    which never did thee know,
upon the kingdomes that have not
    cal'd on thy name also.
7 Because they Iacob have devour'd:
    his habitation
they also wondrously have brought
    to desolation.

(2)

8 Minde not against us former sins,
    let thy mercies make hast
us to prevent: because we are
    neere utterly layd waste.
9 God of our safety, help thou us
    for thy names glory make,
us free also, & purge away
    our sin for thy names sake.
10 Why say the heathen where's their God?
    with heathen let be knowne

PSALM lxxix, lxxx.

before our eyes, the vengeance of
    thy servants bloud out flowne.
11 Before thee let the prisoners sighs
    come up, accordingly
as is thy mighty arme: save those
    that are design'd to dye,
12 And to our neighbours seven fold,
    into their bosome pay,
that their reproach, with which o Lord,
    reproached thee have they.
13 So we thy folk & pasture sheepe,
    will give thee thanks alwayes:
and unto generations all,
    wee will shew forth thy prayse.

Psalme 80
To the chief musician upon Shoshannim
    Eduth, a psalme of Asaph.

O Isr'ells shepheard, give thou eare;
    that Ioseph leadst about
like as a flock: that dwelst betweene
    the Cherubims, shine out.
2 Before Ephr'im & Benjamin,
    Manasseh's tribe also,
doe thou stir up thy strength, & come,
    and to us safety show.
3 O God returne thou us againe,
    and cause thy countenance
to shine forth upon us; so wee
    shall have deliverance.
4 Lord God of hoasts, how long wilt thou
    be wroth at thy folks prayrs?

                                thou

PSALME lxxx.

5 Thou feedst with bread of tears, & them
　　to drink giv'st many teares.
6 A strife unto our neighbours us
　　thou dost also expose:
　and scornefully amongst themselves
　　laugh at us doe our foes.
7 O God of hoasts, turne us againe,
　　& cause thy countenance
　to shine forth upon us, so wee
　　shall have deliverance.

(2)

8 Thou hast brought out of Egipt land
　　a Vine, thou diddest cast
　the heathen people forth, also
　　this *vine* thou planted hast.
9 Before it thou prepared hast
　　a roome where it might stand:
　deep root thou didst cause it to take
　　and it did fill the land.
10 Her shade hid hills, & her boughs did
　　like Cedars great *extend*.
11 Her boughs to th'sea, & her branches
　　she to the floud did send.
12 Why hast thou then her hedges made
　　quite broken downe to lye,
　so that all those doe pluck at her
　　that in the way passe by?
13 The Boare from out the wood he doth
　　by wasting it annoy:
　& wilde beasts of the field doe it
　　devouringly destroy.

V　　　　　　14 wee

14 Wee doe beseech thee to returne
    o God of hoasts, incline
to look from heaven, & behould,
    & visit thou this vine.
15 The vineyard which thou hast also
    with thy right hand set fast,
that branch likewise which for thy selfe
    strongly confirm'd thou hast.
16 It is consumed with the fire
    and utterly cut downe,
perish they doe, & that because
    thy countenance doth frowne.
17 Vpon the man of thy right hand
    let thine hand present bee:
upon the son of man whom thou
    hast made so strong for thee
18 So then from henceforth wee will not
    from thee goe back at all:
o doe thou quicken us, & wee
    upon thy name will call.
19 Lord God of hoasts, turne us againe,
    and cause thy countenance
to shine forth upon us, so wee
    shall have deliverance.

Psalme 81

To the chiefe musician upon Gittith,
    a psalme of Asaph.

SIng unto God who is our strength,
    and that with a loud voyce:
unto him that is Iacobs God

make

PSALME lxxx1.

make yee a joyfull noyse.
2 Take up a psalme of melodie,
    and bring the Timbrel hither:
the Harp *which soundes* so pleasantly
    with Psaltery together.
3 As in the time of the new moone
    with Trumpet sound on high:
in the appoynted time & day
    of our solemnity.
4 Because that unto Israell
    this thing a statute was;
and by the God of Iacob this
    did for a judgement pass.
5 This witnesse he in Ioseph set
    when as through Egipt land
he went: I there a language heard
    I did not understand.
6 I from the burden which he bare
    his shoulder did set free:
his hands also were from the pots
    delivered by mee.

(2)

7 Thou cal'dst in streights, & I thee freed:
    in thunders secret way
I answred thee, I prov'd thee at
    waters of Meribah.   Selah.
8 Heare o my people, & I will
    testifie unto thee:
o Israell, if that thou wilt
    attention give to mee.
9 Any strange god there shall not be

PSALM lxxxi.

in midst of thee at all:
nor unto any forrein god
   thou bowing downe shalt fall.
10 I am the Lord thy God who thee
   from land of Egipt led:
thy mouth ope wide, & thou by mee
   with plenty shalt be fed.
11 My people yet would not give eare
   unto the voyce I spake:
and Israell would not in mee
   quiet contentment take.
12 So in the hardnes of their heart
   I did them send away,
in their owne consultations
   likewise *then* walked they.

(3)

13 O that my people unto mee
   obedient had bin:
and o that Israell he had
   walked my wayes within.
14 I should within a little time
   have pulled downe their foes:
I should have turn'd my hand upon
   such as did them oppose.
15 The haters of the Lord to him
   obedience should have faynd:
but unto perpetuity
   their time should have remaind.
16 And with the finest of the wheat
   have nourisht them should hee:
with honie of the rock I should

                       have

PSALME lxxxii.

have satisfied thee.
Psalme 82
A psalme of Asaph.

THe mighty God doth stand within
  th'assemblie of the strong:
and he it is that righteously
  doth judge the gods among.
2 How long a time is it that yee
  will judge unrighteouslie?
& will accept the countenance
  of those that wicked bee?
3 See that yee doe defend the poore,
  also the fatherlesse:
unto the needy justice doe,
  and that are in distresse.
4 The wasted poore, & those that are
  needy deliver yee;
and them redeeme out of the hand
  of such as wicked bee.
5 They know not, nor will understand,
  in darknes they walk on:
all the foundations of the earth
  quite out of course are gone.
6 I sayd that yee are gods, & sonnes
  of th'highest yee are all.
7 But yee shall dye like men, & like
  one of the princes fall.
8 That thou mayst judge the earth o God,
  doe thou thy selfe advance;
for thou shalt have the nations
  for thine inheritance.

PSALM lxxxiii.

Psalme 83

A psalme or song of Asaph,

O GOD, doe not thou silence keep:
 o doe not thou refraine
thy selfe from speaking, & o God.
 doe not thou dumb remaine.
2 For loe, thine enemies that be
 doe rage tumultuously:
& they that haters be of thee
 have lift the head on hye.
3 Against those that thy people be
 they crafty counsell take;
also against thy hidden ones
 they consultation make.
4 They sayd, lest they a nation be,
 let's cut them downe therefore,
that in remembrance Isr'elss name
 may not be any more.
5 For they together taken have
 counsell with one consent,
and in confederation
 against thee they are bent.
6 The tabernacles of Edom
 and of the Ishmaelites:
the people of the Haggarens
 & of the Moabites.
7 The men of Gebal, with Ammon,
 and Amaleck conspire,
the Philistims, with them that be
 inhabitants of Tyre.
8 Assyria morover is

con-

PSALME lxxxiii

conjoyned unto them:
& help they have administred
unto Lots childerren.
(2)
9 As thou didst to the Middianites,
so to them be it done:
as unto Sisera & Iabin
at the Brook of Kison
10 Who neere to Endor suddenly
were quite discomfited:
who also did become as dung
that on the earth is *spred.*
11 Like unto Oreb, & like Zeeb
make thou their Nobles fall,
yea, as Zeba & Zalmunna
make thou their Princes all.
12 Who sayd, for our possession
Gods houses let us take.
13 My God, thou like a wheel, like straw
before the winde them make.
14 As fire doth burne a wood, & as
the flame sets hills on fire:
15 So with thy tempest them pursue,
& fright them in thine ire.
16 Doe thou their faces all fill full
of ignominious shame:
that so they may o Lord, be made
to seek after thy name.
17 Confounded let them ever be,
and terriblie troubled:
yea, let them be put unto shame,

PSALM lxxxiii, lxxxiv.

and bee extinguished.
18 That men may know; that thou whose name
IEHOVAH is only,
art over all the earth throughout
advanced the most high.

Psalme 84
To the chief musician upon Gittith a psalm
for the sonnes of Korah.

How amiable Lord of hoasts
thy tabernacles bee?
2 My soule longs for Iehovahs courts,
yea it ev'n faints in mee.
Mine heart, my flesh also cryes out
after the living God:
3 Yea ev'n the sparrow hath found out
an house *for hir aboad.*
Also the swallow *findes* her nest
thine Altars *neere unto*
where shee her young layes: Lord of hoasts,
my King, my God also.
4 Blest they that dwell within thy house:
still they will give thee prayse.   Selah.
5 Blest is the man whose strength's in thee,
in whose heart are their wayes.
6 Who as they passe through Baca's Vale
doe make it a fountaine:
also the pooles *that are therin*
are filled full of raine:
7 From strength to strength they go: to God
in Sion all appeare.
8 Lord God of hoasts, o heare my pra'yr,
o Iacobs

PSALME lxxxiv, lxxxv.

o Iacobs God, give eare.　　　Selah.
(2)
9 Behould o God our shield: the face
　　of thine annoynted see.
10 For better's in thy courts a day,
　　then *elswhere* thousands bee:
　I rather had a doore-keeper
　　be it'h house of my God:
　then in the tents of wickednes
　　to settle mine aboad.
11 Because the Lord God is a Sun,
　　he is a shield also:
　Iehovah *on his people* grace
　　and glory will bestow:
　No good thing will he hould from them
　　that doe walk uprightlee.
12 O Lord of hoasts, the man is blest
　　that puts his trust in thee.

Psalme 85

To the chiefe musician, a psalme for the
　　sonnes of Korah.

O LORD, thou hast been to the land
　gracious: Iacobs captiuity
thou hast returned *with thy hand*.
2　Thou *also* the iniquity
　　of thy people hast pardoned:
　　thou all their sin hast covered.　　Selah.
3　Thou all thine anger didst withdraw:
　　from thy fierce indignation
　　thou hast thy selfe turned away.
4　O God of our salvation
　　　　　W　　　　　　convert

PSALM lxxxv, lxxxvi.

    convert thou us; & doe thou make
    thine anger toward us to flake.
5 Shall thy wrath ever be us on?
    wilt thou thine indignation
    draw out to generation?
    and unto generation?
6 Wilt thou not us reviv'd let bee
    that thy folk may rejoyce in thee.

(2)

7 Lord on us shew thy mercy; eke
    thy saving health on us bestow.
8 I'le hark what God the Lord will speak,
    for hee'l speak peace his folk unto,
    and to his Saints: but let not them
    to foolishnes returne agen.
9 Surely his saving health is nigh
    unto all them that doe him feare;
    that in our land may dwell glory.
10 Mercy & truth met *together*,
    prosperity & righteousnes
    embracing did *each other* kiss.
11 Truth springs out of the earth: also
    from heaven looketh righteousnes.
12 Yea, God shall that that's good bestow
    our land eke shall give her increase.
13 Iustice shall goe before his face,
    & in the way her steps shall place.

Another of the same

O LORD, thou favour'd hast thy land:
    Iacobs captivity.
2 Thou hast brought back: thou pard'ned hast
                             thy

PSALME lxxx v.

    thy folks iniquity:
Thou hast close coverd all their sin.
3   Thy wrath away all cast
    thou hast: from fiercenes of thine ire
    thy selfe return'd thou hast.
4 Convert us back, o thou the God
    of our salvation:
    & toward us cause thou to cease
    thine indignation,
5 Wilt thou be angry still with us
    for evermore? what shall?
    thine anger be by thee drawne-out
    to generations all?
6 Wilt thou not us revive? in thee
    thy folk rejoyce shall so.
7 Shew us thy mercy, Lord; on us
    thy saving health bestow.

(2)

8 I'le heare what God the Lord will speak:
    for to his people peace
    hee'l speak, & to his Saints: lest they
    returne to foolishnes.
9 Surely naere them that doe him feare
    is his salvation:
    that glory may within our land
    have habitation.
10 Mercy & truth doe joyntly meet:
    justice & peace doe kisse.
11 Truth springs from earth: & rightousnes
    from heaven looking is.
12 Yea what is good the Lord shall give:

PSALM lxxxv, lxxxvi.

and yeild her fruit our land.
13 Iustice shall 'fore him goe: & make
her steps i'th way to stand.

Psalme 86
A prayer of David.

Bow downe o Lord, thine eare,
  & harken unto mee:
because that I afflicted am,
  also I am needie.
2 Doe thou preserve my soule,
  for gracious am I:
o thou my God, thy servant save,
  that doth on thee rely.
3 Lord pitty me, for I
  daily cry thee unto.
4 Rejoyce thy servants soule: for Lord,
  to thee mine lift I do.
5 For thou o Lord, art good,
  to pardon prone withall:
and to them all in mercy rich
  that doe upon thee call.
6 Iehovah, o doe thou
  give eare my pray'r unto:
& of my supplications
  attend the voyce also.
7 In day of my distresse,
  to thee I will complaine:
by reason that thou unto mee
  wilt answer give againe.

(2)
8 Amongst the gods, o Lord,

none

PSALME lxxxvi.

none is there like to thee:
neither with thine are any work
    that may compared bee.
9   All nations o Lord,
    whom thou hast made, *the same*
shall come & worship thee before:
    and glorify thy Name.
10   Because thou mighty art,
    the things that thou hast done
are wonderfull, thou art thy selfe
    the mighty God alone.
11   Iehovah, unto mee
    o make thy way appeare,
walk in thy truth I will; mine heart
    unite thy name to feare.
12   Withall mine heart I will
    o Lord my God, thee prayse:
& I will glorify thy name,
    for evermore *alwayes*.
13   Because that unto mee
    thy mercy doth excell;
also thou hast delivered
    my soule from lowest hell.

(3)

14   O God, the proud, & troups
    of violent rose 'gainst mee,
after my soule they sought: nor have
    before them placed thee.
15   But Lord thou art a God,
    tender, & gracious;
longsuffring, & in mercy thou

PSALM lxxxvi, lxxxvii.

& truth art plenteous.
16 O turne thou unto mee,
and mercy on mee have:
unto thy servant give thy strength:
thine handmaides son do save.
17 Mee shew a signe for good,
that mine haters may see,
and be asham'd; because Lord, thou
dost help, & comfort mee.

Psalme 87
A psalme or song for the sonnes
of Korah.

AMong the holy hills
is his foundation.
2 More then all Iacobs tents, the Lord
loves the gates of Sion.
3 Things glorious spoken are
o Gods citty, of thee.   Selah.
4 I'le mention Rahab, & Babel,
to them that doe know mee;
Behold Philistia,
Tyrus *citty* likewise,
with Ethiopia; that this man
by birth did thence arise.
5 Also it shall be sayd,
of Sion that borne there
this & that man was, & the high'st
himselfe shall stablish her.
6 Iehovah he shall count,
ev'n at that time when as,
the people he doth number up,

that

PSALME lxxxvii lxxxviii.
that there this man borne was.   Selah
7 Both those that singers are
    as also *there shall bee,*
  those that on instruments doe play:
    all my springs are in thee.

Psalme 88

A song or psalme for the sons of Korah, to
the chief musician upō Mahalath Leannoth,
Maschil of Heman the
Ezrahite.

LORD God of my salvation,
   before thee day & night cryde I.
2 Before thee o let my pray'r come:
  incline thine eare unto my cry.
3 Because my soule is troubled so:
   and my life draws nigh to the grave.
4 Counted with them to'th pit that go:
  I'me as a man that no strength have.
5 Free among those men that be dead,
   like slaine which in the grave are shut;
   by thee noe more remembered:
   and by thy hand off are they cut.
6 Thou hast mee layd i'th pit most low
   in dakrnesses, within deep caves.
7 Hard on mee lyes thy wrath, & thou
  dost mee afflict with all thy waves.   Selah.
8 Men that of mine acquaintance bee
   thou hast put far away mee fro:
   unto them loathsome thou madst mee,
   I am shut up nor forth can go.
9 Because of mine affliction,

mine

PSALM lxxxviii.

mine eye with mourning pines away:
Iehovah, I call thee upon:
& stretch my hands to thee all day;

(2)

10   Shew wonders to the dead wilt thou?
shall dead arise & thee confess?   Selah.
11 I'th grave wilt thou thy kindenes show?
in lost estate thy faithfullnes?
12   Thy works that wonderfull have been
within the dark shal they be knowne?
& shall thy righteousnes *be seene*
in the land of oblivion?
13   But Lord I have cryde thee unto
at morne, my pray'r prevent shall thee.
14 Lord why casts thou my soule thee fro?
why hidest thou thy face from mee?
15   I'me poore afflicted, & to dye
am ready, from my youthfull yeares,
I am sore troubled doubtfully
while I doe beare thy horrid feares.
16   Thy fierce wrath over mee doth goe,
thy terrors they doe mee dismay.
17 Encompasse mee about they doe,
close mee together all the day.
18   Lover & friend a far thou hast
removed off away from mee,
& mine acquaintance thou hast cast
into darksom obscuritee.

Psalme 89
Maschil of Ethan the
Ezrahite.

PSALME lxxxix.

The mercyes of Iehovah sing
   for evermore will I:
I'le with my mouth thy truth make known
   to all posterity.
2 For I have sayd that mercy shall
   for ever be up built;
establish in the very heav'ns
   thy faithfullnes thou wilt.
3 With him that is my chosen one
   I made a covenant:
& by *an oath* have sworne unto
   David mine owne servant.
4 To perpetuity thy seed
   establish-sure I will:
also to generations all
   thy throne I'le build up *still*.   Selah.
5 Also the heav'ns thy wonders Lord,
   they shall with prayse confess;
in the assemblie of the Saints
   also thy faithfullnes.
6 For who can be compar'd unto
   the Lord the heav'ns within?
'mong sonnes of mighty to the Lord
   who is't that's like to him.

(2)

7 I'th Saints assemblie greatly God
   is to be had in feare:
and to be reverenc't of all those
   that round about him are.
8 Lord God of hoasts, what Lord like thee
   in power doth abide?

thy

PSALM lxxxix.

   thy faithfullnes doth compasse thee
     also on every side.
9 Over the raging of the sea,
    thou dost dominion beare:
  when as the waves therof arise,
    by thee they stilled are.
10 Like to one slaine, thou broken hast
    in pieces Rahab quite:
  thou hast disperst thine enemies
    ev'n by thine arme of might.
11 The heav'ns together with the earth,
    thine are they: thine they bee;
  the world, with fullnes of the same,
    founded they were by thee.
12 The North together with the South
    thou didst create the same:
  Tabor together with Hermon,
    rejoyce shall in thy Name.

(3)

13 Thou hast a very mighty arme,
    thy hand it is mighty,
  and also thy right hand it is
    exalted up on high.
14 Iustice & judgement of thy throne
    are the prepared place:
  mercy & truth preventing shall
    goe forth before thy face.
15 O blessed are the people that
    the joyfull sound doe know,
  Lord, in thy countenances light
    they up & downe shall goe:

16 They

PSALME lxxxix.

16 They shall in thy name all the day
    rejoyce exceedingly:
  and in thy righteousnes they shall
    be lifted up on high.
17 Because that thou art unto them
    the glory of their powre:
  our horne shall be exalted high,
    also in thy favour.
18 Because Iehovah is to us
    a safe protection;
  and he that is our Soveraigne,
    is Isr'ells Holy-one.

(4)

19 Then didst thou speake in vision,
    unto thy Saint, & sayd,
  I upon one that mighty is
    salvation have layd:
  One from the folk chose, I set up.
20 David my servant I
  have found: him I annoynted with
    mine oyle of sanctity.
21 With whom my hand shall stablisht be;
    mine arme him strengthen shall.
22 Also the enemy shall not
    exact on him at all:
  Nor shall the Son of wickednes
    afflict him any more.
23 Before him I'le beat downe his foes,
    and plague his haters sore.
24 My mercy, truth, shall be with him;
    & in my name shall be

PSALM lxxxix.

25 his horne exalted. And I'le set
    his hand upon the sea:
I'th rivers also his right hand.
26 He shall cry mee unto,
    thou art my Father: & my God,
    Rock of my health also.
27 Also I will make him to be
    my first begotten one:
higher then those that Princes are,
    who dwell the earth upon.
28 My mercy I will keep for him
    to times which ever last:
also my covenant with him
    it shall stand very fast.

(s)

29 And I will make his seed indure
    to perpetuitee:
his throne likewise it like unto
    the dayes of heav'n shall bee.
30 If that his sons forsake my law,
    & from my judgements swerve:
31 If they my stattutes break, & my
    commandes doe not observe:
32 Then will I visit with the rod
    their bold transgression,
as also their iniquity
    with sore stripes *them upon*.
33 But yet my loving kindenes, it
    I'le not take utterly
away from him: nor will suffer
    my faithfullnes to lye.

34 The

PSALME lxxxix,

34 The covenant I made with him
    by mee shall not be broke:
neither will I alter the thing
    which by my lips is spoke.
35 Once sware I by my holines,
    if I to David lye:
36 His seed asuredly shall last
    to perpetuity:
And like the Sun 'fore mee his throne.
37   It like the moone for aye
    shall be establish't, like a true
    witnesse in heav'n: Selah.

(6)

38 But thou hast cast off, & us had
    in detestation:
exceedingly thou hast been wroth
    with thine annoynted one.
39 Thou hast made voyd the covenant
    of thy servant, his crowne
thou hast prophan'd unto the ground
    by casting of it downe.
40 Thou hast broke all his hedges downe:
    his forts thou ruin'd hast.
41 All those doe make a spoyle of him
    who by the way have past:
Hee's a reproach to his neighbours.
42   Of them that him annoy
thou hast advanced their right hand:
    & made all's foes to joy.
43 The sharp edge also of his sword
    thou hast turn'd backward quite:

PSALM lxxxix.

and in the battell thou haſt not
   made him to ſtand upright.
44 Thou haſt made alſo for to ceaſe
   his glorious renowne:
unto the very earth his throne
   thou alſo haſt caſt downe.
45 And of his youthfull yeares the dayes
   thou haſt diminiſhed;
with very great confuſion
   thou haſt him covered.   Selah.
(7)
46 How long? Iehovah, wilt thou hide
   thy ſelfe for evermore?
burne like unto conſuming fire
   ſhall thy diſpleaſure ſore?
47 To thy remembrance doe thou call
   how ſhort a time have I;
wherefore haſt thou created all
   mens ſonnes to vanity?
48 What ſtrong man is there that doth live,
   & death ſhall never ſee?
from the ſtrong power of the grave
   ſhall he his ſoule ſet free?
49 Thy former loving kindeneſſes
   o Lord, where are they now?
which in thy truth & faithfullnes
   to David thou didſt vow.
50 Lord, the reproach of thy ſervants
   unto remembrance call:
how I it beare in my boſome
   from mighty people all.

                            51 Wher-

PSALME lxxxix, xC.

51 Wherewith thy adversaryes Lord,
    have cast reproach upon,
wherewith they have reproacht the steps
    of thine annointed one.
52 O let Iehovah be blessed
    to all eternitee:
Amen, *so let it be*, also
Amen, *so it shall bee.*

THE
FOVRTH BOOKE

Psalme 90.
A prayer of Moses the man of God.

O LORD, thou hast been unto us
    from generation,
to generation, a place
    of fixed mansion.
2 Before the mountaines were brought forth,
    ere earth & world by thee
were form'd: thou art eternally
    God to eternitee.
3 Thou dost unto destruction
    turne miserable men:
and then thou sayst yee sonnes of men
    doe yee returne agen.
4 For why o Lord, a thousand yeares
    are but within thy sight
as yesterday when it is past:

and

PSALM xC.

and as a watch by night.
5 By thee like as it were a flood
    they quite away are borne,
they like a sleep, & as the grasse
    that grows up in the morne.
6 It in the morning flourisheth,
    it also up doth grow;
it in the ev'ning is cut downe
    it withereth also.
7 Because wee by thine anger are
    consumed speedily:
and by thy sore displeasure wee
    are troubled suddenly.
8 Thou hast set our iniquityes
    before thee in thy sight:
our secret evills are within
    thy countenances light.
9 Because in thine exceeding wrath
    our dayes all passe away:
our years wee have consumed quite,
    ev'n as a tale *are they*.

(2)

10 Threescore & ten yeares are the dayes
    of our yeares which remaine,
& if through strength they fourscore be,
    their strength is grief & paine:
For it's cut off soone, & wee flye
11   away: Who is't doth know
thine angers strength? according as
    thy feare, thy wrath is so.
12 Teach us to count our dayes: our hearts

PSALME xC, xCI.

so wee'l on wisdome set.
13 Turne Lord, how long? of thy servants
   let it repent thee yet?
14 O give us satisfaction
   betimes with thy mercee:
that so rejoyce, & be right glad,
   through all our dayes may wee.
15 According to the dayes *wherin*
   affliction wee have had,
and yeares *wherin* wee have seen ill,
   now also make us glad.
16 Vnto those that thy servants be
   doe thou thy work declare:
also thy comely glory to
   those that thy children are.
17 Let our Gods beauty be on us,
   our handy works also
stablish on us; our handy work
   establish it doe thou.

Psalme 91.

HE that within the secret place
   of the most high doth dwell,
he under the Almightyes shade
   shall lodge himselfe *full well.*
2 My hope he is, & my fortresse,
   I to the Lord will say:
he is my God; & I in him
   my confidence will stay.
3 Surely out of the fowlers snare
   he shall deliver thee,
also thee from the Pestilence

infect-

PSALM xCl.

infectious shall free.

4 He with his feathers hide thee shall,
    under his wings shall bee
thy trust: his truth shall be a shield
    and buckler unto thee.
5 Thou shalt not be dismaide with feare
    for terrour by the night:
nor for the arrow that with speed
    flyeth in the day light:
6 Nor for the Pestilence that doth
    walk in the darknes fast:
nor for the sore destruction
    that doth at noone day wast.

(2)

7 A thousand shall fall at thy side,
    & ten thousand also
at thy right hand, but it shall not
    approach thee neere unto:
8 Only thou with thine eyes this thing
    attentively shalt view:
also thou shalt behold how that
    the wicked have their due.
9 Because Iehovah who hath been
    my safe protection,
ev'n the most high, thou hast him made
    thine habitation.
10 Not any thing that evill is
    there shall to thee befall,
neither shall any plague come nigh
    thy dwelling place at all.
11 Because that he his Angells will

                                   comand

PSALME xCi, xCii.

command concerning thee:
in all thy wayes *where thou dost walk*
  thy keeper for to bee.
12 They shall support thee in their hands:
  lest thou against a stone
13 shouldst dash thy foot. Thou trample shalt
  on th'Adder, & Lion:
The Lion young & Dragon thou
  shalt tread under thy feet.
14 I will deliver him, for hee
  on mee his love hath set:
Because that he hath knowne my **Name**,
  I will him set on high.
15 Vpon mee he shall call in pray'r,
  and answer him will I:
I will be with him when he is
  in troublesome distresse,
& I to him will honour give,
  when I shall him release.
16 With dayes of long continuance
  I'le give to him his fill:
& also my salvation
  declare to him I will.

Psalme 92.

A psalme or song for the
Sabbath day.

IT is a good thing to give thanks
  Iehovah thee unto:
unto thy Name prayses to sing,
  o thou most high also.
2 Thy loving kindenes to shew forth

PSALM xCii.

   within the morning light:
  also thy truth, & faithfullnes,
   to shew forth every night.
3 Vpon a ten string'd instrument,
   and Psaltery upon:
  upon the solemne sounding Harp,
   a meditation.
4 For through thy work, o Lord, thou hast
   mee caused to rejoyce:
  and in the workings of thy hands
   I will triumph with voyce.
5 O Lord, how mighty are thy works:
   thy thoughts are very deepe.
6 The bruitish knows not, nor the foole
   this in his heart doth keepe.
7 When as the wicked doe spring up
   ev'n like the grasse unto,
  & all that work iniquity
   when as they flourish do:
  It's that they then may be destroy'd
   to perpetuity.
8 But thou Iehovah dost abide
   for evermore most high.
9 For loe, thy foes, for loe, o Lord,
   thy foes they perish shall:
  the workers of iniquity
   they shall be scattred all.
          (2)
10 But like the Vnicornes my horne
   thou shalt exalt on high:
  & with fresh oyle in mine old age

                              annoynted

PSALME xCII, xCIII.

annoynted be shall I.
11 Also mine eye shall see my wish
    upon mine enemyes:
mine eare shall heare of wicked ones,
    that up against me rise.
12 Like to the Palme tree flourish shall
    he that is righteous:
like to a Ceadar he shall grow
    that is in Lebanus.
13 They that within Iehovah's house
    are planted *stedfastly*:
within the Courts of our God they
    shall flourish *pleasantly*.
14 Their fruit they shall in their old age
    continue forth to bring:
they shall be fat, yea likewise they
    shall still be flourishing:
15 To shew that upright is the Lord:
    my refuge strong is hee,
also that there is not in him
    any iniquitee.

Psalme 93.

THe Lord reigns, cloth'd with majesty:
    God cloath'd with strength, doth gird
himselfe: the world so stablisht is,
    that it cannot be stir'd.
2 Thy throne is stablished of old:
3   from aye thou art. Their voyce
the flouds lift up, Lord, flouds lift up,
    the flouds lift up their noyse.
4 The Lord on high then waters noyse

                     more

PSALM xCiii, xCiv.

   more strong then waves of sea:
5 Thy words most sure: Lord, holines
     becomes thine house for aye.

Psalme 94

O LORD God, unto whom there doe
    revenges appertaine:
  o God, to whom vengeance belongs,
    clearly shine forth againe.
2 Exalt thy selfe, o thou that art
    Iudge of the earth throughout:
  render a recompence unto
    all those that are so stout.
3 Iehovah, o how long shall they
    that doe walk wickedly?
  how long shall those that wicked are
    rejoyce triumphingly?
4 How long shall those men utter forth
    & speake things that hard bee?
  & shall all such thus boast themselves
    that work iniquitee?
5 Lord, they thy folk in pieces break:
    & heritage oppress.
6 They slay the widdow, & stranger,
    & kill the fatherless.
7 The Lord they say, yet shall not see:
    nor Iacobs God it minde.
8 Learne vulgar Sots: also yee fooles
    when will yee wisdome finde?
9 Who plants the eare, shall he not heare?
    who formes the eye, not see?
10 Who heathen smites, shall he not check?

mans

PSALME xCIV.

mans teacher, knows not hee?
(2)
11 The Lord doth know the thoughts of man,
that they are very vaine.
12 Bleſt man whom thou correctſt, o Lord;
& in thy law doſt traine.
13 That thou mayſt give him quiet from
dayes of adverſity:
untill the pit be digged for
ſuch as doe wickedly.
14 Becauſe Iehovah he will not
his people caſt away,
neither will hee forſake his owne
inheritance for aye.
15 But judgement unto righteouſnes
it ſhall returne agen:
alſo all upright ones in heart
they ſhall purſue it *then*.
16 Againſt the evill doers, who
will up for mee ariſe?
who will ſtand up for mee 'gainſt them
that work iniquityes?
17 Had not the Lord me helpt: my ſoule
had neere in ſilence dwel'd.
18 When as I ſayd, my foot ſlips: Lord,
thy mercy mee upheld.
(3)
19 Amidſt the multitude of thoughts
of mine within my minde,
ſtill from thy conſolations
my ſoule delight doth finde.

20 Shall

20 Shall the throne of iniquity
       have fellowship with thee:
   which frameth molestation
       and that by a decree?
21 They joyntly gathered themselves,
       together they withstood
   the soule of him that righteous is:
       & condemne guiltlesse blood.
22 But yet Iehovah unto mee
       he is a refuge high:
   also my God he is the rock
       of my hopefull safety.
23 Their mischief on them he shall bring,
       & in their wickednes
   he shall them cut off: yea, the Lord
       our God shall them suppress.

Psalme 95.

O Come, let us unto the Lord
       shout loud with singing voyce.
   to the rock of our saving health
       let us make joyfull noyse.
2 Before his presence let us then
       approach with thanksgiving:
   also let us triumphantly
       with Psalmes unto him sing.
3 For the Lord a great God: & great
       King above all gods is.
4 In whose hands are deepes of the earth,
       & strength of hills are his
5 The sea to him doth appertaine,
       also he made the same:

and

PSALME xCv, xCvI.

& also the drye land is his
  for it his hands did frame.
6 O come, & let us worship give,
  & bowing downe adore:
he that our maker is, the Lord
  o let us kneele before.
7 Because he is our God, & wee
  his pasture people are,
& of his hands the sheep: to day
  if yee his voyce will heare,
8 As in the provocation,
  o harden not your heart:
as in day of temptation,
  within the vast desart.
9 Whē mee your fathers tryde, & pro'vd,
  & my works lookt upon:
10 Fourty yeares long I griev'd was with
  this generation:
And sayd, this people erre in heart:
  my wayes they doe not know.
11 To whom I sware in wrath: if they
  into my rest should goe.

Psalme 96.

SIng to the Lord a new song: sing
  all th'earth the Lord unto:
2 Sing to Iehovah, blesse his Name,
  still his salvation show.
3 To'th heathen his glory, to all
  people his wonders spread.
4 For great's the Lord, much to be prays'd,
  above all gods in dread.

        Z   5 Because

PSALM xCvi.

5 Because vaine Idols are they all
    which heathens Gods doe name:
but yet Iehovah he it is
    that did the heavens frame.
6 Honour & comely majesty
    abide before his face:
both fortitude & beauty are
    within his holy place.
7 Yee kindreds of the people *all*
    unto the Lord afford,
glory & mightynes also
    give yee unto the Lord.
8 The glory due unto his name
    give yee the Lord unto;
offer yee an oblation,
    enter his courts also.

(2)

9 In beauty of his holynes
    doe yee the Lord adore:
the universall earth *likewise*
    in feare stand him before.
10 'Mong heathens say, Iehovah reigns:
    the world in stablenes
shall be, unmov'd also: he shall
    judge folk in righteousnes.
11 O let the heav'ns *therat* be glad,
    & let the earth rejoyce:
o let the sea, & it's fullnes
    with roaring make a noyse.
12 O let the field be full of joye,
    & all things there about:

then

PSALME xCvɪ, xCvɪɪ.
then all the trees that be i'th wood
  they joyfully shall shout
13 Before Iehovah, for he comes,
  he comes earths judge to bee.
the world with justice, & the folke
  judge with his truth shall bee.

Psalme 97

THe Lord doth reigne, the earth
  o let heerat rejoyce:
  the many Isles with mirth
  let them lift up their voyce.
2   About him round
  dark clouds there went,
  right & judgement
  his throne doe found.
3 Before him fire doth goe,
  & burnes his foes about.
4 The world was light also
  by lightnings he sent out:
  the earth it saw
  & it trembled.
5 The hills melted
  like wax away
  At presence of the Lord,
  at his presence who is
  of all the earth the Lord.
6 That righteousnes of his
  the heavens high
  they doe forth show:
  all folk also
  see his glory.

Z 2

7 who

PSALM xCvII.

7 Who graven Images
doe serve, on them remaine
let dreadfull shamefullnes:
& who in Idols vaine
themselves doe boast:
with worship bow
to him all you
Gods Angells *hoast*.

8 Sion heard, & was glad,
glad Judahs daughters were,
this cause, o Lord, they had,
thy judgements did appeare.

9 For Lord thou high
all earth set o're:
all Gods before
in dignity.

10 Yee that doe love the Lord,
the evill hate doe yee;
to his Saints soules afford
protection doth hee:
he will for them
freedome command
out of the hand
of wicked men.

11 For men that righteous are
surely there is sowne light:
& gladnes for their share
that are in heart upright.

12 Ioy in the Lord,
yee Iust confesse;
his holynesse

while

PSALME xCviii.

while yee record.
Psalme 9 8.
A Psalme

A New song sing unto the Lord,
   for wonders he hath done:
his right hand & his holy arme
   him victory hath wonne.
2 Iehovah his salvation
   hath made for to be knowne:
his righteousnes i'th heathens sight
   hee openly hath showne.
3 To Isr'ells house of his mercy
   & truth hath mindefull been:
the ends of all the earth they have
   our Gods salvation seene.
4 Vnto Iehovah all the earth,
   make yee a joyfull noyse:
make yee also a cheerfull sound,
   sing prayse, likewise rejoyce.
5 With Harp sing to the Lord; with Harp,
   also with a Psalms voyce.
6 With Trumpets, Cornets sound; before
   the Lord the King rejoyce.
7 The sea let with her fullnes roare:
   the world, & there who dwell.
8 O let the flouds clap hands: let hills
   rejoyce together well
9 Before the Lord, for he doth come
   to judge the earth: rightly
with justice shall he judge the world,
   & folk with equity.

PSALM xCix.

Pſalme 99.

JEHOVAH 'tis that reigns,
   let people be in dread:
  'midſt Cherubs he remaines,
  th'earth let it be moved.
2   Iehovah is
in Sion great,
in highnes ſet
  he is likewiſe
Above all the people.
3 Let them confeſſe thy Name
  ſo great & terrible:
for holy is the ſame.
4   The King his might
doth love juſtice:
thou doſt ſtabliſh
  things that be right:
Iudgement thou doſt, alſo
in Iacob righteouſnes.
5   The Lord our God doe you
ſet up in his highnes,
  & worſhip yee
his footſtoole at:
by reaſon that
  holy is hee.
6   Moſes alſo Aron
among his Prieſts, likewiſe
Samuell all thoſe among
that to his name ſend cryes:
  called they have
the Lord upon,

                      and

PSALME xCix, C.

and he *alone*
   them answer gave.
7 He unto them did speake
it'h cloudy pillar: *then*
they kept his records, eke
his ord'nance he gave them.
8   Lord, thou who art
   our God didst heare,
   & didst answer
      to them impart,
Thou wast a God pard'ning
them, although thou vengeance
upon their works didst bring.
9 The Lord our God advance,
   & bow yee downe
at's holy hill:
for our God's *still*
   the Holy-one.

Psalme 100.
A Psalme of prayse.

MAke yee a joyfull sounding noyse
   unto Iehovah, all the earth:
2 Serve yee Iehovah with gladnes:
before his presence come with mirth.
3 Know, that Iehovah he is God,
who hath us formed it is hee,
& not our selves: his owne people
& sheepe of his pasture are wee.
4 Enter into his gates with prayse,
into his Courts with thankfullnes:
make yee confession unto him,

                    and

PSALM C, CI.

& his name reverently blesse.
5   Because Iehovah he is good,
for evermore is his mercy:
& unto generations all
continue doth his verity.

Another of the same.

Make yee a joyfull noyse unto
Iehovah all the earth:
2 Serve yee Iehovah with gladnes:
before him come with mirth.
3 Know, that Iehovah he is God,
not wee our selves, but hee
hath made us: his people, & sheep
of his pasture are wee.
4 O enter yee into his gates
with prayse, & thankfullnesse
into his Courts: confesse to him,
& his Name doe yee blesse.
5 Because Iehovah he is good,
his bounteous-mercy
is everlasting: & his truth
is to eternity.

Psalme 101.
A psalme of David.

Mercy & judgement I will sing,
Lord, I will sing to thee.
2 I'le wisely doe in perfect way:
when wilt thou come to mee?
I will in midst of my house walk
in my hearts perfectnes:
3 I will not set before mine eyes

matter

PSALME CI, CII.

matter of wickednes:
I hate their worke that turne aside,
  it shall not cleave mee to.
4 Froward in heart from mee shall part,
  none evill will I know.
5 I'le cut him off, that slaundereth
  his neighbour privily:
I cannot beare the proud in heart,
  nor him that looketh high.
6 Vpon the faithfull in the land
  mine eyes shall be, that they
may dwell with mee: he shall mee serve
  that walks in perfect way.
7 Hee that a worker is of guile,
  shall not in my house dwell:
before mine eyes he shall not be
  setled, that lies doth tell.
8 Yea, all the wicked of the land
  early destroy will I:
to cutt off from Gods citty all
  that work iniquity.

Psalme 102

A prayer of the afflicted when he is over-
whelmed, & poureth out his complaint
  before the Lord.

LORD, heare my supplication,
  & let my cry come thee unto:
2 I'th day when trouble is on mee,
  thy face hide not away mee fro:
Thine eare to mee doe thou incline,
  i'th day I cry, soone answer mee:

A 2   3 For

PSALM CII.

3 For as the smoake my dayes consume,
   & like an hearth my bones burnt bee.
4   My heart is smote, & dryde like grasse,
   that I to eate my bread forget:
5 By reason of my groanings voyce
   my bones unto my skin are set.
6   Like Pelican in wildernes,
   like Owle in desart so am I:
7 I watch, & like a sparrow am
   on house top solitarily.
8   Mine enemies daily mee reproach:
   'gainst mee they rage, 'gainst mee they sweare:
9 That I doe ashes eate for bread:
   & mixe my drink with weeping-teare.
10   By reason of thy fervent wrath
   & of thy vehement-disdaine:
   for thou hast high advanced mee,
   & thou hast cast mee downe againe.

(2)

11 My dayes as shaddow that decline:
   & like the withered grasse am I.
12 But thou, Lord, dost abide for aye:
   & thy Name to eternity.
13   Thou wilt arise, & wilt shew forth
   thy tender-mercy on Sion:
   for it is time to favour her,
   yea the set time is now come on.
14 For in her stones thy servants doe
   take pleasure, & her dust pitty.
15 And heathens shall the Lords Name feare:
   & all Kings of th'earth thy glory.

16 when

PSALME CII.

16 When as the Lord shall Sion build
hee in his glory shall appeare.
17 The poor's petition hee'l regard,
& hee will not despise their pray'r.
18 This shall in writing be inroll'd
for the succeeding-after-race:
that people also which shall bee
created, they the Lord may prayse.
19 For from his Sanctuary high
from heavn's the Lord the earth doth see:
20 To heare the groanes of prisoners:
to loose them that deaths children bee.
21 The Lords prayse in Ierusalem:
his Name in Sion to record.
22 when people are together met,
& Kingdomes for to serve the Lord.

(3)
23 He weakned hath i'th way my strength,
& shortened my dayes hath hee.
24 I sayd, in middest of my dayes
my God doe not away take mee:
Thy yeares throughout all ages are.
25 Thou hast the earth's foundation layd
for elder time: & heavens bee
the work which thine owre hands have made.
26 They perish shall, but thou shalt stand:
they all as garments shall decay:
& as a wearing-vestiment
thou shalt thē change, & chang'd are they.
27 But thou art ev'n the same: thy yeares
they never shall consumed bee.

Aa 2   23 Thy

PSALM CII, CIII.

23 Thy servants children shall abide,
    & their seed stablisht before thee.

Psalme 103.
A psalme of David.

O Thou my soule, Iehovah blesse,
    & all things that in me
most inward are, in humblenes
    his Holy-Name blesse ye

2 The Lord blesse in humility,
    o thou my soule: also
put not out of thy memory
    all's bounties, thee unto.

3 For hee it is who pardoneth
    all thine iniquityes:
he it is also who healeth
    all thine infirmityes.

4 Who thy life from destruction
    redeems: who crowneth thee
with his tender compassion
    & kinde benignitee.

5 Who with good things abundantlee
    doth satisfie thy mouth:
so that like as the Eagles bee
    renewed is thy youth.

6 The Lord doth judgement & justice
    for all oppressed ones.

7 To Moses shew'd those wayes of his:
    his acts to Isr'ells sonnes.

(2)

8 The Lord is mercifull also
    hee's very gracious:

                      and

PSALME CIII.

and unto anger hee is flow,
 in mercy plenteous.
9 Contention he will not maintaine
 to perpetuity:
nor he his anger will retaine
 unto eternity.
10 According to our sins *likewise*
 to us hee hath not done:
nor hath he our iniquityes
 rewarded us upon.
11 Because even as the heavens are
 in height the earth above:
so toward them that doe him feare
 confirmed is his love.
12 Like as the East & *West* they are
 farre in their distances:
he hath remov'd away so far
 from us our trespasses.
13 A fathers pitty like unto,
 which he his sonnes doth beare:
like pitty doth Iehovah show
 to them that doe him feare.
14 For he doth know this frame of ours:
 he minds that dust wee bee.
15 Mans dayes are like the grasse: like flowrs
 in field, so flourisheth hee.
16 For over it the winde doth passe,
 & it away doth goe;
also the place wheras it was
 noe longer shall it know.

PSALM CIII, CIV.

17 But yet Gods mercy ever is,
  shall be, & aye hath been
 to them that feare him; and's justice
  unto childrens children.
18 To such as keepe his covenant,
  that doe in minde up lay
 the charge of his commandement
  that it they may obey.
19 The Lord hath in the heavens hye
  established his throne:
 and over all his Royallty
  doth beare dominion.
20 O yee his Angells that excell
  in strength, blesse yee the Lord,
 that doe his word, that harken well
  unto the voyce of 's word.
21 All yee that are the Lords armies,
  o blesse Iehovah *still*:
 & all yee ministers of his,
  his pleasure that fullfill.
22 Yea, all his works in places all
  of his dominion,
 blesse yee Iehovah: o my Soul,
  Iehovah blesse *alone*.

Psalme 104.

THe Lord blesse, o my Soule, o Lord
  my God, exceedingly
 great art thou: thou with honour art
  cloath'd & with majesty.
2 Who dost thy selfe with light, as *if*

it

PSALME CIV.

it were a garment cover:
  who like unto a curtaine doſt
    the heavens ſtretch all over.
3 Who of his chambers layes the beames
  ith waters, & hee makes
the cloudes his Charrets, & his way
  on wings of winde hee takes.
4 His Angells Spirits, his miniſters
  who makes a fiery flame.
5 who earths foundations layd, that ne're
  ſhould be remov'd the ſame.
6 Thou with the deep (as with a robe)
  didſt cover the *dry land*:
above the places mountainous
  the waters they did ſtand.
7 When as that thou rebukedſt them
  away then fled they faſt:
they alſo at thy thunders voyce
  with ſpeed away doe haſt.
8 Vp by the mountaines they aſcend:
  downe by the valleys go,
the place which thou didſt found for them
  untill they come unto.
9 Thou haſt to them a bound prefixt
  which they may not paſſe over:
ſo that they might noe more returne
  againe the earth to cover.
        (2)
10 who ſprings into the valleys ſends,
  which run among the hills.
11 whence all beaſts of the field have drink:
                wilde

PSALM CIV.

wilde asses drink their fills.
12 Heavns fowles dwell by them, which do sing
   among the sprigs with mirth.
13 Hee waters from his lofts the hills:
   thy works fruit fill the earth.
14 For beasts hee makes the grasse to grow,
   herbs also for mans good:
  that hee may bring out of the earth
  what may be for their food:
15 Wine also that mans heart may glad,
   & oyle their face to bright:
  and bread which to the heart of man
  may it supply with might.
16 Gods trees are sappy: his planted
   Cedars of Lebanon:
17 Where birds doe nest: as for the Storke,
   Firres are her mansion.
18 The wilde Goates refuge are the hills:
   rocks Conies doe inclose.
19 The Moone hee hath for seasons set,
   the Sun his setting knows.
(3)
20 Thou makest darknes, & 'tis night:
   when wood beasts creep out all.
21 After their prey young Lions roare:
   from God for food they call.
22 The Sun doth rise, then in their dennes
   they couch, when gone aside.
23 Man to his work & labour goes,
   untill the ev'ning-tide.
24 O Lord, how many are thy works!

in

PSALME CIV.

all of them thou hast wrought
　in wisdome: with thy plenteous store
　the earth is fully fraught.
25 So is this great & spatious sea,
　wherin things creeping bee
beyond all number: beasts of small
　& of great quantitee.
26 There goe the ships: Leviathan,
　therin thou madst to play.
27 These all wayt on thee, that their meate
　in their time give thou may.
23 They gather what thou givest them:
　thy hand thou op'nest wide,
　& they with such things as are good
　are fully satisfyde.
29 Thou hid'st thy face, they troubled are,
　their breath thou tak'st away,
then doe they dye: also returne
　unto their dust doe they.
30 They are created, when thou makst
　thy spirit forth to go:
thou of the earth dost make the face
　to be renew'd also.

(4)
31 The glory of Iehovah shall
　for evermore indure:
in his owne works Iehovah shall
　joyfully take pleasure.
32 The earth doth tremble, when that hee
　upon the same doth look,
the mountaines he doth touch, likewise
　　　　　　Bb　　　　　　　　　　they

they therupon do smoak.
34 Full sweet my meditation
concerning him shall be:
so that I in Iehovah will
rejoyce *exceedinglee.*
35 Let sinners be consum'd from th'earth,
& wicked be no more:
blesse thou Iehovah, o my soule,
prayse yee the Lord *therefore.*

Psalme 105.

O Prayse the Lord, call on his Name.
mong people shew his facts.
2 Sing unto him, sing psalmes to him:
talk of all's wondrous acts.
3 Let their hearts joy, that seek the Lord:
boast in his Holy-Name.
4 The Lord seek, & his strengh: his face
alwayes seek yee *the same.*
5 Those admirable works that hee
hath done remember you:
his wonders, & the judgements which
doe from his mouth *issue.*
6 O yee his servant Abrahams seed:
sonnes of chose Iacob yee.
7 He is the Lord our God: in all
the earth his judgements bee.
8 His Covenant for evermore,
and his comanded word,
a thousand generations to
he doth in minde record,
9 Which he with Abraham made, and's oath

to

PSALME Cv.

10   to Isack. Made it fast,
   a law to Iacob: & Isr'ell
    a Cov'nant aye to last.

(2)

11 He sayd, I'le give thee Canans land:
   by lot, heirs to be there.
12 When few, yea very few in count
   and strangers in't they were;
13 When they did from one nation
   unto another pass:
  when from one Kingdome their goings
   to other people was,
14 *H*e suffred none to doe them wrong:
   Kings checkt he for their sake:
15 Touch not mine oynted ones; none ill
   unto my Prophets make.
16 He cal'd for Famine on the land,
   all staffe of bread brake hee.
17 Before them sent a man: Ioseph
   sold for a slave to bee.
18 *Wh*ose feet they did with fetters hurt:
   in yr'n his soule did lye.
19 Vntill the time that his word came:
   the Lords word did him trye.
20 The King the peoples Ruler sent,
   loos'd him & let him go.
21 He made him Lord of all his house:
   of all's wealth ruler too:
22 At's will to binde his *P*eers: & teach
23 his Ancients skill. Then came
  Isr'ell to Egypt: & Iacob
                    sojourn'd

PSALM C v.

sojourn'd i'th land of Ham.
24 Hee much increast his folk: & made
 them stronger then their foe,
25 Their heart he turn'd his folk to hate
 to's servants craft to show.

(3)

25 Moses his servant he did send:
 & Aaron whom he chose.
27 His signes & wonders them amongst,
 they in Hams land disclose.
28 Hee darknes sent, & made it dark:
 nor did they's word gain-say.
29 Hee turn'd their waters into bloud:
 & he their fish did slay.
30 Great store of Frogs their land brought forth
 in chambers of their Kings.
31 He spake, there came mixt swarmes, & lice
 in all their coasts *he brings*.
32 He gave them haile for raine: & in
 their land fires flame did make.
33 And smote their Vines & their Figtrees:
 & their coast-trees he brake.
34 He spake, & then the Locusts came:
 & Caterpillars, such
 the number of them was as none
 could reckon up how much,
35 And ate all their lands herbs: & did
 fruit of their ground devoure.
36 All first borne in their land he smote:
 the chief of all their powre.

37 with

(4)
37 With silver also & with gold
 he them from thence did bring:
 & among all their tribes there was
 not any one weak ling.
38 Egypt was glad when out they went:
 for on them fell their dread.
39 A cloud for cov'ring, & a fire
 to light the night he spred.
40 They askt, & he brought quailes: did them
 with heav'ns bread satisfy,
41 He op't the rock and waters flow'd:
 flouds ran in places dry.
42 For on his holy promise, hee
 and's servant Abraham thought.
43 With joye his people, and with songs
 forth he his chosen brought.
44 He of the heathen people did
 the land on them bestow:
 the labour of the people they
 inherited also:
45 To this intent that his statutes
 they might observe *alwayes*:
 also that they his lawes might keepe.
 doe yee Iehovah prayse.

Psalme 106.

Prayse yee the Lord, o to the Lord
 give thanks, for good is hee:
for his mercy continued is
 to perpetuitee.
2 Who can the Lords strong acts forth tell?

PSALM CVI.

or all his prayse display?
3 Blest they that judgement keep: & who
doth righteousnes alway.
4 With favour of thy people, Lord,
doe thou remember mee:
and mee with that salvation
visit which is of thee:
5 To see thy chosens good, to joy
in gladnes of thy nation:
that with thine owne inheritance
I might have exultation.
6 As our fore-fathers so have wee
sinned erroniously:
wee practis'd have iniquity,
wee have done wickedly.

(2)

7 Our fathers did not understand
thy wonders in Egypt,
nor was thy mercyes multitude
in their remembrance kept:
But at the sea at the red sea
8 vext him. Yet for his owne
Names sake he sav'd them: that he might
his mighty powre make knowne.
9 The red sea also he rebuk't,
and dryed up it was:
so that as through the wildernes,
through depths he made them pass.
10 And from the hand of him that did
them hate, he set them free:
and them redeemed from his hand

that

that was their enemee.
11 The waters covered their foes:
  of them there was left none.
12 They did believe his word; they sang
  his prayses therupon.

(3)

13 They soone forgot his words; nor would
  they for his counsell stay:
14 But much i'th wildernes did lust;
  i'th desart God tryde they.
15 And he their suite them gave; but sent
  leannes their soule into.
16 They envi'd Moses in the camp,
  Aaron Gods Saint also.
17 The opned earth, Dathan devour'd;
  and hid Abirams troup.
18 And fire was kindled in their rout:
  flame burnt the wicked up.
19 In *H*oreb made a calfe; also
  molt image worshipt they.
20 They chang'd their glory to be like,
  an oxe that eateth hay.
21 They God forgot their saviour; which
  in Egipt did great acts:
22 *W*orks wondrous in the land of *H*am:
  by th'red sea dreadfull facts.
23 And sayd he would them waste; had not
  Moses stood (whom he chose)
  'fore him i'th breach, to turne his wrath,
  lest that hee should waste *those*.

PSALM CVI.

(4)

24 Yet they despis'd the pleasant land:
   nor did believe his word:
25 But murmur'd in their tents: the voyce
   they heard not of the *Lord*.
26 To make them fall i'th desart then,
   'gainst them he lift his hands.
27 'Mongst nations eke to fell their seed,
   and scatter them i'th lands.
28 And to Baal-Peor they joyn'd themselves:
   ate offrings of the dead.
29 Their works his wrath did thus provoake:
   the plague amongst them spread.
30 Then Phineas rose, & judgement did:
   and so the plague did stay.
31 Which justice to him counted was:
   to age and age for aye.

(5)

32 At th'waters of contention
   they angred him also:
   so that with Moses for their sakes,
   it *very* ill did go:
33 Because his spirit they provoakt:
   with's lips to speake rashly.
34 The nations as the Lord them charg'd,
   they stroyd not utterly:
35 But were amongst the Heathen mixt,
   and learn'd their works to do:
36 And did their Idols serve; which them
   became a snare unto.
37 Yea, unto divills, they their sonnes

and

PSALME CVI.

and daughters offered.
38 And guiltleſſe bloud, bloud of their ſons
& of their daughters ſhed,
Whom unto Canans Idols they
offred in ſacrifice:
the land with bloud abundantly
polluted was likewiſe.
39 Thus with the works were they defylde
which they themſelves had done:
and they did goe a whoring with
inventions of their owne:

(6)

40 Therefore againſt his folk the wrath
was kindled of the Lord:
ſo that he the inheritance
which was his owne abhorr'd.
41 And he gave them to heathens hand;
their haters their lords were.
42 Their foes thral'd them; under their hand
made them the yoake to beare.
43 Oft he deliverd them; but they
provoakt him bitterly
with their counſell, & were brought low
for their iniquity.
44 Yet, he regarded their diſtreſſe;
when he did heare their plaint.
45 And he did to remembrance call
for them his Covenant:
And in his many mercyes did
46 repent. And made them bee
pitty'd of all that led them forth

Cc

into

into captivitee.
47 Save us, o Lord our God, & us
 from heathens gath'ring rayse
to give thanks to thy Holy-Name:
 to triumph in thy prayse.
48 The Lord the God of Israell
 from aye to aye blest bee:
and let all people say Amen.
 o prayse Iehovah yee.

THE

FIFT BOOKE

Psalme 107.

O Give yee thanks unto the Lord,
 because that good is hee:
because his loving kindenes lasts
 to perpetuitee.
2 So let the Lords redeem'd say: whom
 hee freed from th'enemies hands:
3 And gathred them from East, & *West*,
 from South, & Northerne lands.
4 I'th desart, in a desart way
 they wandred: no towne finde,
5 to dwell in. Hungry & thirsty:
 their soule within them pinde.
6 Then did they to Iehovah cry
 when they were in distresse:
who did them set at liberty

out

PSALME CvII.

out of their anguishes.
7 In such a way that was most right
   he led them forth also:
that to a citty which they might
   inhabit they might go.
8 O that men would Iehovah prayse
   for his great goodnes *then*:
& for his workings wonderfull
   unto the sonnes of men.
9 Because that he the longing soule
   doth throughly satisfy:
the hungry soule he also fills
   with good abundantly.

(2)

10 Such as in darknes' and within
   the shade of death abide;
who are in sore affliction,
   also in yron tyde:
11 By reason that against the words
   of God they did rebell;
also of him that is most high
   contemned the counsell.
12 Therefore with molestation
   hee did bring downe their heart:
downe did they fall, & none their was
   could help to them impart.
13 Then did they to Iehovah cry
   when they were in distress:
who did them set at liberty
   out of their anguishes.
14 He did them out of darknes bring,

PSALM CVII.

also deaths shade from under:
 as for the bands that they were in
he did them break asunder.
15 O that men would Iehovah prayse
 for his great goodnes *them*:
and for his workings wonderfull
 unto the sonnes of men.
15 For he hath all to shivers broke
 the gates that were of brasse:
& hee asunder cut each barre
 that made of yron was.

(3)

17 For their transgressions & their sins,
 fooles doe affliction beare.
18 All kinde of meate their soule abhorres:
 to deaths gate they draw neare.
19 Then did they to Iehovah cry
 when they were in distress:
who did them set at liberty
 out of their anguishes.
20 He, sent his word, & therewithall
 healing to them he gave:
from out of their destructions
 he did them also save.
21 O that men would Iehovah prayse,
 for his great goodnes *them*:
& for his workings wonderfull
 unto the sons of men.
22 And sacrifices sacrifice
 let them of thanksgiving:
& while his works they doe declare

let

PSALME CVII.

let them for gladnes sing.
(4)
23 They that goe downe to'th sea in ships:
   their busines there to doo
24 in waters great. The Lords work see,
   it'h deep his wonders too.
25 Because that he the stormy winde
   commandeth to arise:
   which lifteth up the waves therof,
26 They mount up to the skyes:
   Downe goe they to the depths againe,
   their soule with ill doth quaile.
27 They reele, & stagger, drunkard like,
   and all their witt doth faile.
28 Then did they to Iehovah cry
   when they were in distress:
   and therupon he bringeth them
   out of their anguishes.
29 Hee makes the storme a calme: so that
   the waves therof are still.
30 Their rest then glads them; he them bring
   to'th hav'n which they did will.
31 O that men would Iehovah prayse
   for his great goodnes *then*:
   & for his workings wonderfull
   unto the sons of men.
32 Also within the peoples Church
   him let them highly rayse:
   where Elders are assembled, there
   him also let them prayse.

Cc 3   33 Hee

(5)
33 He rivers to a defart turnes,
    to drought the fpringing well:
34 A fruitfull foyle to barrennes;
    for their fin there that dwell.
35 The defart to a poole he turnes;
    and dry ground to a fpring.
36 Seates there the hungry, who prepare
    their towne of habiting,
37 Vineyards there alfo for to plant,
    alfo to fow the field;
  which may unto them fruitfull things
    of much revenue yield.
33 Alfo he blefseth them, fo that
    they greatly are increaft:
  and for to be diminifhed
    he fuffers not their beaft.
39 Againe they are diminifhed
    & they are brought downe low,
  by reafon of their prefsing-ftreights,
    affliction & forrow.
(6)
40 On Princes he contempt doth powre;
    and caufeth them to ftray
  i'th folitary wildernes,
    wherin there is no way.
41 Yet hee out of affliction
    doth make the poore to rife:
  & like as if it were a flock
    doth make him families.
42 The righteous fhall it behold,

                                and

PSALME CvII, CvIII.

and he shall joyfull bee:
in silence stop her mouth also
 shall all iniquitee.
43 Who so is wise, & who so will
 these things attentive learne:
the loving-kindenes of the Lord
 they clearely shall discerne.

Psalme 108.
A song or psalme of David.

O GOD, my heart's fixt, I'le sing; prayse
 sing ev'n with my glory.
2 Awake thou Psaltery & Harp;
 I will awake early.
3 O thou Iehovah, thee will I
 the people prayse among:
within the midst of nations
 thee will I prayse with song.
4 For o're the heav'ns thy mercys great;
 to'th skyes thy truth doth mount.
5 Or'e heav'ns o God, be lift, all earth
 let thy glory surmount:
6 That thy beloved people may
 be set at libertee:
with thy right hand salvation give,
 & doe thou answer mee.

(2)

7 God hath in his *owne* holines
 spoken, rejoyce I shall:
of Shechem I'le division make;
 & mete out Succoths vale.
8 Mine Gilead, mine Manasseh is,

and

PSALM C viii. C ix

& Ephraim also hee
  is of my head the strength: Iudah
    shall my law-giver bee.
9 Moab my wash-pot, I will cast
    over Edom my shoo:
  I'le make a shout triumphantly
    over Philistia too.
10 Who is it that will bring me to
    the citty fortifyde?
  who is it that into Edom
    will be to mee a guide?
11 Wilt not thou doe this thing, o God,
    who didst us cast thee fro?
  & likewise wilt not thou o God,
    forth with our armies go?
12 From trouble give us help; for vaine
    is mans salvation.
13 Through God wee shall do valiantly;
    for hee'l our foes tread downe.

Psalme 109.

To the chief musician, a psalme
of David.

GOD of my prayse, hold not thy peace,
  For mouth of the wicked,
& mouth of the deceitfull are
    against mee opened:
Gainst mee they speake with lying tongue.
3   And compasse mee about
  with words of hate; & mee against
    without a cause they fought.
4 They for my love mine enemies are:

                                but

PSALME CIX.

but I my prayer make.
5 And ill for good rewarded mee
    & hate for my loves fake.
6 A wicked perfon over him
    doe thou make for to fit,
also at his right hand doe thou
    let Satan ftand at it.
7 When he is judged, let him then
    condemned be therin:
and let the prayr that hee doth make
    be turned into fin.
8 Few let his dayes bee: & let his
    office another take.
9 His children let be fatherleffe,
    and's wife a widow make.
10 Let's children ftill be vagabonds,
    begge they their bread alfo:
out of their places defolate
    let them a feeking go.

(2)

11 Yea, let th'extortioner catch all
    that doth to him pertaine:
and let the ftranger fpoyle what he
    did by his labour gaine.
12 Let there not any bee that may
    mercy to him expreffe:
nor any one that favour may
    his children fatherleffe.
13 The ifhue alfo let thou be
    cut off that from him came:
it'h following generation

Dd   out

PSALM C ix,

    out blotted be his name.
14 Remembred with the Lord be his
    fathers iniquitee:
  and of his mother never let
    the sin out blotted bee.
15 Before Iehovah let them bee
    continually put:
  that from out of the earth he may
    the mem'ry of them cut.
16 Because that he remembred not
    compassion to impart,
  but did pursue the needy poore:
    to slay the broke in heart.

(3)

17 As he did cursing love, so let
    cursing unto him come:
  as he did not in blessing joy,
    so be it far him from.
18 With cursing like a robe as hee
    cloath'd him: so let it go
  like water to his bowels, and
    like oyle his bones into.
19 Garment like let it to him be,
    himselfe for to aray:
  and for a girdle, wherewith hee
    may gird himselfe alway.
20 Thus let mine adversaryes bee
    rewarded from the Lord:
  also of them against my soule
    that speak an evil word.

PSALME CIX.
(4)
21 But God the Lord, for thy Names sake,
o doe thou well for mee:
because thy mercy it is good,
o doe thou set mee free.
22 For poore & needy I: in mee
my heart's wounded also.
23 Like falling shade I passe: I'me tost
Locust like to & fro.
24 Through fasts my knees are weak: my flesh
it's fatnes doth forsake.
25 And I am their reproach: they look
at mee, their heads they shake.
26 Help mee, o Lord my God: after
thy mercy save thou mee:
27 That they may know this is thy hand:
Lord that i'ts done by thee.
28 Let them curse, but o doe thou blesse;
when as that they arise
let them be shamed, thy servant
let him rejoyce likewise.
29 Mine adversaryes o let them
with shame be cloath'd upon:
& themselves cloath as with a cloak
with their confusion.
30 I'le to Iehovah with my mouth
give thanks exceedingly:
yea him among the multitude
with prayse I'le glorify.
31 For hee shall stand at right hand of
the poore & needy one:

PSALM C ix, C x.

from those that doe condemne his soule
   to give salvation.
Psalme 110.
A psalme of David.

THe Lord did say unto my Lord,
   sit thou at my right hand:
till I thine enemies make a stoole
   wheron thy feet may stand.
2 The Lord the rod shall of thy strength
   send from out of Sion:
in middest of thine enemies
   have thou dominion.
3 Willing thy folk in thy dayes powre,
   in holy beautyes bee:
from mornings womb; thou hast the dew
   of thy youth unto thee.
4 Iehovah sware, nor will repent,
   thou art a Priest for aye:
after the order that I of
   Melchizedeck did say.
5 The Lord who is at thy right hand.
   wounding shall strike through Kings
in that same day wherin that hee
   his indignation brings.
6 Hee shall among the heathen judge,
   and fill with bodies dead
great places, & o're many lands
   he shall strike through the head.
7 Out of the torrent he shall drink
   i'th way *hee passeth by*:
because of this therefore hee shall

                               lift

PSALME Cxr.

lift up his head on hye.
Pfalme 111.

PRayse yee the *L*ord: with my whole heart
Iehovah prayse will I:
i'th private meetings of th'upright,
and publicke affembly.
2 Great are the Lords works: fought of all
that in them have pleafure.
3 Comely & glorious is his work:
aye doth his juftice dure.
4 To be remembred he hath made
his doings merveilous:
full of compaffion is the Lord
as well as gracious.
5 Meate hath hee given unto them
that fearers of him bee:
he evermore his covenant
doth keepe in memoree:
6 The power of his works hee did
unto his people fhow:
that he the heathens heritage
upon them might beftow.
(2)
7 Both verity & judgement are
the working of his hands:
yea very faithfull alfo are
each one of his commands.
8 For ever & for evermore
they ftand in ftablenes:
yea they are done in verity
alfo in uprightnes.

Dd 3   9 Redemption

PSALM CXI. CXII.

9 Redemption to his folk he sent,
    that covenant of his
for aye he hath ordaind: holy
    and reverend his Name is.
10 Of wisdome the begining is
    Iehovahs feare: all they
that doe his will have prudence good:
    his prayse indures for aye.

Psalme 112.

PRayse yee the Lord. blest is the man
    that doth Iehovah feare,
that doth in his commandements
    his spirit greatly cheare.
2 The *very* mighty upon earth
    shall be that are his seed:
they also shall be blessed that
    from th' upright doe proceed.
3 And there shall be within his house
    both wealth & much rich store:
his righteousnes it also doth
    indure for evermore.
4 In midst of darknes there doth light
    to upright ones arise:
both gracious, & pittyfull,
    righteous he is likewise.

(2)

5 A good man hee doth favour show
    & ready is to lend:
and with descretion his affayres
    he carryes to an end.
6 That man shall not assuredly

                 for

PSALME CXII, CXIII.

for ever moved bee:
the righteous man he shall be had
  in lasting memoree.
7 By evill tydings that he heares
  he shall not be afrayd:
his trust he putting in the Lord,
  his heart is firmly stayd.
8 His heart is sure established,
  feare shall not him surprise,
untill he see what hee desires
  upon his enemies.
9 He hath disperst, hath giv'n to poore:
  his justice constantly
indureth: & his horne shall be
  with honour lifted hye.
10 The wicked shall see, & be griev'd;
  gnash with his teeth shall hee
and melt away: and their desire
  shall faile that wicked bee.

Psalme 113.

THe Lord prayse yee, prayse yee the Lord
  his servants Gods Name prayse.
2 O blessed be Iehovahs Name,
  from henceforth & alwayes.
3 From rising to the setting sun:
  the Lords Name's to be praysd.
4 The Lord all nations is above:
  o're heav'ns his glory raysd
5 Who is like to, the Lord our God?
  who upon earth doth dwell.
6 Who humble doth himselfe to view,

in

PSALM CXIII, CXIV.

in heav'n, in earth as well.
7 The needy from the dust he lifts:
   the poore lifts from the dung.
8 That hee with princes may him set:
   his peoples Peeres among.
9 The barren woman he doth make
   to keepe house, & to bee
a joyfull mother of children:
   wherefore the Lord prayse yee.

Psalme 114.

VVHen Isr'ell did depart
   th'Egyptians from among,
and Iacobs house from a people
   that were of a strange tongue:
2 Iudah his holy place:
   Isrell's dominion was.
3 The sea it saw, & fled: Iordane
   was forced back to pass.
4 The mountaines they did leap
   upwards like unto rams:
the litle hills also they did
   leap up like unto lambs.
5 Thou sea what made thee flye?
   thou Iordane, back to go?
6 Yee mountaines that yee skipt like rams:
   like lambs yee hills also?
7 Earth at Gods presence dread;
   at Iacobs Gods presence:
8 The rock who turnes to waters lake:
   springs he from flint sends thence.

PSALME CxV.

Psalme 115

Not to us, not unto us, Lord,
　　but glory to thy Name afford:
for thy mercy, for thy truths sake.
2 The heathen wherefore should they say:
where is their God now gone away?
3　　But heavn's our God his seat doth make:
Hee hath done whatsoe're he would.
4　Their Idols are silver & gold:
　　the handy work of men they were.
5 Mouths have they, speachlesse yet they bee:
eyes have they, but they doe not see.
6　Eares have they but they doe not heare:
Noses have they, but doe not smell.
7 Hands have they, but cannot handell,
　　feet have they but they doe not go:
And through their throat they never spake.
8 Like them are they, that doe them make:
　　& all that trust in them are so.
9 Trust in the Lord o Israell,
he is their help, their shield as well.
10　O Arons house the Lord trust yee:
Hee is their help, & hee their shield.
11 Who feare the Lord, trust to him yield:
　　their help also their shield is hee.

(2)

12 The Lord hath mindefull been of us,
he'le blesse us, he'le blesse Isr'ells house:
　　blessing he'le Arons house afford.
13 He'le blesse Gods fearers: great & small.
14 You & your sons, the Lord much shall
　　　　　　Ee　　　　　　　　increase

PSALM Cxv, Cxvi.

15 increase still. You blest of the Lord
16 which heav'n & earth made. Heav'ns heav'ns
   the Lords: but th'earth mens sons gives hee. (bee
17 The Lords prayse dead doe not afford:
   Nor any that to silence bow.
18 But wee will blesse the Lord both now
      and ever henceforth. prayse the Lord.

Psalme 116.

I Love the Lord, because he doth
   my voice & prayer heare.
2 And in my dayes will call, because
   he bow'd to mee his eare.
3 The pangs of death on ev'ry side
   about beset mee round:
  the paines of hell 'gate hold on mee,
   distresse & griefe I found.
4 Vpon Iehovahs Name therefore
   I called, *& did say*,
  deliver thou my soule, o Lord,
   I doe thee humbly pray.
5 Gracious the Lord & just, our God
   is mercifull also.
6 The Lord the simple keeps: & hee
   sav'd mee when I was low.
7 O thou my soule doe thou returne
   unto thy quiet rest:
  because the Lord to thee himselfe
   hath bounteously exprest.
8 For thou hast freed my soule from death,
   mine eyes from teares, from fall
9 my feet. Before the Lord i'th land

PSALME CXVI.

of living walk I shall.

(2)

10 I did believe, therefore I spake:
 afflicted much was I.
11 That every man a lyar is
 I did say hastily.
12 What shall I render to the Lord,
 to mee for's benefits all.
13 I'le take the cup of saving health
 & on the Lords Name call.
14 In presence now of all his folk,
 I'le pay the Lord my vowes.
15 Of his Saints, in Iehovahs sight
 the death is pretious.
16 I am thy servant, truly Lord
 thine owne servant am I:
I am the son of thy hand-maide,
 my bands thou didst untye.
17 Of thanksgiving the sacrifice
 offer to thee I will:
Iehovahs Name I earnestly
 will call upon it still.
18 Vnto Iehovah I will pay
 the vowes were made by mee,
now in the presence of all them
 that his owne people bee.
19 Within the Courts of the Lords house,
 ev'n in the midst of thee
o thou *citty* Ierusalem:
 o prayse Iehovah yee.

Psalme 117.

PSALM C xvii, C xviii.

AL nations, prayse the Lord; him prayse
all people. For his mercies bee
great toward us: also always
the Lords truth lasts. the Lord prayse yee.
Another of the same.

AL nations, prayse the Lord; all folk
prayse him. For his mercee
is great to us; & the Lords truth
aye lasts. the Lord prayse yee.

Psalme 118.

O Give yee thanks unto the Lord,
because that good is hee;
because his loving kindenes lasts
to perpetuitee.

2 For ever that his mercie lasts
let Israell now say.

3 Let Arons house now say, that his
mercie indures for aye.

4 Likewise let them now say, who of
Iehovah fearers bee;
his loving kindenes that it lasts
to perpetuitee.

5 I did lift up my voice to God
from out of streitnes great;
the Lord mee answerd, & mee plac't
in an inlarged seat.

6 The Lord's for mee, I will not feare
what man can doe to mee.

7 Iehovah takes my part with them
that of mee helpers bee:
Therefore upon them that mee hate

my

PSALME CXVIII.

my wishes see shall I.
8 'Tis better to trust in the Lord:
then on man to rely.
(2)
9 'Tis better to trust on the Lord:
then trust in Princes put.
10 All nations compast mee; but them
in Gods Name I'le off cut.
11 They compast mee about, yea they
mee compassed about:
but in Iehovahs Name I will
them utterly root out.
12 They compast mee like Bees, are quencht
like as of thornes the flame:
but I will utterly destroy
them in Iehovahs Name.
13 Thou didst thrust sore to make mee fall:
the Lord yet helped mee.
14 The Lord my fortitude & song:
& saving health is hee.
15 The tabernacles of the just
the voice of joye afford
& of salvation: strongly works
the right hand of the Lord.
16 The right hand of Iehovah is
exalted up on hye:
the right hand of Iehovah is
a working valiantly.
(3)
17 I shall not dye, but live: & tell
what things the Lord worketh.

PSALM CXVIII.

18 The Lord did sorely chasten mee:
    but gave mee not to death.
19 O set wide open unto mee
    the gates of righteousnes:
I will goe into them, & will
    Iehovahs praise confess.
20 This same Iehovahs gate at which
    the just shall enter in.
21 I'le praise thee, for thou hast mee heard,
    and hast my safety bin.
22 The stone which builders did refuse
    head corner stone now lyes.
23 This is the doing of the Lord:
    it's wondrous in our eyes.

(4)

24 This is the very day the which
    Iehovah hee hath made:
wee will exceedingly rejoyce,
    & in it will be glad.
25 Iehovah I doe thee beseech,
    salvation now afford:
I humbly thee intreat, now send
    prosperity, o Lord.
26 Hee that comes in Iehovahs Name
    o let him blessed bee:
out of Iehovahs house to you
    a blessing with doe wee.
27 God he Iehovah is, and hee
    light unto us affords:
the sacrifices binde unto
    the altars hornes with cords.

Thou

PSALME CxvIII, CxIX.

28 Thou art my God, & I'le thee prayse,
  my God I'le set thee hye.
29 O prayse the Lord, for he is good,
  and aye lasts his mercy.

Psalme 119.
א   (1)   Aleph

ALL-blest are men upright of way:
  walk in Iehovahs law who do.
2 Blest such as doe his records keepe:
  with their whole heart him seek also.
3 And that work no iniquitie:
  but in his wayes doe walke *indeed*.
4 Thou hast giv'n charge, with diligence
  unto thy precepts to give heed.

5 Ah that to keepe thy statutes: *so*
  my wayes addressed were by thee.
6 When I respect thy precepts all,
  then shall I not ashamed bee.
7 Whē I thy righteous judgements learne
  with hearts uprightnes I'le thee prayse.
8 Forsake thou mee not utterly:
  I will observe thy statute-wayes.

ב   (2)   Beth

9 By what may 'young man cleanse his way?
  by heeding it as thy word guides.
10 With my whole heart thee have I sought:
  thy lawes let mee not goe besides.
11 I in my heart thy word have hid:
  that I might not against thee sin.
12 Thou o Iehovah, blessed art:
  thine owne statutes instruct mee in.

13 All

PSALM CXIX.

13 All the just judgements of thy mouth
  declared with my lips have I.
14 I in thy testimonyes way
  joy more then in all rich plenty.
15   In thy precepts I'le meditate:
  and have respect unto thy wayes.
16 My selfe I'le solace in thy lawes:
  and not forget what thy word *sayes*.

      ג   (3)   Gimel

17   Confer this grace thy servant to,
  that I may live thy word to keep.
18 Vnveile mine eyes, that I may see
  out of thy law the wonders *deep*.
19 I am a stranger in the earth:
  do not thy precepts from me hide.
20 My soule is broken with desire
  unto thy judgements time & tide.

21   Thou hast rebuk'd the proud, acurst
  which doe frō thy commandments swerve.
22 Roll off from mee reproach & scorne:
  for I thy records doe observe.
23   Ev'n Princes sate & 'gainst mee spake;
  but on thy lawes thy servant mus'd.
24 Thy records also are my joyes:
  and for men of my counsell *us'd*.

      ד   (4)   Daleth

25   Downe to the dust my soule cleav's fast:
  o quicken mee after thy word.
26 I show'd my wayes & thou mee heardst:
  thy statutes learning mee afford.
27   Thy precepts way make mee to know:

PSALME CxIX.

so I'le muse on thy wondrous wayes.
28 My soule doth melt for heavines:
according to thy word mee rayse.
29   The way of lying from mee take:
and thy law grant mee graciously.
30 The way of truth I chosen have:
thy judgements *fore mee* layd have I.
31   Thy testimonies cleave I to;
o Lord, on mee shame do not cast.
32 Then shall I run thy precepts way,
when thou mine heart enlarged hast.

     ח   (5)   He.
33 Enforme mee Lord, in thy laws path;
and I will keep it to the end.
34 Skill give mee, & thy law I'le keep:
yea with my whole heart it attend.
35   Cause mee to tread thy precepts path;
because therin delight I do.
36 Vnto thy records bend my heart;
& covetousnes not unto.
37   From vaine sights turne away mine eyes:
and in thy way make mee to live.
38 Confirme thy word thy servant to,
who to thy feare himselfe doth give.
39   My slander which I feare remove;
because thy judgements good they bee.
40 Loe for thy precepts I have lon'gd:
o in thy justice quicken mee.

     ו   (6)   Vau.
41 Finde mee out let thy mercies Lord:
thy saving health as thou hast sayd.

              F f

PSALM CXIX.

42 So I my taunters answer shall,
 for on thy word my hope is stayd.
43 Nor truths-word quite frō my mouth take:
 because thy judgements I attend.
44 So I thy law shall alway keep,
 to everlasting without end.

45 And I will walk at libertie,
 because I doe thy precepts seek.
46 Nor will I blush, when before Kings
 I of thy testimonies speak.
47 In thy commands, which I have lov'd,
 also my selfe delight I will.
48 And lift my hands to thy commands
 belov'd: & minde thy statutes still.

G   (7)   Sajin.
49 Good to thy servant make the word,
 on which to hope thou didst mee give.
50 This was my comfort in my griefe,
 because thy word doth make mee live.
51 The proud have much derided mee:
 yet have I not thy law declinde.
52 Thy judgements Lord, that are of old,
 I did recall, & comfort finde.

53 Horrour hath taken hold on mee:
 for lewd men that thy law forsake.
54 I, in my pilgrimages house,
 of thy statutes my songs doe make.
55 By night remembred I thy Name,
 o Lord: & I thy law observe.
55 This hath been unto mee, because
 I from thy precepts did not swerve.

          Hee

PSALME CxIx.

ה (8) Heth.

57 Hee, ev'n the Lord, my portion is,
I said that I would keep thy word.
58 With my whole heart thy face I begg'd:
thy promis'd mercies mee afford.
59 I thought upon my waies, & turn'd
my feet into thy testaments.
60 I hasted, & made no delaies
to keepe with heed thy commandments.
61 The bands of wicked men mee robb'd:
of thy law I am not mindeless.
62 Ile rise at midnight thee to praise;
for judgements of thy righteousnes.
63 Companion am I to all them,
that feare thee, & thy laws doe heed.
64 Thy mercie fills the earth, o Lord:
teach mee the lawes thou hast decreed.

ט (9) Teth.

65 Iehovah, with thy servant thou
after thy word, right-well hast done.
66 Good taste & knowledge, teach thou mee,
for I believe thy precepts on.
67 Before I was chastis'd, I stray'd:
but I thy word observ'd have now.
68 Thou art good, & art doing good:
thy statutes teach mee, oh doe thou.
69 The proud against mee forg'd a lye:
thy laws I'le keepe with my hearts-might.
70 The heart of them is fat as grease:
but in thy law I doe delight.
71 It's good for mee, I was chastis'd:

Ff 2

that

PSALM CXIX.

that so thy statutes learne I should.
72 Better to mee is thy mouths-law,
then thousands of silver & gold.

   K ' (10) Iod.
73 Know make mee, & I'le learn thy lawes:
thy hands mee formed have, & made.
74 Who feare thee, mee shall see, & joy:
because hope in thy word I had.
75 Thy judgements Lord, I know are just;
& faithfully thou chastnedst mee.
76 As thou hast to thy servant spoke,
now let thy grace my comfort bee.
77 Send mee thy grace, that I may live;
for thy law as my joy I chuse.
78 Shame proud ones, that mee falsly wrong:
but I will in thy precepts muse.
79 Let them that feare thee turne to mee;
and such as have thy records knowne.
80 Let my heart bee in thy lawes sound
that so I shame may suffer none.

   L ⊃ (11) Caph.
81 Look for thy word I doe, *when as*
my soule doth faint for help from thee.
82 Mine eies have failed for thy word,
saying, when wilt thou comfort mee?
83 I like a smoake-dride-bottle am;
yet doe I not thy laws forgoe.
84 what are thy servants daies? when wilt
on my pursuers judgement doe?
85 The proud have digged pits for mee,
which doe not unto thy law sute.

All

PSALME CXIX.

86 All thy comands are truth: help mee,
    they wrongfully mee perfecute.
87 They nigh had wafted mee on earth,
    but I thy laws did not forfake.
88 To keep the records of thy mouth,
    mee in thy mercie lively make.

        ל (12)   Lamed.
89 Made faft i'th heavens is thy word,
    o Lord, for ever to endure.
90 From age to age thy faithfullnes:
    thou form'dft the earth, & it ftands-fure.
91 As thou ordain'dft, they ftill abide;
    for all are fervants thee unto.
92 Had not thy law been my delight:
    Then had I perifht in my wo.
93 Thy ftatutes I will ne're forget:
    becaufe by them thou quicknedft mee.
94 Thine owne am I, fave mee, becaufe
    I fought thy precepts ftudiouflee.
95 The wicked watch mee, mee to ftroy:
    but I thy teftimonies minde.
96 Of all perfection, end I fee:
    but very large thy law *I finde*.

        מ (13)   Mem.
97 Now how much doe I love thy law?
    it is my ftudy all the day.
98 Thou mad'ft mee wifer then my foes
    by thy rule: for it's with mee aye.
99 I'me wifer then my teachers all:
    for thy records my ftudy are.
100 I more then ancients underftand;

                                  becaufe

PSALM CXIX.

because I kept thy laws with care.
101 From each ill path my feet I stay'd:
that so I might thy word observe.
102 Because thou hast instructed mee,
I did not from thy judgements swerve.
103 How sweet are thy words to my taste?
to my mouth more then honie they.
104 I from thy precepts wisdome learne:
therefore I hate each lying way.

O נ (14) Nun.
105 Of my feet is thy word the lamp:
and to my path the shining light.
106 Sworne have I, & will it performe,
that I will keep thy judgements right.
107 I am afflicted very much:
Lord quicken mee after thy word.
108 Accept my mouths free-offrings now:
& mee thy judgements teach o Lord.
109 My soule is alwaies in my hand:
but I have not thy law forgot.
110 The wicked laide for mee a snare:
yet from thy laws I strayed not.
111 Thy records are mine heritage
for aye: for my hearts joy they bee.
112 I bent my heart still to performe
thy statues to eternitee.

P ס (15) Samech.
113 Pursue-I doe with hatred, all
vaine thoughts: but love thy law doe I.
114 My covert & my shield art thou:
I on thy word wait hopefully.

Bee

PSALME CxIx.

115 Depart from mee, lewd men, that I
may keepe my Gods commandements.
116 By thy word stay mee, & I live:
nor shame mee for my confidence.
117 Susteine mee, & I shall be safe:
and in thy law still I'le delight.
118 thou tread'st downe all that from thy laws
doe stray: for false is their deceit.
119 All th'earths lewd ones like drosse thou- (stroyd'st
therefore thy records love I do.
120 For feare of thee my flesh doth quake:
I doe thy judgements dread also.

ע (16) Hajin.

121 Quite to oppressors leave mee not:
I judgement doe, & righteousnes.
122 thy servants suretie be for good:
let not the proud ones mee oppress.
123 Mine eyes for thy salvation faile:
as also for thy righteous word.
124 In mercie with thy servant deale:
& thy lawes-learning mee afford.
125 I am thy servant, make mee wise,
thy testimonies for to know.
126 Time for thee Lord it is to work,
for men thy law doe overthrow.
127 Therefore doe I thy precepts love,
above gold, yea the finest gold.
128 All false paths hate I: for thy rules
of all things, are all right, I hold.

ד (17) Pe.

129 Right-wondrous are thy testimonies:
there-

PSALM C xix.

therefore my soule keeps them with care.
130 The entrance of thy words gives light:
and makes them wise that simple are.
131   I gape & pant for thy precepts;
because I longed *for the same*.
132 Look on mee, & such grace mee show,
as thou dost them that love thy Name
133   My steps by thy word guide: & let
no wickednes beare rule in mee.
134 From mens oppression mee redeem:
and thy laws-keeper will I bee.
135   Make thy face on thy servant shine:
and mee to learne thy statutes cause.
136 Mine eies run floods of waters downe:
because they doe not keep thy laws.

S   ♃   (18)   Tzade.
137 Sincerely-just art thou, o Lord,
thy judgements upright are also.
138 Thy testimonies thou commandst
are right, yea, very faithfull too.
139   My zeale consumed mee, because
mine enemies thy words forget.
140 Thy word it is exceeding pure:
therefore thy servant loveth it.
141   Small am I, & contemptible:
yet thy commands forget not I.
142 Thy justice, justice is for aye:
also thy law is verity.
143   Distresse & anguish seas'd on mee:
yet thy commands delights mee give.
144 Thy records justice lasts for aye:

                              also

PSALME Cxx.

make thou mee wise, & I shall live.

        ק (19) Koph.

145 To mee that cry with my whole heart
    Lord heare: thy statutes keep I will.

146 I unto thee did cry: save mee,
    & I shall keep thy records still.

147 The dawning I prevent, & cry:
    I for thy word doe hopefull-waite.

148 Mine eyes prevent the night-watches,
    in thy word for to meditate.

149 Lord, of thy mercy heare my voice:
    after thy judgements quicken mee.

150 Who follow mischiefe, they draw nigh:
    who from thy law afarre off bee.

151 But o Iehovah, thou art neere:
    and all thy precepts verity.

152 I long since of thy records knew:
    thou laid'st them for eternity.

        ר (20) Resch.

153 View mine affliction, & mee free:
    for I thy law doe not forget.

154 Plead thou my cause, & mee redeem:
    for thy words sake alive mee set.

155 Salvation from lewd men is far:
    sith they thy laws to finde ne're strive.

156 Great are thy bowell- mercies Lord:
    after thy judgements mee revive.

157 Many my foes and hunters are:
    yet I not from thy records swerve.

158 I saw transgressors, & was griev'd,
    for they thy word doe not observe.

PSALM CXIX.

159 See Lord, that I thy precepts love:
graunt, of thy bounty live I may.
160 Thy word's beginning it is truth:
and all thy right judgements for aye.

VV ՞ (21) Schin.

161 Without cause Princes mee pursue:
but of thy word my hearts in awe.
162 As one that hath much booty found,
so I rejoyce doe in thy law.
163 Lying I hate, & it abhorre:
but thy law dearly love doe I.
164 Seven times a day I prayse thee, for
the judgements of thine equity.
165 Great peace have they that love thy law:
& such shall finde no stumbling-stone.
166 I hop't for thy salvation, Lord:
and thy commandments I have done.
167 My soule thy testimonies keeps:
and them I love exceedinglee.
168 I keep thy rules & thy records:
for all my waies before thee bee.

Y ת (22) Thau.

169 Yield Lord, my cry, t'approach thy face:
as thou hast spoke, mee prudent make.
170 Let my request before thee come:
deliver mee for thy words sake.
171 My lips shall utter forth *thy* prayse:
when thou thy lawes hast learned mee.
172 My tongue shall forth thy word resound:
for all thy precepts justice *bee*.

173 To help mee let thy hand be neere:

for

for thy commandments chose have I.
274 I long for thy salvation, Lord:
   and my delights in thy law ly.
275   Let my soule live, & shew thy prayse:
   help mee also thy judgements let.
276 Like lost sheep strayd, thy servant seeke:
   for I thy laws doe not forget

Psalme 120.
A song of degrees.

VNto the Lord, in my distresse
   I cry'd, & he heard mee.
2 From lying lipps & guilefull tongue,
   o Lord, my soule set free.
3 What shall thy false tongue give to thee,
   or what on thee confer?
4 Sharp arrows of the mighty ones,
   with coales of juniper.
5 Woe's mee, that I in Mesech doe
   a sojourner remaine:
   that I doe dwell in tents, which doe
   to Kedar appertaine.
6 Long time my soule hath dwelt with him
   that peace doth much abhorre,
7 I am for peace, but when I speake,
   they ready are for warre.

Psalme 121.
A song of degrees.

I To the hills lift up mine eyes,
   from whence shall come mine aid.
2 Mine help doth from Iehovah come,
   which heav'n & earth hath made.

PSALM CXXI, CXXII.

3 Hee will not let thy foot be mov'd,
  nor slumber; that thee keeps.
4 Loe hee that keepeth Israell,
  hee slumbreth not, nor sleeps.
5 The Lord thy keeper is, the Lord
  on thy right hand the shade.
6 The Sun by day, nor Moone by night,
  shall thee by stroke *invade*.
7 The Lord will keep the from all ill:
  thy soule hee keeps alway,
8 Thy going out, & thy income,
  the Lord keeps now & aye.

Psalme 122.
A song of degrees.

I Ioy'd in them, that to mee syd
  to the Lords house go wee.
2 Ierusalem, within thy gates,
  our feet shall standing bee.
3 Ierusalem, it builded is
  like unto a citty
together which compacted is
  within it selfe closely.
4 Whether the tribes, Gods tribes ascend
  unto Isr'ells witnes;
that they unto Iehovahs Name
  may render thankfullnes.
5 For there the judgements thrones, the thrones
  of Davids house doe sit.
6 O for Ierusalem her peace
  see that yee pray for it:
Prosper they shall that doe thee love.

7 peace

PSALME CXXII, CXXIII, CXXIV.

7 Peace in thy fortresses
　o let there be, prosperity
　　within thy Pallaces.
8 For my brethren & for my friends,
　I'le now speake peace to thee.
9 I'le for our God Iehovahs house,
　seek thy felicitee.

Psalme 123.
A song of degrees.

O Thou that sittest in the heav'ns,
　I lift mine eyes to thee.
2 Loe, as the servants eyes unto
　hand of their masters *bee*:
As maides eyes to her mistresse hand,
　so are our eyes unto
the Lord our God, untill that hee
　shall mercy to us show.
3 O Lord be mercifull to us,
　mercifull to us bee:
because that filled with contempt
　exceedingly are wee.
4 With scorne of those that be at ease,
　our soule's fill'd very much:
also of those that great ones are,
　ev'n with contempt of such.

Psalme 124.
A song of degrees. of David.

HAd not the Lord been on our side,
　may Israell now say,
2 Had not God been for us, when men
　did rise against us they:

Gg 3　　　　　　3 The

PSALM Cxxiv, Cxxv.

3 They had then swallow'd us alive,
   when their wrath on us burn'd.
4 Then had the waters us o'rewhelmd,
   the streame our soule or'e turnd.
5 The proud waters then, on our soule
   had passed on their way:
6 Blest be the Lord, that to their teeth
   did not give us a prey.
7 Our soule, as bird, escaped is
   out of the fowlers snare:
 the snare asunder broken is,
   and wee delivered are.
8 The succour which wee doe injoye,
   is in Iehovahs Name:
 who is the maker of the earth,
   and of the heavens frame.

psalme 125.
A song of degrees.

THey that doe in Iehovah trust
   shall as mount Sion bee:
 which cannot be remo'vd, but shall
   remaine perpetuallee.
2 Like as the mountaines round about
   Ierusalem doe stay:
 so doth the Lord surround his folk,
   from henceforth ev'n for aye.
3 For lewd mens rod on just mens lot
   it shall not resting bee:
 lest just men should put forth their hand
   unto iniquitee.
4 To those Iehovah, that be good,

gladnes

PSALME Cxxv, Cxxvi. &c

gladnes to them impart:
as also unto them that are
   upright within their heart.
5 But who turne to their crooked wayes,
   the Lord shall make them go
with workers of iniquity:
   but peace be Isr'ell to.

psalme 126.
A song of degrees.

WHen as the Lord return'd againe
   Sions captivitee:
at that time unto them that dreame
   compared might wee bee.
2 Then was our mouth with laughter fill'd,
   with singing then our tongue:
the Lord hath done great things for them
   said they, t'heathens among.
3 The Lord hath done great things for us,
   wherof wee joyfull bee.
4 As streames in South, doe thou o Lord,
   turne our captivitee.
5 Who sow in teares, shall reape in joy.
6   Who doe goe forth,& mourne,
bearing choise seed, shall sure with joye
   bringing their sheaves returne.

psalme 127.
A song of degrees for Solomon.

IF God build not the house, vainly
   who build it doe take paine:
except the Lord the citty keepe,
   the watchman wakes in vaine.

PSALM CXXVII, CXXVIII.

2 I'ts vaine for you early to rise,
   watch late, to feed upon
 the bread of grief: so hee gives sleep
   to his beloved one.
3 Loe, the wombes fruit, it's Gods reward
   sonnes are his heritage.
4 As arrows in a strong mans hand,
   are sons of youthfull age.
5 O blessed is the man which hath
   his quiver fill'd with those:
 they shall not be asham'd, i'th gate
   when they speake with their foes.

Psalme 128.
A song of degrees.

Blessed is every one
   that doth Iehovah feare:
   that walks his wayes along.
2 For thou shalt eate *with cheare*
   thy hands labour:
 blest shalt thou bee,
 it well with thee
   shall be therefore.
3 Thy wife like fruitfull vine
 shall be by thine house side:
 the children that be thine
 like olive plants abide
   about thy board.
4 Behold thus blest
   that man doth rest,
     that feares the Lord.
5 Iehovah shall thee blesse

from

PSALME CxxvIII, CxxIx.

from Sion, & shalt see
Ierusalems goodnes
all thy lifes dayes that bee.
6   And shalt view well
thy children then
with their children,
    peace on Isr'ell.

Psalme 129.
A song of degrees.

From my youth, now may Isr'ell say,
  oft have they mee assaild:
2 They mee assaild oft from my youth,
  yet 'gainst mee nought prevaild.
3 The ploughers plough'd upon my back,
  their furrows long they drew:
4 The righteous Lord the wickeds cords
  he did asunder-hew.
5 Let all that Sion hate be sham'd,
  and turned back together.
6 As grasse on house tops, let them be,
  which ere it's grown, doth wither:
7 Wherof that which might fill his hand
  the mower doth not finde:
nor therewith hee his bosome fills
  that doth the sheaves up binde.
8 Neither doe they that passe by, say,
  Iehovahs blessing bee
on you: you in Iehovahs Name
  a blessing wish doe wee.

Psalme 130.
A song of degrees.

H h

PSALM Cxxx, Cxxxi.

LORD, from the depth I cryde to thee.
  My voice Lord, doe thou heare:
unto my supplications voice
  let be attent thine eare.
3 Lord, who should stand? if thou o Lord,
  shouldst mark iniquitee.
4 But with thee there forgivenes is:
  that feared thou maist bee.
5 I for the Lord wayt, my soule wayts:
  & I hope in his word.
6 Then morning watchers watch for morn,
  more my soule for the Lord.
7 In God hope Isr'ell, for mercy
  is with the Lord: with him
8 there's much redemption. From all's sin
  hee Isr'ell will redeem.

Psalme 131.

A song of degrees, of David.

MY heart's not haughty, Lord,
  nor lofty are mine eyes:
in things too great, or high for mee,
  is not mine exercise.
2 Surely my selfe I have
  compos'd, and made to rest,
like as a child that weaned is,
  from off his mothers *brest*:
  Im'e like a weaned child.
3 Let Israell then stay
with expectation on the Lord,
  from henceforth and for aye.

Psalme 132.

A song

PSALME CXXXII.

A song of degrees.

Remember David, Lord,
and all's affliction:
2 How to the Lord he swore, & vow'd
to Iacobs mighty one.
3 Surely I will not goe
my houses tent into:
upon the pallate of my bed,
thither I will not go.
4 I will not verily
give sleep unto mine eyes:
nor will I give to mine eye-lidds
slmber *in any wise,*
5 Vntill that for the Lord
I doe finde out a seate:
a fixed habitation,
for Iacobs God so great.
6 Behould, at Epratah,
there did wee of it heare:
ev'n in the plain-fields of the wood
wee found it *to be there.*
7 Wee'l goe into his tents:
wee'l at his footstoole bow.
8 Arise, Lord, thou into thy rest:
and th'Arke of thy strength *now.*
9 Grant that thy priests may be
cloathed with righteousnes:
o let thy holy ones likewise
shout forth for joyfullnes.
10 Let not for Davids sake   2 *part.*
a servant unto thee,

PSALM CxxxII.

the face of thine annoynted one
   away quite turned bee.
11 The Lord to David sware
   truth, nor will turne from it;
thy bodyes fruit, of them I'le make
   upon thy throne to sit.
12 If thy sons keep my law,
   and covenant, I teach them;
upon thy throne for evermore
   shall sit their children then.
13 Because Iehovah hath
   made choise of *mount* Sion:
he hath desired it to bee
   his habitation.
14 This is my resting place
   to perpetuity:
here will I dwell, and that because
   desired it have I.
15 Blesse her provision
   abundantly I will:
the poore that be in her with bread
   by mee shall have their fill.
16 Her Priests with saving health
   them also I will clad:
her holy ones likewise they shall
   with shouting loud be glad.
17 The horne of David I
   will make to bud forth there:
a candle I prepared have
   for mine annoynted *deare.*
18 His enemies I will

                            with

with shame apparrell them:
but flourishing upon himselfe
shall be his Diadem:

Psalme 133.

A song of degrees, of David.

How good and sweet o see,
i'ts for brethren to dwell
together in unitee:
2 It's like choise oyle *that fell*
the head upon,
that downe did flow
the beard unto,
beard of Aron:
The skirts of his garment
that unto them went downe;
3 Like Hermons dews descent,
Sions mountaines upon,
for there to bee
the Lords blessing,
life aye lasting
commandeth hee.

Annother of the same.

How good it is, o see,
and how it pleaseth well,
together ev'n in unitee
for brethren soe to dwell:
2 I'ts like the choise oyntment
from head, to'th beard did go,
downe Arons beard: downeward that went
his garments skirts unto.
3 As Hermons dew, which did

PSALM CXXXIV, CXXXV.

on Sions hill descend:
for there the Lord blessing doth bid,
 ev'n life without an end.

Psalme 134.
A song of degrees.

O All yee servants of the Lord,
  behold the Lord blesse yee;
yee who within Iehovahs house
  i'th night time standing bee.
2 Lift up your hands, and blesse the Lord,
   in's *place* of holines.
3 The Lord that heav'n & earth hath made,
   thee out of Sion bless.

Psalme 135.

THe Lord praise, praise ye the Lords Name:
  the Lords servants o praise him yee.
2 That in the Lords house stand: *the same*
   i'th Courts of our Gods house who bee.
3 The Lord prayse, for the Lord is good:
   for sweet its to his Name to sing.
4 For Iacob to him chose hath God:
   & Isr'ell for his pretious thing.
5 For that the Lord is great I know:
   & over all gods, our Lord keeps.
6 All that he wills, the Lord doth do:
   in heav'n, earth, seas, & in all deeps.
7 The vapours he doth them constraine,
   forth from the ends of th'earth to rise;
   he maketh lightning for the raine:
   the winde brings from his treasuries.

PSALME CXxxv.
(2)

8 Of Egipt he the first borne smit:
and that of man, of beasts also.
9 Sent wondrous signes midst thee, Egipt:
on Pharoah, on all's servants too.
10 Who smote great natiōs, flew great Kings:
11 Slew Sihon King of th'Amorites,
Og also one of Bathans kings:
all kingdomes of the Cananites,
12 And gave their land an heritage:
his people Isr'ells lot to fall.
13 For aye thy Name, Lord, through each age
o Lord, is thy memoriall.
14 For his folks judge, the Lord is hee:
and of his servants he'le repent.
15 The heathens Idols silver bee,
& gold: mens hands did them invent.
16 Mouths have they, yet they never spake:
eyes have they, but they doe not see:
17 Eares have they, but no hearing take:
& in their mouth no breathings bee.
18 They that them make, have their likenes;
that trust in them so is each one.
19 The Lord o house of Isr'ell bless;
the Lord blesse, thou house of Aaron.
20 O house of Levi, blesse the Lord:
who feare the Lord, blesse ye the Lord.
21 From Sion blessed be the Lord;
who dwells at Salem praise the Lord.
Psalme 136.

psalme

PSALM CXXXVI.

O Thank the Lord, for hee is good:
   for's mercy lasts for aye.
2 Give thanks unto the God of gods:
   for's mercy is alway.
3 Give thanks unto the Lord of lords:
   for's mercy lasts for aye.
4 To him who only doth great signes:
   for's mercy is alway.
5 To him whose wisdome made the heav'ns:
   for's mercy &c.
6 Who o're the waters spread the earth:
   for's mercy &c.
7 Vnto him that did make great lights:
   for's mercy &c.
8 The Sun for ruliug of the day:
   for's mercy &c.
9 The Moone and Stars to rule by night:
   for's mercy &c.
10 To him who Egipts first-borne smote:
   for's mercy &c.
11 And from amongst them Isr'ell brought:
   for's mercy &c.
12 With strong hand, & with stretcht-out arme:
   for's mercy &c.
13 To him who did the red sea part:
   for's mercy &c.
14 And throngh i'ts midst made Isr'ell goe:
   for's mercy &c.
15 But there dround Pharoah & his hoast:
   for's mercy &c.
16 His people who through desart led:

for's

PSALME CXXXVI, CXXXVII.

for's mercy &c.
17 To him which did smite mighty Kings:
 for's mercy &c.
18 And put to slaughter famous Kings:
 for's mercy &c.
19 Sihon King of the Amorites:
 for's mercy &c.
20 And Og who was of Bashan King:
 for's mercy &c.
21 And gave their land an heritage:
 for's mercy &c.
22 A lot his servant Israell to:
 for's mercy &c.
23 In our low 'state who minded us:
 for's mercy &c.
24 And us redeemed from our foes:
 for's mercy &c.
25 Who giveth food unto all flesh:
 for's mercy lasts for ay.
26 Vnto the God of heav'n give thanks:
 for's mercy is alway.

Psalme 137.

THe rivers on of Babilon
 there when wee did sit downe:
yea even then wee mourned, when
 wee remembred Sion.
2 Our Harps wee did hang it amid,
 upon the willow tree.
3 Because there they that us away
 led in captivitee,
Requir'd of us a song, & thus

PSALM CxxxvII, CxxxvIII.

askt mirth: us waste who laid,
sing us among a Sions song,
   unto us then they said.
4 The lords song sing can wee? being
5   in strangers land. Then let
loose her skill my right hand, if I
   Ierusalem forget.
6 Let cleave my tongue my pallate on,
   if minde thee doe not I:
if chiefe joyes or'e I prize not more
   Ierusalem my joy.
7 Remember Lord, Edoms sons word,
   unto the ground said they,
it rase, it rase, when as it was
   Ierusalem her day.
8 Blest shall hee bee, that payeth thee,
   daughter of Babilon,
who must be waste: that which thou hast
   rewarded us upon.
9 O happie hee shall surely bee
   that taketh up, that eke
thy little ones against the stones
   doth into pieces breake.

Psalme 138.
A psalme of David.

With all my heart, I'le prayse thee *now*:
   before the gods I'le sing to thee.
2 Toward thine holy Temple bow,
   & praise thy Name for thy mercee,
      & thy truth: for thy word thou hye
   or'e all thy Name dost magnify.

3 I'th

PSALME CxxxvIII.

3 It'h day I cride, thou anſwredſt mee:
with ſtrength thou didſt my ſoule up-beare.
4 Lord, all the earths kings ſhall praiſe thee,
the word when of thy mouth they heare.
5 Yea, they ſhall ſing in the Lords wayes,
for great's Iehovahs glorious prayſe.
6 Albeit that the Lord be hye,
reſpect yet hath he to the low:
but as for them that are lofty,
he them doth at a diſtance know.
7 Though in the midſt I walking bee
of trouble thou wilt quicken mee,
Forth ſhalt thou make thine hand to go
againſt their wrath that doe me hate;
thy right hand ſhall me ſave alſo.
8 The Lord will perfect mine eſtate:
thy mercy Lord, for ever ſtands:
leave not the works of thine owne hands.

Another of the ſame.

WIthall my heart, I'le thee confeſs:
thee praiſe the gods before.
2 The Temple of thine holines
towards it I'le adore:
Alſo I will confeſſe thy Name,
for thy truth, & mercy:
becauſe thou over all thy Name
thy word doſt magnify.
3 In that ſame day that I did cry,
thou didſt mee anſwer make:
thou ſtrengthnedſt mee with ſtrength, which I
within my ſoule *did take.*

4 O Lord, when thy mouths words they heare
    all earths Kings shall thee praise.
5 And for the Lords great glory, there
    they shall sing in his wayes.
6 Albeit that the Lord be high,
    yet hee respects the low:
  but as for them that are lofty
    hee them far off doth know.
7 Though I in midst of trouble go,
    thee quickning mee I haue:
  thy hand thou wilt cast on my foe,
    thy right hand shall mee save.
8 The Lord will perfect it for mee:
    thy mercy ever stands,
  Lord, doe not those forsake that bee
    the works of thine owne hands.

Psalme 139.

To the chief musician, a psalme
of David.

O LORD, thou hast me searcht & knowne.
    Thou knowst my sitting downe,
  & mine up-rising: my thought is
    to thee afarre off knowne.
3 Thou knowst my paths, & lying downe,
    & all my wayes knowst well.
4 For loe, each word that's in my tongue,
    Lord, thou canst fully tell.
5 Behinde thou gird'st mee, & before:
    & layst on mee thine hand.
6 Such knowledge is too strange, too high,
    for mee to understand

7 where

PSALME CxxxIx,

7 Where shall I from thy presence go?
　　or where from thy face flye?
8 If heav'n I climbe, thou there, loe thou,
　　if downe in hell I lye.
9 If I take mornings wings, & dwell
　　where utmost sea-coasts bee.
10 Ev'n there thy hand shall mee conduct:
　　& thy right hand hold mee.
11 That veryly the darknes shall
　　mee cover, if I say:
　then shall the night about mee be
　　like to the lightsome day.
12 Yea, darknes hideth not from thee,
　　but as the day shines night:
　alike unto thee both these are,
　　the darknes & the light.
13 Because that thou possessed hast
　　my reines: *and* covered mee
　within my mothers wombe thou hast.
14 　My prayse shall be of thee,
　Because that I am fashioned
　　in fearfull wondrous wise:
　　& that thy works are merveilous,
　　my soule right well descries.

(2)

15 From thee my substance was not hid,
　　when made I was closely:
　& when within th'earths lowest parts
　　I was wrought curiously.
16 Thine eyes upon my substance yet
　　imperfected, did look,

Ii 3

and

PSALM CxxxIx.

& all the members that I have
   were written in thy booke,
What dayes they should be fashioned:
   none of them yet were come.
17 How pretious are thy thoughts to mee,
   o God? how great's their summe?
18 If I should count them, in number
   more then the sands they bee:
& at what time I doe awake,
   still I abide with thee.
19 Assuredly thou wilt o God,
   those that be wicked slay:
yee that are bloody men, therefore
   depart from mee away.
20 Because that they against thee doe
   speake wickedly *likewise*:
thy Name they doe take up in vaine
   who are thine enemies.
21 Thy haters Lord, doe I not hate?
   & am not I with those
offended grievously that doe
   up-rising thee oppose?
22 Them I with perfect hatred hate:
   I count them as my foes.
23 Search mee o God, & know my heart:
   try mee, my thoughts disclose:
24 And see if any wicked way
   in mee there bee at all:
& mee conduct within the way
   that last for ever shall.
      Palme 140

PSALME CxL.

To the chief musician, a psalme
of David,

LORD, free mee from the evill man:
from violent man save mee.
2 Whose hearts thinke mischief: every day
for war they gathred bee.
3 Their tongues they have made to be sharp
a serpent like unto:
the poyson of the Aspe it is
under their lipps *also*.   Selah.
4 Keepe mee, Lord, from the wickeds hands,
from violent man mee save:
my goings who to overthrow
in thought projected have.
5 The proud have hid a snare for mee,
cords also: they a net
have spred abroad by the way side:
grins for mee they have set.   Selah.
6 Vnto Iehovah I did say,
thou art a God to mee:
Lord, heare the voice of my requests,
which are for grace to thee.

(2)

7 O God, the Lord, who art the stay
of my salvation:
my head by thee hath covered been
the day of battell on.
8 Those mens desires that wicked are,
Iehovah, doe not grant,
their wicked purpose furher not,
lest they themselves doe vaunt.

PSALM Cxl, Cxlr.

9 As for the head of them that mee
    doe round about inclose,
  o let the molestation
    of their lips cover those.
10 Let burning coales upon them fall,
    into the fire *likewise*
  let them be cast, into deepe pits,
    that they no more may rise.
11 Let not i'th earth establisht bee
    men of an evill tongue:
  evill shall hunt to overthrow
    the man of violent wrong.
12 The afflicteds cause, the poore mans right,
    I know God will maintaine:
13 Yea, just shall praise thy Name: th'upright
    shall 'fore thy face remaine.

Psalme 141.
A psalme of David.

O GOD, my Lord, on thee I call,
    doe thou make hast to mee:
  and harken thou unto my voice,
    when I cry unto thee.
2 And let my pray'r directed be
    as incense in thy sight:
  and the up-lifting of my hands
    as sacrifice at night.
3 Iehovah, oh that thou would'st set
    a watch my mouth before:
  as also of my lips with care
    o doe thou keepe the dore.
4 Bow not my heart to evill things;

PSALME Cxli,

    to doe the wicked deed
with wicked workers: & let not
    mee of their dainties feed.
5 Let juſt-men ſmite mee, kindenes 'tis;
    let him reprove mee eke,
it ſhall be ſuch a pretious oyle,
    my head it ſhall not breake:
For yet my pray'r's ev'n in their woes.
6   When their judges are caſt
    on rocks, then ſhall they heare my words,
for they are ſweet to taſte.
7 Like unto one who on the earth
    doth cutt & cleave the wood,
ev'n ſo our bones at the graves mouth
    are ſcattered abroad.
8 But unto thee o God, the Lord
    directed are mine eyes:
my ſoule o leave not deſtitute,
    on thee my hope relyes.
9 O doe thou keepe mee from the ſnare
    which they have layd for mee;
& alſo from the grins of thoſe
    that work iniquitee.
10 Together into their owne nets
    o let the wicked fall:
untill ſuch time that I eſcape
    may make from them withall.

      Pſalme 142.
Maſchil of David, a prayer when
    he was in the cave.

PSALM CXLII.

Unto Iehovah with my voice,
   I did unto him cry:
unto Iehovah with my voice
   my sute for grace made I.
2 I did poure out before his face
   my meditation:
before his face I did declare
   the trouble mee upon.
3 O'rewhelm'd in mee when was my spirit,
   then thou didst know my way:
I'th way I walkt, a snare for mee
   they privily did lay.
4 On my right hand I lookt, & saw,
   but no man would mee know,
all refuge faild mee: for my soule
   none any care did show.
5 Then to thee Lord, I cryde, & sayd,
   my hope thou art *alone*:
& in the land of living ones
   thou art my portion.
6 Because I am brought very low,
   attend unto my cry:
from my pursuers save thou mee,
   which stronger bee then I.
7 That I thy Name may praise, my soule
   from prison oh bring out:
when thou shalt mee reward, the just
   shall compasse mee about.
      Psalme 143.
    A psalme of David.

PSALME CxlIII.

LORD, heare my prayr, give eare when I
  doe supplicate to thee:
 in thy truth, in thy righteousnes;
  make answer unto mee.
2 And into judgement enter not
  with him that serveth thee;
 for in thy sight no man that lives
  can justified bee.
3 For th'enemie hath pursude my soule,
  my life to'th ground hath throwne:
 & made mee dwell i'th dark like them
  that dead are long agone.
4 Therefore my spirit is overwhelmd
  perplexedly in mee:
 my heart also within mee is
  made desolate to bee.
5 I call to minde the dayes of old,
  I meditation use
 on all thy words: upon the work
  of thy hands I doe muse.
6 I even I doe unto thee
  reach mine out-stretched hands:
 so after thee my soule doth thirst
  as doe the thristy lands.   Selah.
        (2)
7 Hast, Lord, heare mee, my spirit doth faile,
  hide not thy face mee fro:
 lest I become like one of them
  that downe to pit doe go.
8 Let mee thy mercy heare i'th morne,
  for I doe on thee stay,

Kk 2   wherin

PSALM CxlIII, CxlIV.

wherin that I should walk cause mee
   to understand the way:
For unto thee I lift my soule.
9   O Lord deliver mee
   from all mine enemies; I doe flye
     to hide my selfe with thee.
10 Because thou art my God, thy will
     oh teach thou mee to doe,
   thy spirit is good: of uprightnes
     lead mee the land into.
11 Iehovah, mee o quicken thou
     ev'n for thine owne Names sake;
   And for thy righteousnes my soule
     from out of trouble take.
12 Doe thou also mine enemies
     cut off in thy mercy,
   destroy them that afflict my soule:
     for thy servant am I.

Psalme 144.
A psalme of David.

O Let Iehovah blessed be
    who is my rock of might,
who doth instruct my hands to war,
   and my fingers to fight.
2 My goodnes, fortresse, my hye towre,
     & that doth set mee free:
   my shield, my trust, which doth subdue
     my people under mee.
3 Iehovah, what is man, that thou
     knowledge of him dost take?
   what is the son of man, that thou

acount

PSALME Cxliv.

account of him doſt make?
4 Man's like to vanity: his dayes
   paſſe like a ſhade away.
5 Lord, bow the heav'ns, come downe & touch
   the mounts & ſmoake ſhall they.
6 Lightning caſt forth, & ſcatter them:
   thine arrows ſhoor, them rout,
7 Thine hand o ſend thou from above,
   doe thou redeeme mee out:
   And rid mee from the waters great:
   from hand of ſtrangers brood:
8 Whoſe mouth ſpeaks lyes, their right hand is
   a right hand of falſehood.

(2)

9 O God, new ſongs I'le ſing to thee:
   upon the Pſaltery,
   and on ten ſtringed inſtrument
   to thee ſing praiſe will I.
10 It's hee that giveth unto Kings
   ſafety victorious:
   his ſervant David he doth ſave
   from ſword pernitious.
11 Rid mee from hand of ſtrange children,
   whoſe mouth ſpeakes vanity:
   & their right hand a right hand is
   of lying falſity:
12 That like as plants which are growne up
   in youth may be our ſons;
   our daughters pallace like may be
   polliſht as corner ſtones:
13 Our garners full, affording ſtore

PSALM CxLiv, Cxlv.

of every sort of meates;
  our cattell bringing thousands forth,
    ten thousands in our streets:
14 Strong let our oxen bee to work,
    that breaking in none bee
  nor going out: that so our streets
    may from complaints bee free.
15 O blessed shall the people be
    whose state is such as this:
  o blessed shall the people be,
    whose God Iehovah is.

Psalme 145.
Davids psalme of praise.

MY God, o King, I'le thee extoll:
    & blesse thy Name for aye.
2 For ever will I praise thy Name;
    and blesse thee every day.
3 Great is the Lord, most worthy praise:
    his greatnes search can none.
4 Age unto age shall praise thy works:
    & thy great acts make knowne.
5 I of thy glorious honour will
    speake of thy majesty;
  & of the operations
    by thee done wondrously.
6 Also men of thy mighty works
    shall speake which dreadfull are:
  also concerning thy greatnes,
    it I will forth declare:
7 Thy great goodnesses memory
    they largely shall expres:

and

PSALME CxlV.

and they shall with a shouting voice
   sing of thy righteousnes.
8 The Lord is gracious, & hee is
   full of compassion:
slow unto anger, & full of
   commiseration.
9 The Lord is good to all: or'e all *part* (2)
   his works his mercies bee.
10 All thy works shall praise thee, o Lord:
   & thy Saints shall blesse thee,
11 They'le of thy kingdomes glory speake:
   and talk of thy powre *hye*;
12 To make mens sons his great acts know:
   his kingdomes majesty.
13 Thy Kingdome is a kingdome aye:
   & thy reigne lasts alwayes.
14 The Lord doth hold up all that fall:
   and all downe-bow'd ones rayse.
15 All eyes wayt on thee, & their meat
   thou dost in season bring.
16 Opnest thy hand, & the desire
   fill'st of each living thing.
17 In all his wayes the Lord is just:
   & holy in's works all.
18 Hee's neere to all that call on him:
   in truth that on him call.
19 Hee satisfy will the desire
   of those that doe him feare:
Hee will be safety unto them,
   and when they cry he'le heare.
20 The Lord preserves each one of them

                          that

PSALM CxlV, CxlvI.

that *lovers of* him bee:
  but whosoever wicked are
    abolish them doth hee.
21 My mouth the prayses of the Lord
    by speaking shall express:
  also all flesh his holy Name
    for evermore shall bless.

Psalme 146.

THe Lord praise: praise(my soule) the Lord.
    So long as I doe live
  I'le praise the Lord; while that I am,
    praise to my God I'le give.
3 Trust not in Princes; nor mans son
    who can no succour send.
4 His breath goe's forth, to's earth he turnes,
    his thoughts that day doe end.
5 Happie is hee that hath the God
    of Iacob for his ayd:
  whose expectation is upon
    Iehovah his God stayd.
6 Which heav'n, earth, sea, all in them made:
    truth keeps for evermore:
7 Which for th'oppressed judgement doth,
    gives to the hungry store,
8 The Lord doth loose the prisoners.
    the Lord ope's eyes of blinde,
  the Lord doth raise the bowed downe;
    the Lord to'th just is kinde.
9 The Lord saves stangers, & relievs
    the orphan, & widow:
  but hee of them that wicked are

                  the

PSALME Cxlvi, Cxlvii.

the way doth overthrow.
10 The Lord shall reigne for evermore,
thy God, o Sion, hee
to generations all shall reigne:
o prayse Iehovah yee.

Psalme 147.

PRayse yee the Lord, for it
is good praises to sing,
to our God for it's sweet,
praise is a comely thing.
2   Ierusalem
the Lord up-reares,
outcasts gathers
    of Isre'll *them*.
3 The broke in heart he heales:
& up their wounds doth binde.
4 The stars by number tells:
hee calls them all by kinde.
5   Our Lord great is,
& of great might,
yea infinite
    his knowledge 'tis.
6 The Lord sets up the low:
wicked to ground doth fling.
7 Sing thanks the Lord unto
on Harp, our Gods praise sing.
8   Who clouds the skyes,
to earth gives raines:
who on mountaines
    makes grasse to rise.
9 Beasts, hee & ravens young

when

PSALM Cxlvii.

when as they cry feeds then.
10 Ioyes not in horses strong:
nor in the leggs of men.
11   The Lord doth place
his pleasure where
men doe him feare,
  & hope on's grace.
12 Ierusalem, God praise:
Sion thy God confess:
13 For thy gates barres he stayes:
in thee thy sons doth bless.
14   Peace maketh hee
in borders thine:
with wheat so fine
  hee filleth thee.
15 On earth sends his decree:
swiftly his word doth pass.
16 Gives snow like wool, spreds hee
his hoare frost ashes as.
17   His yce doth cast
like morsels to:
'fore his cold who
  can stand stedfast?
18 His word sends, & them thaws:
makes winde blow, water flows.
19 His word, Iacob; his laws,
& judgements Isr'ell shows.
20   Hee hath so done
no nation to,
judgements also
  they have not knowne.
   Hallelujah,

psalme

PSALME CxlvIII.

Psalme 148. Hallelujah.

FRom heav'n o praise the Lord:
　him praise the heights within.
2　All's Angells praise afford,
　　all's Armies praise yee him.
3　　O give him praise
　Sun & Moone *bright*:
　all Stars of light,
　　o give him praise.
4　Yee heav'ns of heav'ns him praise:
　or'e heav'ns yee waters *cleare*.
5　The Lords Name let them praise:
　for hee spake, made they were.
6　　Them stablisht hee
　for ever & aye:
　nor shall away
　　his made decree.
7　Praise God from th'earth *below*:
　yee dragons & each deepe.
8　Fire & haile, mist & snow:
　whirl-windes his word which keepe.
9　　Mountaines, also
　you hills all yee:
　each fruitfull tree,
　　all Cedars too.
10　Beasts also all cattell:
　things creeping, foules that flye.
11　Earths kings, & all people:
　princes, earths judges *hye*:
　　doe all the same.
12　Young men & maids:

Ll 2　　　　　　　　old

PSALM CxlvIII, Cxlix.

old men & babes.
13   Praise the Lords Name,
For his Name's hye only:
  his glory o're earth & heav'n.
14 His folks horne he lifts hye
  the praise of all's Saints, ev'n
    the sons who bee
  of Israell,
  his neere people,
    the Lord praise yee.

Psalme 149.

PRaise yee the Lord: unto the Lord
  doe yee sing a new song:
  & in the congregation
    his praise the Saints among.
2 Let Israell now joyfull bee
    in him who him hath made:
  children of Sion in their King
    o let them be full glad.
3 O let them with *melodious* flute
    his Name give praise unto:
  let them sing praises unto him
    with Timbrell, Harp also.
4 Because Iehovah in his folk
    doth pleasure greatly take:
  the meek bee with salvation
    ev'n beautifull will make.
5 Let them the gracious Saints that be
    most gloriously rejoyce:
  & as they lye upon their beds
    lift up their singing voyce.

6 let

PSALME CxLx, Cl.

6 Let their mouths have Gods praise: their hand
   a two edg'd sword also:
7 On heathen vengeance, on the folk
   punishment for to do:
8 Their kings with chaines, with yron bolts
   also their peers to binde:
9 To doe on them the judgement writ:
   all's Saints this honour finde.
           Hallelujah.

Psalme 150.

PRaise yee the Lord. praise God
  in's place of holines:
 o praise him in the firmament
  of his great mightines.
2 O praise him for his acts
  that be magnificent:
 & praise yee him according to
  his greatnes excellent.
3 With Trumpet praise yee him
  that gives a sound so hye:
 & doe yee praise him with the Harp,
  & sounding Psalterye.
4 With Timbrell & with Flute
  praise unto him give yee:
 with Organs, & string'd instruments
  prais'd by you let him bee.
5 Vpon the loude Cymballs
  unto him give yee praise:
 upon the Cimballs praise yee him
  which hye their sound doe raise.

PSALM CI.

6 Let every thing to which
the Lord doth breath afford
the praises of the Lord set forth:
o doe yee praise the Lord.

FINIS

An admonition to the Reader.

THe verses of these psalmes may be reduced to six kindes, the first wherof may be sung in very neere fourty common tunes; as they are collected, out of our chief musicians, by *Tho. Ravenscroft.*

The second kinde may be sung in three tunes as *Ps.* 25. 50. & 67. in our english psalm books.

The third. may be sung indifferently, as *ps.* the 51. 100. & ten comandements, in our english psalme books. which three tunes aforesaid, comprehend almost all this whole book of psalmes, as being tunes most familiar to us.

The fourth. as *ps.* 148. of which there are but about five.

The fift. as *ps.* 112. or the *Pater noster*, of which there are but two. *viz.* 85. & 138.

The sixt. as *ps.* 113, of which but one, *viz.* 115.

Faults escaped in printing.

Escaped.	Right
psalme 9. vers 9. oprest.	opprest.
v. 10. knowes.	know.
pf. 18. n. 29. the.	thee.
n. 31. 3 part wanting.	3 part.
pf. 19. v. 13. let thou- kept back.	kept back o let.
pf. 21. n. 8. the Lord.	thine hand.
pf. 143. n. 6. Ieven I.	moreover I.

The rest, which have escaped through over-sight, you may amend, as you finde them obvious.

Notes on the Reproduction

The process used for the production of this facsimile of the Bay Psalm Book of 1640 was line offset, with negatives made from an original copy of the Prince Collection in the Boston Public Library (No. 3 of the list printed in *The Enigma of the Bay Psalm Book*, p. 82). The pages were photographed, in exact size, by precision cameras in the shop of the Meriden Gravure Company at Meriden, Connecticut. Since the original copy, like all extant copies, contains a number of poorly printed pages, it seemed desirable to reproduce such pages from the second copy of the Prince Collection (No. 4 of the list).

The first facsimile of the Bay Psalm Book, published in 1903, was produced from the incomplete copy belonging to E. Dwight Church and now in the Huntington Library, using also the Lenox copy of the New York Public Library. In his Introduction, Wilberforce Eames, the foremost American bibliographer of his time, did not specify the pages prepared from the Lenox copy, mentioning as such only the first three leaves of the Preface. Yet the noting of substitutions may be useful. In the present facsimile the following pages were photographed from the second Prince copy: **v, A4v, F2, O3, S4, S4v, Tv, V3v (catchword retained from the first copy), V4, Aa, Aav, Aa2v, Aa4, Cc, Cc4v, Dd2, Dd2v, Ee, Eev, Ff4v, Ii3, Ll2. The catchwords of pages **2, D4, and R3v were also taken from the second Prince copy.

The presswork of the Bay Psalm Book was very uneven; Stephen Day at times thinned out the ink and at others splashed it over the forme, causing blotches and strong show-through. He probably never washed

The Bay Psalm Book

his type; signs of dried ink stuck between the letters are conspicuous throughout the book. The wet sheets must have attracted dust; and the fox-marks seem to have favored the edges of the letters as if the type, crushing the fiber of the paper, had rendered such areas especially sensitive. In making the present facsimile, these blemishes have been removed by careful opaquing, without retouching the negatives otherwise.

The earlier facsimile was produced from line cuts, that is, from plates prepared by etching; and, because of inept handling and the sponginess of the paper, the letters spread and became flat and heavy. No effort seems to have been made to clear the print of the ancient dirt. In contrast, the new facsimile has remarkable freshness and vitality.

Bibliographers may have preferred the reproduction of a single copy, with all its shortcomings, by the collotype process. The inclusion of the weak, barely legible, pages undoubtedly would have better revealed the quality of Day's printing. But even then only the characteristics of a particular copy would have been shown; for each copy has its own peculiar defects. It would have been unwarranted, therefore, to spoil the interest of the book for all but a few specialized scholars who can always examine the original copies. Still less could be said for perpetuating the damage wrought by time and usage.

The proofs were compared, letter by letter, with the original pages. For the correctness of the reproduction the writer testifies.

ZOLTÁN HARASZTI

BOSTON, MASSACHUSETTS
August 1956